Women Write Back

Irish and Catalan Short Stories in Colonial Context

IRENE BOADA-MONTAGUT

IRISH ACADEMIC PRESS
DUBLIN • PORTLAND, OR

First published in 2003 in by
IRISH ACADEMIC PRESS
44, Northumberland Road, Dublin 4, Ireland

and in the United States of America by
IRISH ACADEMIC PRESS
c/o ISBS, 5824 N.E. Hassalo Street, Portland
Oregon 97213-3644

Website: www.iap.ie

British Library Cataloguing in Publication Data
A catalogue record of this book is available from the British Library.
ISBN 0-7165-2749-9

Library of Congress Cataloging-in-Publication Data
A catalog record of this book is available from the Library of Congress.

Typeset by Carrigboy Typesetting Services, County Cork
Printed by MPG Books Ltd., Bodmin, Cornwall

Contents

Acknowledgements

I WOULD LIKE to thank Dr Kathleen McCracken for her help during the time I was writing this work. Her support, encouragement and guidance have been vital. I will always remember her for her trust and belief in me from the first time we met. I would also like to thank Dr August Bover, a teacher and a friend, who, many years ago, in beautiful Western Canada, gave me the confidence to think of pursuing my dream of going to university. I will always thank him for that moment and for his help and friendship down the years. My gratitude also to the University of Ulster for facilitating my research and providing a supportive framework over the years. I am indebted to the Comissionat per a Universitats i Recerca, Generalitat de Catalunya, for the provision of a grant which made it possible for me to take time off work and pursue this study on a full-time basis.

I must express my appreciation of Dr Jennifer Fitzgerald of Queen's University, Belfast, who opened my eyes to literary criticism and life during the first two years I spent in Belfast. I have also had valuable conversations about literature and received much help from Professor J.W. Foster, Dr Rosa González, Dr Kathleen McNerney, Dr Leon Litvack, Professor Jackie Hurtley, Dr Maria Campillo, Dr Carme Arnau, Dr Arthur Aughey and Dr Dominic Keown, and also from the writers Colm Tóibín, Marta Pessarrodona and Isabel-Clara Simó. Especially, I would like to thank Professor Ailbhe Smyth. Reading her work has been both deeply stimulating and a source of inspiration for my own efforts. Knowing her in recent years has been an enriching experience.

Unes gracies especials a la meva mare, al meu pare, germana Laura i germans Estanis i Lluís. Also I am especially thankful to my friends who gave me unfailing support and encouragement when I needed it, which was quite often. They are many, but I want to mention in particular Prócoro Hernández, Esther Aliaga, Tess Moran, Karin White, John Kane, Carme Rodés, Sinéad Monks, and Ricard Torres.

I am more than grateful to Líam Kennedy, who has been patient enough to help me with the difficulties I had, especially with the English language.

Go raibh míle maith agat. Although I failed to dispel his scepticism regarding postcolonial theory, we have had fascinating conversations about Irish culture and history, including the similarities and contrasts with the Catalan experience. Without his encouragement and loving support, this piece of work would not have been possible. This book is dedicated to him.

'Edward colonised her territory. Everywhere she looked in Ireland reminded her of him. He had taken over every place and every object in her life'

Eilís Ní Dhuibhne

'*M'agradaria poder deixar de plantejar-me la meva nació o el meu sexe com a problema*'
(I would like to be able to stop thinking of my nation or my sex as a problem)

Isabel-Clara Simó

'Write! Write is for you, you are for you, your body is yours. Take it.'
Hélène Cixous

'The Empire Writes back to the Centre.'
Salman Rushdie

Introduction

Sometimes, as I sat in the Biblioteca de Catalunya in the 14th-century hospital building, I had to blink to make sure that I was not in the National Library in Dublin.

Colm Tóibín[1]

IT IS customary to compare Ireland with England, which is hardly surprising in view of the long and intimate political relationship between the two countries. Whether it is a question of relative economic progress, political freedoms or cultural production, the neighbouring island has always been seen as a seemingly natural point of reference. These comparisons, even when not carrying the weight of historic recrimination, run the risk of being hackneyed and hence less than illuminating. There is some merit, therefore, in breaking away from this claustrophobic comparison.

Catalonia, another European region, has important features in common with Ireland in terms of its socio-cultural development: both were colonial societies at one time; both have had experiences of bilingualism; both existed in the shadow of a political and cultural giant and responded to this position of cultural subordination in literature as well as in politics, and both experienced a cultural revival during the second half of the nineteenth century. Both nations are often referred to in terms of the Catalan or Irish 'problem', from the perspective of the Spanish and British states respectively. In both cases literature was exploited in the service of a nationalist ideology. Coincidentally, the popular poems 'A Nation Once Again' (1848), by Thomas Davis, and 'La Pàtria' (Ode to the Fatherland) (1833), by B.C. Aribau, were written in the same period. The political ethos of the major political parties in Ireland and Catalonia is imbued with nationalism of one kind or another.[2] Moreover, within each society, there has been a fair degree of self-questioning which runs along roughly parallel lines. What does Irishness mean? What does it mean to be Catalan, both in the past and in the present? In literature, problems of identity are reflected in problems of definition and classification. Is Anglo-Irish literature Irish? Can writings in Spanish, by Catalan writers, be regarded as truly Catalan?

1

Such similarities forcefully struck the Irish writer Colm Tóibín, who spent some years in Barcelona. He highlights both connections and parallels:

> Some of the connections between Catalonia and Ireland during this period of nation-inventing were obvious: the Catalans founded a political party in the early Twenties called *Nosaltres Sols*, a direct translation of *Sinn Féin*, Ourselves Alone. There were poems in Catalan on the death of Terence MacSwiney on hunger strike in 1921. A stirring poem had been written in Catalan in 1848 which inspired a generation of nationalism; in the same year in Ireland Thomas Davis wrote the song 'A Nation Once Again'. Both Catalan and Irish politicians could, and still can, play tricks with the arithmetic of the Cortes in Madrid and the Mother of Parliaments in Westminster . . . But it was the general shape and atmosphere of Catalan cultural politics between 1890 and 1910 which constantly reminded me of Ireland. The foundation of the Barça football club, and its role in creating waves of Catalan emotion, was close to that of the Gaelic Athletic Association in Ireland, founded in the same period.[3]

One can think of further links. A short-lived political party was established in Valencia called *Joventut Obrera Nacionalista* (Nationalist Labour Youth), which drew explicitly on the Irish nationalist experience. Moreover, some Catalan political activists took refuge in Ireland in the mid-1930s. From Ireland they issued nationalist pamphlets, thereby connecting nationalist politics in the two societies.[4]

Until 1921 all of Ireland was part of the British world. This reality had profound implications for Ireland and, to a lesser degree, for Britain. The outcome of the manifold interactions between the two societies was both culturally enriching and also a source of division and conflict within Ireland. To an outsider from a Catalan background, this diversity of experience, and some of the contradictions, are immediately familiar. Catalonia has had to learn to live with biculturalism, for example. Like Ireland, it was a small society which, in the early modern period, was incorporated forcibly into a larger imperial state.

There are also differences, of course. In the Catalan case the indigenous language survived, and now flourishes, and has long been the primary marker of identity. In the Irish case the Irish language has been largely lost, and religious affiliation is a more important sign of ethnic identity. Not all of Ireland became part of the newly independent state in 1921–22. Northern Ireland remained within the United Kingdom, a frontier society deeply divided along ethnic, religious and national lines.[5] These divisions have given rise to intense conflict and violence since the 1970s, although the level has varied through time, being particularly pronounced during the first and last quarters of the present century.

Having mentioned the question of Northern Ireland, it is as well to say that this work is only incidentally concerned with questions of northern nationalism and Ulster unionism. Ulster unionism in particular seems to be relatively neglected in literary explorations of Irish culture. My neglect of this hugely significant and complex aspect of British and Irish culture in Ireland is not intended as a deliberate affront. It is merely to recognise that the enterprise undertaken here is sufficiently ambitious in itself to stretch my own capabilities. Having said that, there is a limited engagement with northern themes, and I would like to return to a more systematic analysis of Unionist traditions and their Catalan counterparts in some future work.

The existence of antagonistic political and cultural formations on the island of Ireland has no direct parallel in the Catalan case, although there has been violence in Catalonia. The Civil War in Catalonia (1936–9) killed 75,000 people and was particularly bloody in Catalonia. Around 60,000 Catalans were exiled to France and Latin America.[6] While there have been instances of conflict between native-born Catalans and Spanish-speaking immigrants to Barcelona, since the Second World War integration has worked well and the tensions have been of a qualitatively different kind from the deep-seated ethnic divisions apparent in Northern Ireland. The tradition of *pactisme* (compromise) within Catalan nationalism, it may be suggested, has taken precedence over that of political violence.

There is a further difference that tends to set the countries apart, one which is of basic importance to cultural production. This is the matter of the language spoken and its place in the global system of communication and commerce. English is now the most powerful language in the world, whereas Catalan is a minority language in Europe with, at most, some nine million speakers. Being able to publish in one or the other language is obviously a different story. The opportunities for publishing in English are much greater and the potential rewards greater still. For example, some of the women writers analysed in this book, such as Edna O'Brien or Mary Dorcey, are well known in Britain, North America and probably in many other countries. But even though she has been translated widely, one of the best writers in Catalonia, Mercè Rodoreda, greatly admired by Gabriel Garcia Márquez, is largely ignored by non-Catalan speakers. She is also ignored elsewhere in the Spanish State.

This book explores contemporary Irish and Catalan short stories by women writers within the frame of postcolonial and feminist theories. Studying women's writing from a feminist perspective should not present too many problems, but one might wonder if the use of postcolonial theory is legitimate or illuminating in relation to these two European societies. Let us explore this a little further. First of all, colonisation is a broad term. It was not an identical process in the different parts of the affected world but, according to Ania Loomba: 'everywhere it locked the original inhabitants and the newcomers into the most complex and traumatic relationships in human history'.[7] Loomba gives a generic definition: 'colonialism can be defined as the conquest and control of other people's land and goods . . . Modern colonialism did more than extract tribute, goods and wealth from the countries that it conquered – it restructured the economies of the latter, drawing them into a complex relationship with their own.'[8]

The latter point is important in the study of literature under a post-colonial frame. The focus of this book is to look at the relationship of the postcolonial individual within herself – her insecurities, fears, her experience in a world which has little to do with herself and which is alien – and how that is reflected in her literary production. Ireland and Catalonia have also been colonised.[9] Each has suffered from an imperial aggression which has not allowed them to develop and express themselves freely and they still find themselves undergoing a process of decolonisation. In the process, the cultures of Catalonia and Ireland have been burdened by anxieties and preoccupations which reflect the violent origins and reality of colonisation.

The Irish and the Catalan cases also come from different historical experiences. While there was general expansion in the Irish economy between the 1740s and 1815, the accompanying population explosion and deepening poverty after the end of the French wars prepared the way for the catastrophe of the Great Famine of the 1840s. Many historians are now sceptical of the traditional view that the political union of Britain and Ireland in 1801 led directly to the decline of the Irish economies in the nineteenth century. But there seems little doubt that the political and cultural personality of the island was diminished and the Irish language almost disappeared in favour of the English one.[10] In marked contrast, Catalonia developed a strong economy after it was defeated by the Spanish state in 1714 and condemned, as a result, to live without the features which constituted its personality: political institutions, its native language and other cultural moorings. Catalonia became the most industrialised and the wealthiest community in Spain, yet remained powerless politically and culturally. During the eighteenth century, in reaction to the Spanish aggression, forms of collective Catalan awareness persisted. These developed into a national consciousness during the course of the nineteenth century and survived the vicissitudes of the twentieth century. Even though the native language was banned, people still used it. The language survived, being part of a wider national consciousness, and became the major sign of national identity. After the Spanish Civil War, the main Catalan political institutions – those which had been in existence before the war – were transferred abroad and remained there for the duration of the Francoist dictatorship. Those facts show the failure of the assimilationist policies pursued by the Spanish state towards Catalonia.

Despite the existence of differentiated cultures and languages within its boundaries, the Spanish state never had a policy of plurality. Quite the reverse. According to the historian Ferrer i Gironès, Catalonians have not been able to participate fully in the politics of the central government, even in the contemporary democratic era. It would be difficult, for instance, to imagine a president of the central government who was Catalan. This is part of what Ferrer i Gironès calls *'Catalanofòbia'*,[11] which could be described as a dislike, sometimes even hatred, directed by Spaniards towards Catalan people. According to this historian, the main reason for *'catalanofòbia'* was the assimilative imperial aims of the Castile kingdom first, and what later became the Spanish state. These involved the abolition of the Catalan constitution and laws, the drive to control the Catalan public revenue system and the cultural and linguistic colonisation of Catalan citizens.[12] The Catalan language was feared by the Spanish government and treated as a dialect. Perhaps the surprising thing is how effectively the culture and language were maintained in the face of imperial disapproval. Catalan is one of the very few languages in western Europe which has survived on a wide scale without the support of its own state. Most of the other minority languages in western and northern Europe, which lack a state of their own, have died or are under serious threat, such as Gaelic in Ireland and Scotland, Welsh, the Basque language, Galician, Breton, Occitan and Sardinian.

The discriminatory policies of the British towards the Irish, and the accompanying mental sets, are probably responsible for the phenomenon of nationalism in Ireland as well.[13] The British and the Spanish states, like the French and the Italian ones, were centralist states and disliked any sort of difference which could threaten their unity and 'greatness'. The truth of the matter is that these two small nations, Ireland and Catalonia, persisted in maintaining their identity. Like other postcolonial nations, they pursued a process of resistance and national invention, which, at the beginning of a new millennium, is still alive.

Going back to postcolonial theory, in postcolonial societies, the individuals are frozen into a hierarchical relationship in which the subordinate group is locked into position by the assumed moral superiority of the dominant group – a superiority which is reinforced when necessary by the use of physical force.[14] As a result, most colonies were obliged to use violence in order to achieve independence. An example of oppression in Catalonia and the Basque Country is that, nowadays, self-determination is banned in both communities by law. That means those two nations are not allowed the possibility of becoming independent, should they so wish.

This book is based on a metaphor in which women are defined as colonised beings. In this context, we could establish a parallelism with women and independent nations. Women in developed countries have achieved some rights, such as access to education, some presence in the workforce and some sort of economic independence, though they still remain unequal to men in relation to pay and promotion. Continuing this metaphor, we could compare this independence with the independence achieved by the former colonies. However, independence does not mean that the process of decolonisation has ended. It is a long process. According to one of the best guides written on postcolonialism so far, the term 'postcolonial' is used to 'cover all the culture affected by the imperial process from the moment of colonisation to the present day. This is because there is a continuity of preoccupations throughout the historical process initiated by European imperial aggression.'[15] The frozen hierarchical relationship remains. In patriarchal societies, the social discrimination against women is hidden by 'normality'. This misogyny 'in the air' naturally creates a sense of inferiority among women. There is still a lot of resistance to women being in positions of power and having egalitarian relationships with their partners and within their families. Women are seen by some as mere appendages of men; they are of little consequence in their own right. Maria Aurèlia Capmany offers the following summary depiction: '*una dona és un silenci on puguis sentir-te, un espai buit on instal.lar-te, una dona és només un vehicle de la teva continuïtat*' (a woman is a space of silence where you can hear yourself, an empty space where you can settle, a woman is only a vehicle of your continuity).[16]

After centuries of oppression, individuals become less sure about their culture, their language, their identity as a group, even about themselves. The effect is huge, leaving the individual wondering: Who am I? What is my culture? Is my culture inferior to that of the metropolitan one? Indeed, according to Simon During, in postcolonial countries 'one finds a crisis of emptiness'[17] which leads to an 'identity imperative'. Here again we find a striking parallel with the condition of women who feel lost, for example, in unhappy marriages. The nameless protagonist in 'La sang del castell' (The blood of the castle) describes her feelings of sadness and confusion in the morning after her wedding night:

> *Pujo cansada la costa, fugint del meu temps futur, fora del meu present, esmaperduda, sense saber qui sóc ni on buscar la meva identitat . . . un castell que a cada passa em sembla més llunyà. Llunyà com jo mateixa que no em retrobaré mai.*

(I struggle up the hill, running away from my future, out of my present, lost, without knowing who I am or where to find my identity. My identity – it is a castle which recedes into the distance as I walk towards it. Far away like myself and I will never find myself again.[18]

More so than a corpus of postcolonial texts, we could regard postcolonial theory as 'a reading practice'[19] and a way into revising time-encrusted concepts and literary canons. Christine Froula says: 'the opening of the canon entails not only the inclusion of women's texts but the revision of the venerated male texts themselves and, more importantly, of the cultural and institutional authority they enact'.[20] Nowadays women want to change the literary canon, which traditionally has been male-centred and has excluded women's values and writing. The Catalan writer Carme Riera notes the machismo of some critics, for example those who failed to see the eroticism in her book *Epitelis tendríssims* (Tender Epitheliums) just because it is not about male eroticism. She believes that 'the type of eroticism which is the insinuation of desire, more than of its realisation, is feminine, and that this distinction may make it difficult for some male critics to respond to her work'.[21]

Even though it will be a long time before women's writing is valued as it should be, feminist approaches thus far have contributed much to the endeavour. In a similar way, postcolonial theory has increased mainstream appreciation and study of marginalised literatures. It has encouraged academics and writers to reconsider in a more critical way the claims of cosmopolitan literature and, in so doing, has changed the literary canon. The authors of *The Empire Writes Back* explain how postcolonial theory is subversive because it questions Eurocentric assertions. The same can be said of feminism in relation to patriarchal assertions:

> Directly and indirectly, in Salman Rushdie's phrase, the 'Empire writes back' to the imperial 'centre', not only through nationalist assertion, proclaiming itself central and self-determining, but even more radically by questioning the bases of European and British metaphysics, challenging the world-view that can polarise centre and periphery in the first place. In this way,

concepts of polarity, of 'governor and governed, ruler and ruled' . . . are challenged as an essential way of ordering reality.[22]

Postcolonial literature is, therefore, politically engaged. Not only is it about the imaginative and creative responses to domination,[23] it questions the nature of domination and the bases of Western metaphysics. It is about 'challenging the world-view that can polarise centre and periphery'.[24] As a result, such polar concepts as 'governor and governed, ruler and ruled' are challenged as an essential way of ordering reality. In a parallel way, for French feminism, it is crucial to challenge the basic polarity of man–woman. Julia Kristeva does not see any other option but to deconstruct the binary oppositions of masculinity and femininity.[25]

Thus it emerges that feminism and postcolonialism share a common interest: 'to invert the structures of domination, substituting, for instance, a female tradition or traditions in place of a male-dominated canon'.[26] The willingness to engage critically with women's roles in the world induces some women to take a more generalised view of oppression. In fact, feminism was reborn together with Marxism as a general and committed fight against oppression. A Catalan poet, Maria Mercè Marçal, author of a popular poem '*Divisa*' (Motto), contends that all kinds of oppression must be fought against, as they reinforce each other and are all equally unfair: '*A l'atzar agraeixo tres dons, haver nascut dona / de classe baixa i nació oprimida / I el tèrbol atzur de tres voltes rebel*' (I am grateful to fate for three gifts: to have been born a woman, from the working class and an oppressed nation. And the turbid azure of being three times a rebel).[27]

Although not adopted uncritically here, postcolonial theory should provide a useful theoretical vantage point for the study of the two societies. Colin Graham finds postcolonial theory useful precisely because it turns its attention to gender, class, ethnicity, race and localised history. 'Marginalised' perspectives from each of these areas can be employed to fracture the homogeneity of the nationalist discourse, which pervades so much writing on Catalonia as well as on Ireland.[28]

In order to make those enormous changes, the postcolonial text becomes itself a site of struggle for linguistic control. The connections between power and truth, trapped in the language, are crucial as defined by Foucault: 'The discourse of the post-colonial is therefore grounded on a struggle for power, that power focused in the control of the metropolitan language. Power is invested in the language because it provides the terms in which truth itself is constituted.'[29] However, there is a danger of copying the metropolitan model: 'The struggle for power over truth in some senses "mimics" the metropolitan impulse of dominance'.[30] That explains why it is so important to be aware of how those mechanisms of power work in order not to mimic them but to create new ones. Thus, 'only by stressing the way in which the text transforms the societies and institutions within which it functions . . . can such a mimicry be avoided and replaced by a theory and practice which embraces difference and absence as material signs of power rather than negation, of freedom not subjugation, of creativity not limitation'.[31]

Postcolonial literatures have commonalties in style. They tend to show insecurities and confusion because they arise out of a past of intolerance. There is a strong desire to find new truths, new realities. Often, post-colonial individuals write just because they are postcolonial and they pick up on some anomalies in the culture in which they grew up and which they want to correct. For example, the Catalan poet, Narcís Comadira, says he writes simply because he is Catalan and in his youth he discovered that his language was banned. He decided to contribute and used his energies towards the 'normalisation' of his culture.[32] Another Catalan writer, Montserrat Roig, proclaims her wish to produce a 'perfect novel as a contribution to Catalan culture'.[33] The poet Nuala Ní Dhomhnaill writes in Irish because it is her first love, even if it is harder to win a reputation in a minority language.

Another of the features of the postcolonial condition is the sense of victimhood. In Ireland, the historian Líam Kennedy talks about the Irish MOPE syndrome (the sense of being the Most Oppressed People Ever).[34] A somewhat similar observation has been made by the Catalan writer, Marta Pessarrodona. He says that Catalan people are pessimistic and that Catalonia is not so much a country as *'una manera de queixar-se'* (a way of complaining).[35] More directly, the singer, poet and musician, Lluís Llach, argues that Catalonia has done little else but express its victimhood. He notes that the Catalan anthem is one of very few composed in a minor key to express sadness. The legend says that the Catalan flag was made by a man who was dying and he used the blood of his four fingers to trace its form. This explains why it has four red stripes. Moreover, the National Day of Catalonia celebrates its major historical defeat. Llach concludes that Catalonia is a defeated country and that Catalans have been losers in history. Being losers has some advantages: perhaps 'we are tolerant because we are losers', he says.[36] The Catalan politician and economist, Ernest Lluch, who would subscribe to a more moderate nationalist position, claims that defeat has been the normal reality for the Catalan people and is what has led them to 'a collective psychology which tends towards pessimism as a permanent state'. He thinks it is crucial that politicians change this collective feeling which can lead to difficulties and still greater pessimism. Lluch suggests that Catalan people should forget what they are never going to get.[37] There is something else which seems to show a collective feeling of pessimism and that is the question of the possible future loss of the Catalan language. Linguists, sociologists and nationalist politicians often refer to the future of the Catalan language in an era of globalisation and they do it with a touch of fear in their voices.

Being a Catalan or an Irish woman implies being 'doubly colonised', in the sense used here, and confers on their writing elements of a 'double pessimism'. Anne Charlon makes the point that female Catalan characters in the writings of the 1960s and 1970s come across as frustrated, with feelings of confusion in a world which is hostile to them. This sense of hopelessness is rife because the possibilities of escape are so limited. This is not surprising as many women could not work outside their homes then, and education directed them to marriage as an only and necessary path to follow. Even success at university was considered bad for women. Love relationships were not satisfactory either. In the face of such life circumstances, pessimism, sometimes bordering on despair, was only natural.[38]

It is time to draw out more explicitly some of the parallels between postcolonial subjects and women in patriarchal society. Both share a subservient status within the society in which they find themselves.[39] They each possess the characteristic of 'otherness'. Their minds – some would argue their very psychology – are dominated and colonised by male power systems and imperious male modes of thought. It is hardly surprising, therefore, that women writers and critics have elaborated on these themes and connections. In the words of Ann Owens Weekes: 'women, like colonised peoples, have had to repress their desires, women's fiction has been subject to the same kinds of repression as women themselves, repression which forced early writers to encode their concerns in a muted voice'.[40] In support of her view, she quotes Elizabeth Janeway, who notes that: 'Cut off from authority, wealth, and overt decision making . . . women resemble the Gaelic-Irish of the eighteenth century'.[41] Weekes also draws on the historian Karl Bottigheimer who argues: 'Excluded from landed wealth, from political life, from the "official church", the Irish erected a counter-culture, not so much rebellious as evasive, a strategy, like women's, decreed by their similar repression, and one whose end was also survival'.[42]

The Irish poet Nuala Ní Dhomhnaill takes a long-term perspective on women and postcolonial Ireland:

As we aborigines are just now getting back to what we were going on
about before the Norman invasion, likewise we female aborigines are
beginning to get back to what we were going on about before we were
interrupted by the male side of the psyche that caused Christianity and
witch-burning. We are going back to where the sibyl was interrupted in
mid-sentence by the invasions.[43]

In literature, it may be said, the postcolonial and the woman's text is a
space of resistance. It seeks to break tradition and the text becomes a 'site
of struggle' where women 'write back' to their metropolitan centre which
is the patriarchal text. Thus the colonised woman writer has space to
manoeuvre, to reject an ideology of domination and destruction and,
under appropriate circumstances, she has the opportunity to be creative
and fight back. It is of course true that both women and colonised peoples
have been forced to articulate their experiences in the language of their
oppressors. This point is made explicitly in *The Empire Writes Back*:
'Women, like post-colonial peoples, have had to construct a language of
their own when their only available "tools" are those of the "coloniser"'.[44]
Having no language other than that of the coloniser's, 'writing back' is not
an easy venture. According to Ashcroft *et al*:

> Women in many societies have been relegated to the position of 'other',
> marginalised and, in a metaphorical sense, 'colonised', forced to pursue
> guerrilla warfare against imperial domination from positions deeply
> embedded in, yet fundamentally alienated from, that imperium. They share
> with colonised races and peoples an intimate experience of the politics of
> oppression and repression, and like them they have been forced to articulate
> their experiences in the language of their oppressors.[45]

Writers in the postcolonial tradition and women writers question
dominant assumptions and try to create alternatives in their own writing.
But this is in more recent times. The historical experience, as Ailbhe Smyth
observes is that women in Ireland have been silenced. The traditional view
of Ireland as a woman, weak and victimised as in the *Cathleen Ní Houlihan*
tradition, converts Ireland and women to 'the other' and weakens both:

> That is how 'men like to imagine her' and she has no space, no voice, no
> right to imagine herself differently – or even to imagine at all. As symbol,
> 'woman' is allowed no history, no story, no capacity for change – she is a
> given. Her particularity is overwhelmed by the primary demands of the
> nation. To be free, therefore, Irish women must find some way of extri-
> cating themselves from the double burden of patriarchy and colonisation,
> whether consciously identified or not.[46]

In this journey back, women face resistance by men, which can in turn spill over easily into violence. Violence is the last and fatal consequence of both postcolonial power and male aggression. A common theme in Irish women's writing, Ann Owens Weekes notes, is the link between domestic and political violence:

> The Rackrent men in Maria Edgeworth's *Castle Rackrent* are equally appalling as husbands and as landlords. E.OE. Somerville and Martin Ross present an unappealing and amoral character in *The Real Charlotte*, but depict her nevertheless as a victim of an unjust society. The Eden of Anglo-Ireland, as Elizabeth Bowen presents it in *The Last September*, depends upon Anglo-Irish women and the Gaelic-Irish population accepting without question the word of domestic or colonising fathers. The security of the Gaelic-Irish society in Kate O'Brien's *Without My Cloak* also rests upon the sacrifice of women, as does the independent state posited in *The Land of Spices*. The Gaelic-Irish warriors of 1922 and 1979 are both equally willing to exploit women in Julia O'Faolain's *No Country for Young Men*. And domestic repression reflects national repression in almost all Jennifer Johnston's work, most overtly in *Shadows on Our Skin*.[47]

It is noticeable that recourse to feminist and postcolonial theories is much more highly developed in Irish than in Catalan literature.[48] There are few feminist studies, in relation to literature or history, emanating from Catalonia. Those which do exist have been carried out primarily by foreign academics, most notably, the Irish Mary Nash, the North Americans Kathleen McNerney and Geraldine C. Nichols, and the French critic Anne Charlon. Catalan universities do not have departments of women's studies. Of more fundamental significance, there has existed and there still exists a resistance towards feminism in Catalonia. Feminism is seen as a radical ideology espoused by extremists. As a result of this marginalisation, it is not perceived as an attractive or potentially useful theoretical perspective in literary studies.

It is surely no coincidence, then, that the neglect of women writers has been more pronounced in Catalonia than in Ireland. In her book *Double Minorities of Spain*,[49] the critic Kathleen McNerney has collected the biographies of 421 women writers from Catalonia. Only three of these 421 women have received any mention in conventional criticism: Isabel de Villena (1430–90), Caterina Albert 'Víctor Català' (1869–1966) and Mercè Rodoreda (1908–83). A Catalan short-story writer, Carme Riera, referring to her most successful book, says:

> *El que més recordo és la gran indiferència que vaig sentir per part de la crítica. Vaig publicar* Te deix . . . *l'any 1975 i, fins al 1977, no va aparèixer cap crítica del llibre.*

A les escriptores, ens han perdonat molt la vida. Hem tingut èxit de vendes, però la crítica ha continuat considerant que la qualitat era menor.

(The thing I recall the most is the great sense of indifference I received from critics. I published *I Give You, My Love, the Sea as a Token* in the year 1975 and there was no criticism of my book until 1977. Critics have spared women writers' lives. We have been successful at selling but critics still believe that our quality was less.)[50]

McNerney points out that these writers have been marginalised by prejudice in relation to both their sex and their language.[51] 'Spanish' has traditionally meant the Castilian language, and 'Spanish literature' has meant literature written in Castilian. The other languages of the state, the languages 'at the margins', tend to be ignored by the 'centred peoples'.[52] These forms of dismissal have encouraged nationalist movements in Catalonia, the Basque Country and Galicia, according to McNerney.[53]

But the walls of prejudice exist within Catalan society as well. According to Mary Nash, in Catalonia it is very difficult for women to get into powerful positions. When a woman talks in the public sphere she is generally not listened to closely. Power is still very much under male control.[54] The situation appears to be worse than in Ireland where, for instance, women account for fifty per cent of the jobs in the mass media and are better represented in public life more generally.

Catalan studies have not been opened up to theory in any sustained way, as indicated earlier. Lately people are timidly starting to use the term 'colonisation' as applied to the Catalan experience.[55] Certainly there is an unease among Catalan intellectuals and writers in dealing with an unpleasant past. A Catalan writer, Víctor Mora, complains that more research should have been devoted to the Francoist period:

si s'hagués parlat de les coses tal com cal ... explicant que va ser el franquisme i la lluita contra Franco, possiblement ara no hi hauria tants nous nazis.

(If people had talked more about it ... explaining what francoism was and the struggle against Franco, probably now there would not be so many new Nazis.)[56]

Modern Spain was dominated by a fascist dictatorship for forty years, one of whose main concerns was to repress any form of culture which was not Spanish and expressed in the Spanish language. Thus the state was hostile to the Catalan, the Basque and the Galician cultures. This is well summed up in the famous Francoist statement: *'España antes roja que rota'* (Spain will be red before it is broken). As in other fascist regimes, the exclusive mission of women was conceived in terms of being housewives and having as many children as possible. Prizes for the most numerous families were very popular during the forty years of the regime (1939–75). Needless to say, being a female writer and writing in Catalan was to swim against the tide.

Irish society was also deeply conservative during those years, though in different ways. Having achieved political independence, Ireland went through a period of self-immersion in order to 'invent' a national culture, a process which extends back into the nationalist struggles of the nineteenth century. Writing at a tangent to the official ideology was not easy, particularly for women. Many felt the need to leave, such as Kate O'Brien, Edna O'Brien and the historian Mary Nash who moved to Barcelona.

Not only was it difficult for women to write but, in addition, the subject matter of their writing, which was different from that of male writing, had difficulty being accepted within the masculine canon. Women's writing is frequently a literature of confession, as Edna O'Brien relates: 'My work is very close to my life, not necessarily to the smaller events but to the main story'.[57] The importance of the autobiographical in women's writing has been, at times, the reason for its marginalisation, according to Nuala O'Faolain:

> it is the absence of realism from our great literary tradition which obliterates women. Because realism is the only mode available to women writers who want to write to and of women. I do not mean that women could not and do not avail themselves of non-realist devices, but I do mean that the core of women's writing has always been confessional and has, in the last few decades, become autobiographical. Its ultimate realisation would be a realism based on personal realisation: but the ultimate in this or any other form of expression is only a guide here.[58]

Expanding the canon is surely one of the more important objectives of postcolonial and feminist theories, as applied to literature. It is now time to examine the relationship of women to the canon in the respective cultures.

The first chapter introduces the genre of the short story in Catalonia and Ireland. The short story has received comparatively little attention from critics who have tended to see it as a minor genre, one in which a writer serves an apprenticeship before going on to write something 'serious' – a novel or a play. Yet in Ireland and Catalonia the short story has had particular popularity. In the Irish case, the genre has been linked to the oral tale, whereas in the Catalan case the more obvious link has been with the struggle for survival of the Catalan language. As a minority culture, and one subject to institutionalised displeasure, the prospects of being a full-time professional writer in Catalan literature were limited to say the least.

The short story, as it happens, is a popular genre among women writers. One explanation for this may have to do with time. Many women, because of their domestic role, have little leisure time at home, especially if they have children. Female writers, like Mary Lavin and Mary Beckett, wrote in the company of their children (we do not find many male writers doing so). There are other possible explanatory factors. French feminists, for example, often use poetry to express their ideas and, like poetry, the short story is a very malleable genre, open to what Julia Kristeva calls the semiotic language. This is in contrast to the novel or drama which is closer to the symbolic order. In this sense, the short story gives greater freedom to the writer. Thus in a collection of short stories, the writer can offer a great plurality of viewpoints – what Edna O'Brien has called 'lantern slides'.[59] This diversity may conceivably be of particular value to women who, if one is to believe Luce Irigaray, seek out plurality.[60] Though not obviously so, postcolonial theory also offers new vantage points from which to analyse the short genre.

The second chapter deals with power relations within marriage. While the situation for women has undoubtedly changed over time in the sense that marriage and procreation are not the only missions women have in life, women are still under greater pressure than men to be successful in the domestic sphere. They are still entrusted with emotional communication within families and the bulk of domestic chores. As a result, women have less time and energy to invest in themselves and in their own careers as compared to men. In many instances, but again more so in the past, they are economically dependent within marriage. This is the only chapter, it may be noted, in which analysis of Catalan and Irish short stories is combined. This is because there is a marked similarity between the views of Catalan and Irish women writers on marriage. This allows a simultaneous treatment of the two literatures, something which proved unmanageable in other chapters. In the subsequent chapters significant points of contrast as well as similarity emerged, whose origins lay in different historical experiences, and which dictated a different strategy of presentation.

In Chapter Two it is suggested that the resemblance between women and colonised peoples is perhaps closer still in the case of *married* women, where the institution of marriage might be conceived as the key colonising device. Certainly in much female writing marriage is portrayed as a repressive arrangement as far as wives are concerned. Wives are frequently disempowered beings subject to the authority, sometimes the whim, of their lords and husbands. As a result, we find powerless, lonely and victimised women. They are burdened by the pressure of family, marriage, society and work. As a consequence, their confidence is eroded and they suffer identity crises. The nature of these crises, it might be suggested, bears some similarity to those experienced by countries which have been colonised. Edna O'Brien, for example, mixes these themes in her story, 'Honeymoon'. About her new husband, who is not Irish, she says:

> He was not a native and sometimes she got the feeling that he had no pity for those people, her people, who had for so long lived in subjugation and who like her were ashamed to confront themselves. He was twice her age, and she obeyed him in everything, even in the type of shoes she was to wear – completely flat shoes which as it happened gave her a pain in her instep.[61]

O'Brien is drawing parallels between the colonial experience of the Irish and the woman who, subservient to her husband, experiences physical pain. Ironically, this happens on their honeymoon, a time that is expected to be happy. She notices also that both the 'colonised Irish' and the 'colonised woman' are lacking in confidence. They are both powerless.

The third chapter, 'Towards a Feminisation of Nationalism', traces women's involvement with nationalism, including its violent manifestations, and the representation of nationalism in short stories. In Edna O'Brien's stories we are made aware of the contemporary importance of history for the Irish, and she herself has articulated her nationalist views on Northern Ireland on several occasions. The Belfast writer, Mary Beckett, has given voice to the nightmare of living in the middle of the conflict. Julia O'Faolain develops a perceptive analysis in 'It's a Long Way to Tipperary', ironically drawing out the contradictions of an Irish officer returning home, having fought in the British army in the two world wars.

Catalan writers have also shown a strong interest in nationalism but in a different way. This was through the act of using the Catalan language as their literary language, even though at times this was neither prestigious nor profitable. The commitment shown to the Catalan language has been remarkable, because it has meant renouncing the much larger audience of the Spanish-speaking world. Interestingly, Catalan and Irish writers are equally impatient with the patriarchal image of the nation as a woman who needs to be saved or died for. In all the stories explored in this work, women writers react strongly against violence, whether national or domestic in origin.

The fourth chapter examines the subject of 'decolonising language'. In Catalonia the native language has been maintained, whereas in Ireland the Irish language has been largely lost. The result has been major and differing consequences for the two societies. Imposing names and languages has been an important part of the process of colonisation and, perhaps less obviously, also a means of oppressing women. From a feminist perspective, language is a phallogocentric construction. Women need to change language, it is contended, in order to be able to find equality. Dale Spender asserts that:

> This monopoly over language is one of the means by which males have ensured their own primacy, and consequently have ensured the invisibility or 'other' nature of females, and this primacy is perpetuated while women continue to use, unchanged, the language which we have inherited.[62]

Irish writers whose work is explored in this study include Edna O'Brien, Julia O'Faolain, Mary Beckett, Eilís Ní Dhuibhne, Anne Devlin, Angela Bourke, Mary Dorcey, Clare Boylan and Katy Hayes. The Catalan writers include Caterina Albert 'Víctor Català', Mercè Rodoreda, Carme Riera, Isabel-Clara Simó, Montserrat Roig, Núria Pompeia, Maria Àngels Anglada and Imma Monsó. These are leading practitioners of the genre of the short story in Ireland and Catalonia. Each writer deals extensively with love, marriage, nationalism and language, which are the themes of central concern to my study. The range of writers is wide, so as to give space to a variety of viewpoints and to leave open the possibility of shifts in perspective over time. In relation to the latter, for example, it would not be surprising if the influence of the women's movement was such as to change or colour the representation of women on the part of newer, younger writers. We shall see.

Before launching into the main body of the work, it is worth making a few general observations regarding the critical literature as it currently stands. Studies of the Irish or the Catalan short story are not plentiful, few adopt a comparative perspective, and none (so far as I know) use Irish and Catalan literatures as mutual reference points. The present book, which adopts an explicitly comparative approach, will hopefully prove fruitful in terms of opening up some fresh perspectives. Finally, by engaging with different areas of marginality – the genre of the short story, the gender of women, the status of the postcolonial society – the book itself is a statement of the importance of the margins. By focusing its attention in this way, it seeks to destabilise conventional hierarchies of ideas and categories, in the process celebrating the subordinate, the marginal, the excluded.

CHAPTER ONE

The short story in Ireland and Catalonia: a postcolonial genre?

He descobert que el conte es un gran gènere.
(I have discovered that the short story is a great genre.)
Mercè Rodoreda[1]

INTRODUCTION

THE SHORT story in Ireland and Catalonia forms the raw material of this book. More specifically, the focus is on the genre of the short story as practised by women writers. This chapter will explore various aspects of the short story, including the characteristic conditions under which it is produced, its popularity as a medium for women's writing and its resonance in the contexts of postcolonial societies. Some of the issues are intrinsically elusive – the relationship between genre and gender, or the influence of the postcolonial condition on the choice of genre – but no less worth pursuing for all that.

By way of beginning, it may be helpful to consider the genre in a wider context than that of Ireland and Catalonia. In terms of European literature, short-story writing has been a striking feature of literary production in many societies, notably Russia and France. Equally striking, though somewhat paradoxical in view of the popularity of the genre, has been its relative neglect by literary critics. It has often been considered as a minor or a learning genre. It is as if the short-story writer invites the reproach of being one who is just not capable of producing a more complete work, with the novel as the obvious reference point. Still, length alone should not be the distinguishing criterion of merit: poetry ranks higher in the hierarchy of literary production. Somehow, short stories appear less worthy of serious critical scrutiny than novels, drama and poetry.

One notes also that short-story writers themselves have confessed to feeling under pressure to produce novels. The Catalan short-story writer Ernest Martínez Ferrando is a case in point. One of his sympathetic reviewers, Díez Canedo, rounded off an article about Martínez Ferrando's stories in 1919 by saying: '*Martínez nos debe ahora la "novedad grande" que se le puede exigir a muy pocos*' (Martínez now owes us the 'big novelty' which can be required of the very few).[2] Some years later, the Catalan writer C.A. Jordana was making a similar point: '*Qualsevol dia l'Ernest Martínez Ferrando ens sorprendrà amb una obra perfecta*' (Some day, now, Ernest Martínez Ferrando will surprise us with a perfect piece of work). By this he meant a novel.[3] Vicent Alonso adds that, in general, when a writer has produced one or two novels s/he is referred to as a novelist even if the main output remains the short genre.[4] This is notably the case in relation to such fine writers Mercè Rodoreda or Caterina Albert. Writing about Mercè Rodoreda in 1998, the critic Jaume Aulet judged: '*és bàsicament una novel.lista que se serveix del conte com a gènere més aviat subsidiari i d'exercitació, cosa que no vol dir que no arribi a obtenir resultats importants*'.[5] (She is basically a novelist who makes use of the rather subsidiary and learning genre of the short story, but this does not mean that she does not manage to pull off achievements). In her book on Catalan female writers, Anne Charlon refers to all of them as novelists, even if some of them are good short-story writers, as if by using that term she was somehow dignifying their work. Regrettably, and this is more true of Catalan literary studies, prejudices against the short narrative form persist.

One can only speculate about the reasons for the notion that the short story is a minor genre. One possibility is the historic association between the short story and the children's tale. In fact, one of the Catalan terms for a short story is '*conte*', which also means tale, and which suggests '*orature*' and fantastic elements. Orature is, as a matter of fact, a common narrative technique in postcolonial literature. In European culture, oral literature has been devalued as 'uncivilized' or 'primitive' and less 'abstract', whereas the written word has been accorded a privileged position.[6] Ian Reid, however, believes that despite being the most widely read of all modern genres, the short story is marginalised because of a different set of associations: the genre has been closely linked with magazine publishing. Many short stories first saw the light of day in popular or semi-popular magazines. Reid recalls: 'Magazine publication expanded hugely during the nineteenth century, tending to encourage stereotypes, mannerisms, gimmickry and the like. Consequently critics are sometimes reluctant to take the short story seriously as a substantial genre in its own right.'[7] While it is true that novels were sometimes serialised in magazines also (one thinks of the works of Charles Dickens, for example), the association was less pronounced. The comparative newness of the genre, at least in its modern form, may also be relevant. Elizabeth Bowen, with pardonable exaggeration, called the short story 'a young art', and 'a child of this century'.[8]

Turning from general to more specific musings, we can at least agree that short-story writing has enjoyed great popularity in Catalonia and Ireland. In the introduction to his *Irish Short Stories*, Valentin Iremonger observes: 'The Irish genius, always predominantly lyrical, has in this century expressed itself peculiarly well through the medium of the short story; it has also expressed itself with alarming frequency in that genre'.[9] David Marcus has made similar points in his many anthologies of Irish short stories. On the Catalan side, the critic Joan Triadú holds that the short story and poetry are the most popular genres in Catalan literature, but adds gratuitously that the former is a minor genre.[10] It may well be that, in view of the earlier discussion, the term 'alarming frequency' may not be wholly innocent. The short story has been less valued in Catalonia than in Ireland. Still, in terms of reception, the short story has enjoyed a wide popularity since the period of cultural revival in the late nineteenth century. Interestingly, a cultural revival happened in both Ireland and Catalonia at approximately the same time, suggesting these in turn were currents within a wider European flood of cultural change.

A simple, partly economic explanation for the popularity of the short story in the two societies is that it is easier and cheaper to publish short stories, in comparison to novels, for instance. But there may be deeper, more complex reasons. In his introduction to *The Lonely Voice*, a volume dedicated to the short story, Frank O'Connor coined a phrase – 'the submerged population group' – to refer to the Irish.[11] According to O'Connor, the short story not only attracts marginalised individuals and groups but also Ireland itself could be conceived to be marginalised in much the same way. He goes on to claim: 'without the concept of a normal society the novel is impossible'.[12] Translated into Catalan, we could talk about the 'abnormality' of both nation and language. The assumption here seems to be that Ireland was not a 'normal' country, hence it had produced comparatively few novelists.[13] Perhaps because it had been colonised, because it had lost its indigenous language and other cultural moorings, Ireland (or Catalonia) had evolved historically in a way which had left it as less than 'normal'. Part of that legacy might have been a lack of self-confidence on the part of writers who would otherwise have aspired to writing novels. Read in this way, O'Connor's argument has the flavour of contemporary post-colonial thought: 'The post-colonial text is itself a site of struggle for linguistic control, as the power which it makes manifest is yielded up to the appropriating discourse. This struggle, as we have shown, extends to the disputes concerning theme, form, genre definition, implicit systems of manner, custom, and value.'[14]

Similar lines of reasoning might be deployed in relation to Catalonia by highlighting its colonial heritage. This necessarily leads us to explore the particular political and cultural histories of the two societies in an attempt to identify the conditions which have given rise to the pre-eminence of the short story in the two societies.

HISTORICAL CONTEXTS

Catalonia

The War of the Spanish Succession (1701–14), which put the House of Bourbon on the throne, led to the annexation of Catalonia and its subordination to a centralised Spanish state. The new king, Philip V, banned the use of Catalan in Catalonia, Valencia and the Balearic Islands. In the words of the historian Albert Balcells, Philip V 'abolished all Catalan political institutions by right of conquest, and imposed Castilian laws, absolutism, and centralism . . . Catalonia's former political system was replaced by one in which royal authority was all-encompassing . . . Catalonia became a country overburdened by taxation in comparison with Castile'.[15] One of the historic ironies, however, is that Catalonia went on to become the first region in Spain to industrialise, thereby creating an indigenous bourgeoisie which was to play a major role in the cultural revival of the nineteenth century. The aims of this revival movement were far reaching: to claim (or reclaim) the centrality of the language in Catalan cultural life and to recover Catalonia's political institutions.

Historians seem to agree that the rise of national feeling was a reaction to the authoritarian exercise of power by the military and political authorities centred in Madrid, building on traditions of conquest and loss, and encouraged by the rise of nationalisms elsewhere in Europe. Despite what we might call the political and cultural colonisation endured by the people of Catalonia since the beginning of the eighteenth century, Catalan was still the language spoken by the majority at the end of the nineteenth century. This contrasts with the case of Ireland, where Irish had largely died out by 1900, apart from some remote districts in the west. Nonetheless, the situation of the native language in Catalonia was fraught with difficulty and its future was far from assured. In terms of the language itself, it lacked a grammatical infrastructure. Much of the thrust of the cultural revival was, therefore, directed at issues of language and literature.

Catalan *Modernisme* (in English, art nouveau), around 1888–1911, was a striking artistic current in the development of modern Catalonia, embracing such great architects as Antonio Gaudí; Puig i Cadafalch and Domènech i Muntaner painters such as Joan Cases and Santiago Russiñol, and writers like Joan Maragall, Caterina Albert and Miquel Costa i Llobera. The term suggests the Catalan wished to achieve the modernisation of a nineteenth-century culture considered archaic and provincial in order to create a modern national culture. It was an effort to experiment, to innovate, and to open up to European culture:

> Associated with the growth of political Catalanism (Catalan Nationalism), awareness increased that only by becoming cosmopolitan and abreast of the latest advances abroad would Catalan culture shake off its provincial complexion, thus to attain a higher degree of differentiation and independence from perceived deficiencies in the official Spanish-Castilian culture centred in Madrid.[16]

During this period, Catalan nationalism was expressing itself more intensively through culture than politics, although politics was also going to play an important part in the national revival.

Catalan *Modernisme* was an eclectic movement but Naturalism and Symbolism were its vital sources. It was critical of a materialistic society and attributed to art and to the artist-intellectual a messianic function. An interest in rural themes and settings – what has been called *Ruralisme* – formed part of its mission and can be related to the growth of nationalism and its quest for historic roots.

> Ultimately it is etymology which explains the primary energy of Modernisme in relation to its counterparts abroad: a question of creating, within the exhilaration of the Catalan context, a *new* art, a *modern* art seen as appropriate to the dawning of a new era, and to a reaffirmation of Catalan-ness.[17]

To explain the nature of Catalan nationalism, Colm Tóibín quotes a Catalan architect and politician, Josep Puig i Cadafalch, who was an important figure in Catalan *Modernisme*: 'The most important thing we have done is that we have made a modern art, taking our traditional art as a basis, adorning it with new material, solving contemporary problems with a national spirit'.[18] Tóibín points out that there were many things in common between Ireland and Catalonia during this particular period in particular:

The fetishisation of certain parts of the landscape – Montseny, for example, or the Canigo – bore a great resemblance to the sanctity of the Aran Islands and the Blasket Islands in Ireland. The attempt by Yeats and Lady Gregory and Douglas Hyde to surround the Gaelic past with holiness had loud echoes in the efforts by Catalan architects and artists, from Gaudí to Miró, to establish the Romanesque tradition as quintessentially Catalan while the rest of Spain was Moorish. And the attempt, too, by Yeats and Synge, and indeed Joyce, to embrace modernity and Europe as a way of keeping England at bay was close to Domenech's use of iron and steel and modern systems while Spain slept.[19]

The revival took a more sharply political turn during the first quarter of the twentieth century with the rise of a new literary movement known in Catalonia as *Noucentisme*. More practically-minded than the idealistic *Modernisme*, the aim was to create some stability in the Catalan language, culture and literary aesthetics. *Noucentisme*, despite being (or perhaps because it was) a cultural vehicle for a nationalist political ideology, had some success in this respect. Noucentistes organised a number of outstanding events such as the First International Conference of the Catalan Language (1906) and, in the following year, the Institute of Catalan Studies, which still exists, was created. A major, if belated, step in the maintenance of the language – the creation of a standard grammar – was realised in 1913. This was several centuries after its French and Spanish equivalents.

On a political level, some limited forms of local democracy were instituted in 1914, the first since centralised power and control were imposed two centuries earlier. This experiment did not, however, last long. In 1923 the Spanish dictator, Primo de Rivera, crushed these embryonic political developments, fearing their separatist potential. The political setbacks of *Noucentisme* plunged its cultural wing into crisis also, but opposition to the dictatorship was maintained, being expressed through the medium of culture as much as political activity. The legacy of Noucentisme has been fundamental to twentieth-century Catalonia.

In 1931, following further political upheavals, an autonomous Catalan Government was re-established. This gave a powerful, if short-lived, stimulus to Catalan culture and artistic endeavour. Tragically, within a short space of years, war intervened. During the Civil War (1936–39), Catalan artists and writers came to the fore as advocates for the republican side and in defence of the Catalan cause.[20] Despite the disruptions of the war, it proved possible to convene a literary conference, the Second International Conference of Antifascist writers, which took place in 1937.

The development of Catalan culture and literature after the Civil War was heavily constrained by the difficult political and social circumstances in which the country found itself. Catalan society might be said to have experienced a double repression – one specific, the other more general. One was directed against reds (republicans and left-wing elements) and the other against Catalonians in general, simply because of their nationality. Their collective 'crime' was to have challenged the 'unity of the fatherland' (Spain).[21] In terms of this imagery, one might say the military power, or masculine coloniser, had sought to achieve the 'return of the lost daughter' (Catalonia), the feminine colonised.

The repression was not only political but cultural. The Catalan lanuage was banned once again from the public sphere. This was the case, for example, at all levels of education. It applied also to the press and radio where Spanish was substituted. Catalan cultural institutions were suppressed, including publishing houses. Indicative of the new cultural order were statements from the authorities, the police in particular, such as 'Hable usted en cristiano' (use the Christian language), or 'Hable el idioma del imperio' (use the language of the empire). The immediate consequence was that Catalonia lost many of the material resources for the production and reproduction of its culture. Effectively, many of the gains of the previous fifty years in reconstructing the cultural life of Catalonia were being systematically dismantled. Moreover, among the many dead were artists and authors; some of the survivors switched to writing in Spanish, others turned to silence (a form of 'interior exile'). Others still were numbered among the 60,000 Catalan people forced into exile, principally in France and Latin America. France itself was not a safe refuge: some of these exiles were subsequently killed during the German occupation of France, including the president of the Catalan government who was deported to Spain by the Gestapo and executed in 1940.

Efforts to impose the Spanish language and Spanish cultural forms proceeded apace during the forty years of the Francoist dictatorship. A tight censorship, based on a law enacted in 1938, curbed freedom of expression in the cultural and political spheres. This was based on fascist and Nazi models and was not seriously amended until 1966. The Catalan language was derided as little more than a regional dialect. Obviously no state resources were available for the promotion of distinctively Catalan forms of artistic expression. Not only was the language increasingly confined to private spaces, but upper-class and middle-class people, especially in urban areas, began to change their family language to Spanish. They felt ashamed of speaking Catalan and Spanish came to be seen as the high-status medium of expression.

During the 1960s the political and economic situation improved in Spain generally and in Catalonia in particular. In the case of the latter, though, there were some problems in accepting and integrating over a million Andalucian immigrants who came to find work in Catalonia. Catalan resistance to Madrid and Francoism stiffened. Unlike other minority nationalisms, such as the Irish, this took a primarily cultural rather than a militantly political form. Communists, socialists, radical intellectuals, some members of the Catholic Church as well as artists met together to promote their common cause. The point of unity and mobilisation was Catalan culture. They created organisations such as cultural groups, literary magazines and publishing companies to promote Catalan culture. While many writers lived in exile, there were also those survivors of the 1930s and the 1940s within Catalonia who were only too glad to contribute to the stirrings of revival as spaces for artistic expression opened up. For these, a sense of cultural nationalism was both a source of inspiration and motivation.

Ireland

Let us now look at the Irish case. The colonial conquest of Ireland was completed in the seventeenth century. Economy and population expanded substantially during the following century. Civil disabilities suffered by Roman Catholics and Dissenters, at first severe, were gradually relaxed though by no means eliminated. The century was generally peaceful, until in the closing decade national and sectarian conflict engulfed parts of the country, most notably Ulster and south Leinster. The Act of Union in 1800, incorporating Ireland into the United Kingdom of Great Britain and Ireland, followed on the heels of these disturbances. The Union set the framework for political and cultural politics on the island for more than a century.

The period between the Union and the Great Famine of the 1840s constitutes the bleakest period in the economic fortunes of the island. Poverty and population grew alarmingly in the decades before 1845, and when potato blight struck in that year and again in 1846 the economy of the numerous cotters and labourers was devastated. By the time the Famine had run its course in 1850, at least a million had died of famine or famine-related diseases and another million had fled the stricken island.

While living standards rose in the fifty years after the Famine, most of Ireland outside the north-east did not industrialise. Thus, when the Irish Free State came into being in 1922, it was economically heavily dependent on agriculture and still experiencing substantial migration. The historian Joe Lee observes that Ireland's economic situation after the British withdrawal was worse than under the British. In *Inventing Ireland*, Declan Kiberd blames colonisation for poor economic performance, but Colm Tóibín suggests a very different interpretation: 'it is just as likely that the way in which Ireland was invented, with so much emphasis on the Gaelic past and foreign occupation and so little on how people lived and what they wanted, meant that economic performance would never be a priority for an Irish government'.[22]

At independence, therefore, according to Terence Brown, 'there was no self-confident national bourgeoisie with control over substantial wealth'.[23] Moreover, he believes the society was lacking in cultural and social innovation. Still, one needs to recall that this self-same society had shown very considerable cultural vitality during the literary and cultural renaissance of the late nineteenth and early twentieth centuries.

The years after independence were characterised by conservatism in the policies of the new state and in society at large. In part this can be attributed to the strongly Catholic ethos of Irish society. More fundamental, perhaps, was the agrarian character of Irish economy and society: in 1926 one out of every two persons still derived their livelihood from the land. The new government made a large effort to recover the Irish language, building on the efforts of the Gaelic League (founded in 1893) and the Irish Ireland movement. Terence Brown, however, sees the effort to protect the language as conservative and authoritarian: 'The revival attempt, therefore, despite its apparent radicalism, can be seen as rather more a reactionary expression of the deep conservatism of mind that governed public attitudes in the period than as a revolutionary movement'.[24] He is also critical of the importance accorded to Irish in the school curriculum, believing that 'Irish at school was promoted at the expense of standards in other subjects'.[25] Yet, in defence of these policies, it could be argued that the campaign to recover the language was important in the context of state building at this particular juncture in Irish history. Moreover, the costs and limits of the language revival campaign are clearer in retrospect. After all, this was at the dawn of a new era, before experience crushed many of the visionary hopes.

The political revolution in Ireland was accompanied by a desire to reconstruct Irish society in cultural as well as economic and political terms. Much was made of the exceptional character of the Irish experience – the fact that Ireland had escaped the Roman yoke, that it had contributed to the re-civilising of Europe during the Dark Ages, that it had successfully resisted assimilation to English ways over a period of seven centuries, that piety and morality among the Catholic Irish were the wonder of the world. Though the loss of Irish was a severe blow, Catholicism had increasingly been substituted as a badge of identity from at least the period of the Famine onwards. But this unique culture was also perceived to be under threat, chiefly (but not exclusively) from alien influences from abroad.

In 1929 the Irish Censorship Board was established. Unlike the Catalan case, this was self-imposed in response to Irish clerical and lay Catholic pressures. During the next four decades the board succeeded in banning hundreds of books, a significant number of which were by Ireland's leading writers. In cultural terms, a fortress Hibernia was being created in which the people were shielded from the worst excesses of the modern world, or so the guardians of Irish virtue believed. For a number of writers this resulted in exile, self-imposed or otherwise, though hardly with the dire consequences that attended such a fate in a number of continental countries. Among them was Samuel Beckett, and also less well-known poets like Denis Devlin, Brian Coffey and Thomas MacGreevy, who moved to Paris in the 1930s.

Many writers and commentators spoke of the repressive intellectual and social climate of de Valera's Ireland (roughly speaking, the three decades after Eamon de Valera and Fianna Fáil came to power for the first time in the general election of 1932). Yet, despite the undoubted stultification of thought, there were stirrings of change from within. In 1940 Seán O'Faoláin founded the periodical *The Bell*, which provided a platform for critical explorations of Irish life and literature. In his journal O'Faoláin attacked censorship and devoted considerable attention to political and social developments outside Ireland. He was scathing in his criticism: 'the period since independence had seen a kind of putsch which had brought an intellectually and culturally impoverished middle class into power'.[26] In his view, Ireland should look at the future and forget the past. O'Faoláin attacked romantic conceptions of that past, believing that 'Ireland was not a cultural unity but a synthesis, even a mosaic, a hybrid society that had developed following the English conquest'.[27] That meant that the Irish had two languages, Irish and English, and that Anglo-Irish literature was indeed Irish literature. These assertions flew in the face of the dominant ideology. He added that they should celebrate the fact that Irish literature in English had won acclaim. What we see here is an anticipation by Seán O'Faoláin of one of the key concepts to emerge in postcolonial writings, that of 'hybridity':

> Both literary theorists and cultural historians are beginning to recognize cross-culturality as the potential termination point of an apparently endless human history of conquest and annihilation justified by the myth of group purity and as the basis on which the postcolonial world can be creatively stabilised.[28]

Other small magazines and papers afforded spaces within the society for critical thought, though admittedly the audiences were limited. Yet the drive for cultural reconstruction, no less than the weak, dissenting forces within Irish Free State society, failed in its primary task of reshaping Irish cultural life in radically new ways. As Brown summarises: 'the twenty-six counties had remained in many aspects a social province of the UK'.[29]

The 1950s has been described as a decade of stagnation and change. Clearly the economy was in crisis and there was a massive exodus of people from rural Ireland in particular. From the 1960s onwards the modern industrialisation of Ireland, achieved to a substantial degree on the back of huge multinational investment, transformed 'de Valera's Ireland'. Some social commentators wondered to what extent Ireland's traditional identity could be retained in the new circumstances. Minor writers might go on celebrating rural folk tradition to satisfy the dominant ideology, but the increasingly secular and modernising society no longer provided the dissenting artist with manifestations of Irish purity, puritanism and repression, which had been sources of inspiration in the past.

In his influential article 'Who are the Irish?', the Ulster-born critic John Wilson Foster contends that the definition of Irishness, coined during the Revival period, has excluded the Ulster Protestant group. According to Foster, the Irish Literary Revival was elitist and republican, embodying an ideology that was anti-Protestant. Irishness meant being Catholic first, but also being native, rural and Gaelic. Being industrialised and of Northern Protestant stock was, then, identified as the opposite, almost the antithesis, of being Irish. Foster suggests no one wants to claim second-class identity. So, instead of claiming Irishness, Ulster Protestants prefer to claim first-class Ulsterness, within or without a constitutional Britishness.[30]

Foster views Ireland as petit-bourgeois and provincial, dominated numerically by small farmers. From these characteristics, the rejection of the Protestants of the north follows. However, this phase of hermeticism was perhaps difficult to avoid in order to 'invent Ireland', to use Declan Kiberd's expression. In the rush to reconstruct itself, nationalist Ireland largely ignored the Protestant minority[31] which remained concentrated in the north-east of the island, other than to denounce ritualistically the 'evils of partition'. Protestants within the Irish Free State, a small and dwindling minority, were not the object of official disapproval, though there was little place for their culture and aspirations within the framework of the new official ideology. Still, it should be remembered, there was an historic association between being Protestant and upholding the union of Britain and Ireland. Thus, perhaps it is not too surprising that during the early phases of decolonisation there was little concern with the sensitivities of Protestants, either within the Irish Free State (later Irish Republic) or in Northern Ireland. Nor can the legacy of colonialism in Ireland, whose origins lay in violence, be easily dismissed. One might sum up by saying that if the term 'Irishness' did not include the Northern Protestants, the term 'Britishness' did not include Irish Catholics.

Foster thinks a redefinition of Irishness is crucial. The Republic must separate Church and state to become a pluralist Ireland. It has to surrender the fiction of a Gaelic-speaking nation and historians must revise and demystify the history of the island. It would be important to expand the definition of Irishness. He gives, as an example, the Dublin poet Paul Durcan who has no problem in saying he is, culturally, British as well as Irish. As Foster says, the situation in Northern Ireland makes one wonder: 'We have to know what being Protestant or Catholic does to us and for us, and how far it produces identity and meaning in our lives'.[32] Questions of identity and meaning are crucial issues for students of postcolonialism.

Terence Brown believes that even more than Irish public/communal life, private life was the primary concern for the writers of the 1960s and 1970s. Sexual and religious themes, working-class experiences and Northern Ireland came increasingly to the fore:

> The familiar figure of twentieth-century Irish fiction, the adolescent young man discovering the all-encompassing nets of religion, nation, and family and seeking to escape the oppressive constraints of Irish society still occurs, but with less frequency.[33]

Yet there were new pressures on writers, not least to offer something helpful in relation to the renewed conflict in Northern Ireland. This crisis burst on an unsuspecting public in 1969 and still dominates much political and cultural discussion on the island. Coupled with this has been a concern with identity, a striving to explore notions of Irishness and Britishness, of nationalism and unionism. Finally, Brown alerts us to a concern with commercialism as a threat to a distinctive collective identity: 'At present of course such a nascent humanism is a fragile dyke against the cultural and social depredations of a rampant commercialism in an Ireland which could lose, before long, any distinctive identity it may once have possessed'.[34] These of course are issues which have ramifications far beyond the shores of Ireland, not least on the Mediterranean coast of Catalonia.

THE POPULARITY OF THE SHORT STORY

Having provided a brief, schematic account of political and cultural change in Catalonia and Ireland, it is appropriate to explore the more specific question of why the genre of the short story has achieved such prominence in both countries. Presumably the answer to this is contained, in part, in the complexities of the respective histories of the two societies. I will begin the discussion by looking first at Catalonia.

The literary critic Joaquim Molas sees a number of general reasons why short stories have been so prominent in Catalan literature from the revival period to the present day.[35] These reasons are characteristic of postcolonial societies which have to struggle to keep their identity, have limited material resources and are lacking in self-confidence. Molas's reasons are both social and political: a small population, the lack of an autonomous and sympathetic political administration and an underdeveloped publishing industry. These conditions made it difficult for professional writers to emerge who might have had the time and the resources to commit themselves to long-term writing projects, such as the novel. Writing for magazines and papers was more feasible. Molas also adds a linguistic reason. Since the 1890s Catalan writers had been trying to create a modern literary language. Both the short story and poetry were more conducive to experimentation with language than was the case with novels. (Joyce's *Finnegan's Wake* may be the exception which proves the rule.) Finally, Molas notes an aesthetic crisis early this century – brought to a head by *Noucentisme* (as we shall see later) – which centred on the crisis of the novel. Lacking the theoretical resources to overcome this problem, the short story increasingly substituted for the novel. Later in the twentieth century, the symbolists were to treat the novel as a kind of a poem and reduce it to a short story, as Edgar Allan Poe, the first to create a universal theory of the short story, explained in *The Poetic Principle*.[36]

Another critic, Jordi Castellanos, sees the Catalan short story in the romantic period as separate from oral literature which, in any case, was in retreat in the face of an industrialising society. In Castellanos' view, the short-story writer was not merely a collector of anonymous popular culture, such as the Grimm brothers and Hans Christian Andersen, but a creator. He tends to downgrade, therefore, the role and influence of oral tradition in the genesis of the Catalan short story but does not deny it.[37] The case may have been different in Ireland (outside Ulster) where, at the end of the nineteenth century, the country was much less industrialised than Catalonia and where the oral tale still exerted a strong influence.[38]

Changing technology in the printing and publishing industry, when allied to rising literacy – profoundly affected the demand for literary work. In relation to the short story, one can say that its form was shaped by one of the great novelties of the nineteenth century – that is, journalism. Papers and magazines were the medium through which many short stories reached a mass readership. In this way, the birth of the short story was inseparable from the emergence of mass literacy and mass readership.

The short story had advantages over many other genres: it was easy to publish, cheap and, unlike the novel, it achieved its artistic object within the confines of limited space. In addition, there was the special quality of the short story: its malleability. It could assimilate old forms, such as folklore, and open up to new ones. It could be adapted to all kinds of subjects. Moreover, it adapted more successfully than the novel to the acceleration and the fragmentation of modern life and new ways of reading. To illustrate this point, Castellanos quotes a critic of that period, Ernest Moline i Brases, who, in 1897, observed:

> *És un senyal dels temps: avui lo periòdic és l'aliment obligat de la immensa majoria; lo llibre ha perdut lectors; los autors d'imaginació, per emmotllar-se al medi, se veuen obligats a presentar sos productes en proporcions dosimètriques i el públic, que viu una vida agitada i neuròtica, llegeix ràpidament les obres, molt agrait de l'atenció que ha tingut l'autor fent-ho curt.*

> (It is a sign of our times: today what is a daily occurrence is compulsory food for the majority; the book has lost readers; writers, in order to adapt themselves to the environment, are obliged to present their products in small helpings and the audience, which has a hectic and neurotic life, reads the books quickly, thankful to the writer who has had the consideration to do it in short form.)[39]

Yet, at the turn of the century, there was a gradual separation between literary creation and journalism, the latter remaining more factual and less concerned with aesthetics. The short story also separated itself from the nineteenth-century literature of manners and became more elaborate. It found a new space in literary magazines, which became important outlets by the end of the century.

A modernist writer, Raimon Caselles, detected two literary inheritances in the Catalan short story. The first was that of Flaubert, who gave poetic attributes to the genre and avoided totality in favour of fragmentation. The second was the legacy of Poe and Baudelaire, who stressed the importance of feelings and sensations. The genre was also enriched by contact with movements in visual art. As a result of the impact of impressionism and symbolism, there was a refusal to engage in detailed description. The key words were synthesis, intensity and suggestion. The short story expressed fragmentation and the ephemeral nature of sensations and emotions. Anecdotes were abandoned in favour of suggestion and imprecision. While the novel was associated with realism, the short story was held to be better adapted to expressing deeper realities: contradiction and doubt rather than certainty, the primacy of aesthetic emotion over analysis, and suggestion in preference to statement.

As we have seen, *Noucentisme* had a political component which, at times, bordered on the intolerant. For instance, it established a hierarchy of genres in which poetry was at the top and the novel was at the bottom, as Maria Campillo points out.[40] This arose from the movement's preoccupation with form and language, and in particular its concern with purifying the Catalan language. The short story was a more convenient vehicle for this than the novel. As a result, during the first quarter of the twentieth century, it was almost impossible to publish novels in Catalonia.

At this point it may be helpful to return to Frank O'Connor's thought that the short story was prominent in those societies which experienced colonisation. In considering this suggestion, one might examine whether the vicissitudes of history and culture also have a bearing in the Catalan case. The struggle to maintain Catalan culture in the face of a hostile metropolitan power certainly induced a sense of insecurity among Catalan intellectuals. Perhaps the culture, and the situation of the language, were not 'normal' enough to be conducive to the production of the novel. Or, as the writer, Josep M. de Sagarra, commented in 1924:

> la vida del nostre poble no tenia potser una personalitat prou definida i prou complexa perque es produís el desitjat moviment novel.listic.

> (the life of our country perhaps did not have a definite and complex enough personality to be able to produce the desired novelistic movement)[41]

The insecurity of the culture had repercussions for the Catalan language. Sagarra also noted the emergence of new possibilities of expression, by implication registering a legacy of problems from the past:

> Avui dia la nostra llengua comença a ésser apta per dir meravelles, per arribar a totes les possibilitats; la prosa d'en Josep Carner demostra això que estic dient.

> (Now our language is beginning to be capable of expressing marvels, to arrive at all kinds of possibilities; Josep Carner's prose proves what I am saying.)[42]

Sagarra's defensive stance that the Catalan language is good enough for literary work may be revealing in a wider context. This lack of confidence about the 'submerged' language could be seen as one of the colonial consequences. Postcolonial countries are often unsure, somehow or other, if their own language or dialect is as good as others:

In contrast to the Irish Revival and *Modernisme*, *Noucentisme* saw *ruralisme*, or the celebration of rural ways and folk culture, as dangerous. It demanded a more urbanised Catalan culture, associating the city with culture and modernity, as well as political effectiveness. As Alan Yates adds, the countryside was viewed as hostile to innovation and new influences, a further deficiency given the enthusiastic internationalism of the movement.[43] Again there is an interesting contrast with the contemporaneous Irish-Ireland movement, which was suspicious of external influences and tended to emphasise native resources and values, though it is true both held in common the urgent need to forge national unity.

The novel in Catalonia was held responsible for perpetuating ruralist mythology by some intellectuals like Gabriel Alomar. Poetry, however, had managed to free itself from the malign inheritance of the rural world. As a result, poetry was seen as the model genre. One should note, though, the timing of the reaction against the novel. This came just after a woman's novel was published, *Solitude* by Caterina Albert 'Víctor Català', which, ironically, is now cited as one of the most accomplished in Catalan literature. One cannot, therefore, rule out the possibility that the initial reaction was motivated, in part, by feelings of misogyny.

Perhaps the popularity of the short story in Ireland has been an escape route from the restrictions of the literary dominance of English high style. John Wilson Foster, in seeking to explain the prominence of the short story in Irish literature, places particular emphasis on the importance of the oral tradition in Irish culture. 'Orature', as we have seen, has been identified as one of the features of postcolonial culture – a postcolonial characteristic. Foster continues:

The relative scarcity of good novels is less significant, in any case, than the fact that so many Irish writers, whether or not they have written successful novels, have produced volumes of fine stories. Since 1965, a quarter century after O'Faoláin's remarks, these have come from Bryan MacMahon, Patrick Boyle, Benedict Kiely, William Trevor, Edna O'Brien, Julia O'Faolain, John McGahern, Neil Jordan, Clare Boylan and Aidan Higgins . . . A fuller explanation would include the persistence among Irish people of the gift of anecdote, of idiomatic flair, of the comic tradition and of the real life 'characters' (an endangered species today) who offer themselves ready-made

for portraiture in the economical short form . . . All this work has that strong
oral element that Frank O'Connor recommended in the short-story . . .
O'Faoláin thought the short story suitable for the enforced, unwanted but
accepted subjectivity of the Irish writer, a more interesting notion if we
remember that it was Moore and Joyce who invented the short story as a
vehicle for what O'Connor called 'the lonely voice'.[44]

In many writers like Carleton, O'Kelly, Colum, Stephens, Corkery,
O'Connor, Mary Lavin and Bryan MacMahon, we find oral vestiges, a
clear testimony to the importance of the oral tradition. Many of these
short-story writers use a conversational style which is close to the Irish folk
tale. In the early phase of the Literary Revival at the beginning of the
twentieth century, many writers looked to the Gaelic folk tradition for
inspiration. This idealisation of the past, or a particular phase of the past,
is a common characteristic of postcolonial countries. It is an understandable, if doomed, attempt to recover a precolonial identity which
might do service in the present and the future.

Declan Kiberd points to some of the strengths of the short story. The
folk tale was impersonal, whereas the short story was personal, credible
and written in private for the solitary reader.[45] In the modern short story,
the teller no longer seeks to escape but rather to confront reality.[46]
Moreover, the genre flourished:

> in those countries where a vibrant oral culture is suddenly challenged by
> the onset of a sophisticated literary tradition. The short story is the natural
> result of a fusion between the ancient form of the folk-tale and the
> preoccupations of modern literature.[47]

The adverb 'suddenly' would suggest that the 'onset' Kiberd has in mind
refers to the sudden arrival of the British literary tradition in largely pre-
literate societies undergoing colonisation. The expectation, therefore,
might be that the short story would flourish in countries which have been
colonised. This brings us back to O'Connor's notion of a 'submerged
population group'. Moreover, Kiberd explains that whereas the great
Anglo-Irish writers of the Literary Revival, such as Yeats and Synge,
excelled in poetry and drama, the short story has been popular among
Catholic writers from the countryside who have been close to the oral
tradition. These writers also experienced the transitional pains to both
modern society and the status of nation state. Thus, in the years in which
the modern Irish nation took shape, the short story was the form which
many writers chose to depict their vision of the emerging Ireland:

Mainly pioneered by the risen people – the O'Kellys, O'Flaherties, O'Faoláins and O'Connors. The genre had a particular appeal for the writers of the emerging Catholic bourgeoisie who hailed from regional towns. For example, O'Faoláin and O'Connor grew up in Cork where the folk story-tellers still existed . . . A genre which was poised between the profane world of contemporary literature and the pious world of the folk. By the nature of its origins, the form was admirably suited to the task of reflecting the disturbances in Irish society as it painfully shed its ancient traditions.[48]

Vivian Mercier considers that because most modern Irish writers possess this awareness of audience, this sense of 'dramatic rapport' between writer and reader, the typical Irish short story is more likely to be a story, not a prose poem, than its counterpart in other literatures.[49] On the other hand, trying to explain why England has good novelists but not short story-writers, Seán O'Faoláin claimed that English readers preferred the social scope of the novel to the more private concerns of the short story. This is because the English way of looking at life is more social and less personal and individual than the French,[50] for example.

Colm Tóibín's masterly exploration of the prominence of the short story has distinct echoes of O'Connor's postcolonial discourse with its emphasis on a broken past. The confusion of the present and despair for the future inhibits the production of the novel but is compatible with short-story writing:

> Six short stories, six lyric poems in a country where history wiped out any hope of us forming a cohesive, safe, secure, well adjusted, class-ridden society. We were left instead with something broken and insecure, a post–colonial society which remained in spirit part of the one-time mother country, and part of America, and part of its own invention . . . How can the novel flourish in such a world? The novel explores psychology, sociology, the individual consciousness; the novel finds a form and a language for these explorations. We require an accepted world for the novel to flourish, a shared sense of time and place . . . What we have come to treasure instead are those small moments in our literature known as short stories. This is the legacy we have chosen to take from Joyce, not the vision and word play of 'Finnegans Wake', but the glimpses of life as it is truly lived in 'Dubliners', the sharpness of the realism, the precision, the detail, the ending of each story in pathos and bitter wisdom and purple prose, the individual in relation to landscape and memory.
>
> Short stories occur in a limited time and a limited place. In our post-colonial societies, it is a perfect form: we need not deal with the bitterness of the past, the confusion of the present or the hopelessness of the future. We can offer merely small instances unassociated with other instances.[51]

William Trevor, by contrast, preferred a more structural interpretation to explain the difference but agrees with Tóibín that a sense of confusion and poverty creates an environment which is prone to produce short stories rather than novels:

> When the novel reared its head Ireland wasn't ready for it . . . In England, for instance, the great Victorian novel had been fed by the architecture of a rich, stratified society in which complacency and hypocrisy, accompanied by the ill-treatment of the unfortunate and the poor, provided both fictional material and grounds for protest. Wealth had purchased leisure and a veneer of sophistication for the up-and-coming middle classes; stability at home was the jewel in the imperial crown. In Ireland there was disaffection, repressed religion, the confusion of two languages, and the spectre of famine.[52]

Short-story writers such as Liam O'Flaherty, Frank O'Connor, Mary Lavin and Seán O'Faoláin developed a strong reaction against the ruling ideology of the new Irish state. The fusion of Catholic and nationalist ideas and ideals was seen as oppressive. They considered Gaelic Ireland had died in the eighteenth century and articulated a need to open up to Europe rather than remain fixated on the past. The reaction of writers like Patrick Kavanagh was mainly through the medium of poetry. In 1942 he wrote the long poem 'The Great Hunger'. This concerns the diminished experience and frustrations of a small farmer. In the poem, sexual starvation is imaginatively associated with the great famine of the 1840s. This link is interesting in that the sexual inhibition of the Irish (with the highest rates of celibacy in Europe in the century after the Famine) has been associated with poverty, emigration and colonisation. These writers depicted a depressing and narrow-minded Irish society:

> We see an Irish provincial world, in Cork, in the small towns, in the countryside, where inhibition is disguised as economic prudence, land hunger and stolid conservatism as patriotic duty, subservience to Church authority as piety. It is a world where intimacies, moments of personal fulfilment, seem wrested from an unyielding oppression. The emotional climate of the Irish short story, particularly in O'Faoláin, O'Connor and Mary Lavin, is one where passion and encounter are matters of fleeting provinces, where disillusionment dogs individual hope and disappointment enforces bitter submission. The Irish short story of the 1930s and forties registered a social reality that flew in the face of nationalistic self-congratulation. Instead of de Valera's Gaelic Eden and the uncomplicated satisfactions of Ireland free, the writers revealed a mediocre, dishevelled, often neurotic and depressed petit-bourgeois society that atrophied for want of a liberating idea. O'Faoláin's image for it, as it was James Joyce's before him, is the entire landscape of Ireland shrouded in snow.[53]

Terence Brown sees the short story as the natural form for the Irish writer who felt little need for literary experiment, and who preferred to explore the new Irish world through the traditional form of the short-story. In other words, the art of short story writing, Irish style, is a conservative act (notwithstanding the view of literary critics who, as noted earlier, see the short story as well adapted to innovation and experimentation): 'The short story is involved with Irish life, peculiarly adapted to its rhythms and moods. Its unquestioning dependence on traditional narrative techniques, implies the writers' own innate conservatism.'[54]

In his introduction to *The Picador Book of Irish Contemporary Fiction*, Dermot Bolger introduces a new element and wonders about censorship as a reason for the production of short stories:

> Looking back at the achievements with the short-story form of Frank O'Connor and Seán O'Faoláin . . . it is hard to know how much the problems of censorship in their own country influenced their bent towards short fiction . . . or how much the society they existed in lent itself more readily towards the short story.[55]

Some years before that, Ian Reid emphasised the romantic influence in the construction of the genre. Reid saw the Irish short story as a child of the romantic movement, in which the lonely hero 'O'Connor's lonely voice' – finds it hard to cope with society, its conventions and its dreariness:

> Short stories do frequently focus on one or two individuals who are seen as separated from their fellow-men in some way, at odds with social norms, beyond the pale. In this respect short stories can properly be called romantic, as O'Connor proposes, or even romantic by virtue of their affinity with those works by Wordsworth, Coleridge, Byron, Nerval and others through which move wanderers, lonely dreamers, and outcast or scapegoat figures. Indeed, since the emergence of the short story as a fully fledged genre in Europe and America coincides, as already noted, with the burgeoning of that protean cultural phenomenon known as Romanticism, there would seem to be a broad basis for the common remark that the short story is in essence a Romantic form: the Romantic prose form. In its normally limited scope and subjective orientation it corresponds to the lyric poem as the novel does to the epic.[56]

It is not easy to offer a definitive answer to the question why short-story writing has occupied such a prominent position in the cultural production of both Ireland and Catalonia. However, the following factors are surely relevant: new aesthetic currents; the difficulty of becoming a professional writer in a minority language (especially in Catalonia); the oral and rural

influence (especially in Ireland); economic factors; the beginning of journalism; the freedom for experimentation, and, of course, the insecurities
of the postcolonial condition which might make the writer feel at home
in a genre which is new, has no tradition and is often regarded as a minor
genre. Now it is time to consider if there might also be a connection
between the gender and the genre.

WOMEN AND THE SHORT STORY

There is some evidence of a connection between women and short-story
writing, although this seems to be more clear in the Irish case than in the
Catalan one.[57] The pressure to write novels, as discussed earlier, may well
have been stronger in Catalonia than in Ireland and this could well explain
why Catalan women writers have thrown themselves into the adventure
of writing novels, with more or less success. In the Irish case, David
Marcus has remarked: 'As far as the writing of short stories is concerned
their [women's] impact has been marked, for it has meant that a whole
new thematic field is being explored and exposed'.[58] Janet Madden-
Simpson is also of the opinion that 'some of the best writing by Irish
women has taken this form'.[59] In Catalonia, the most accomplished
women writers have often used the short story; in some cases it has been
their major form, as for Caterina Albert. The most prestigious prize for
short-story writing, established in 1953, bears her name (or rather her pen-
name 'Víctor Català'), whereas prizes for poetry, the novel and drama have
male writers' names. The critic Carme Arnau emphasises the influence of
the short story on Mercè Rodoreda's novels. Most chapters of Rodoreda's
novels could be read as independent or free-standing short stories.[60]

Frank O'Connor's anticipation of postcolonial theory helps explain why
so many women writers, being 'colonised subjects', are drawn to the short
story.[61] In particular, one of the reasons for this tendency is the preference
women have for oral language, a vital element in postcolonial theorising.
Mary Louise Pratt notes that the short story welcomes oral and non-
standard speech, which allows women to create their own language. In
Pratt's words:

> the short story provides not just the 'small' place for experimentation, but
> also a genre where oral and marginal experience have some tradition of
> being at home, and the form best-suited to reproducing the length of most
> oral speech events. Orality can be counted as one of the important factors
> behind the flourishing of the short stories in the modern literatures of

many Third World nations and peoples, where, not incidentally, it is taken much more seriously as an art form than it is elsewhere.[62]

One of the characteristics of 'submerged groups' is their marginality. Being in this position means that they tend to lack time as well as economic resources. Until recently many women in Ireland and Catalonia had either no salaries or only low earnings, being housewives or part-time workers, athough the situation is changing. Writing short stories, like poetry, required less time than other genres. While exiled in France, the Catalan writer Mercè Rodoreda said:

> *No, no faig ni faré novel.la per ara. No tinc temps. Un conte es pot escriure relativament de pressa . . . La novel.la és massa absorbent. A més he descobert que el conte és un gran gènere.*

> (No, I am not making and I am not going to make a novel for the moment. I have no time. You can write a short story relatively quickly . . . The novel is too demanding. Also I have discovered that the short story is a great genre.)[63]

Generally speaking, it is easier to get published in periodicals: 'Edith Somerville and Violet Martin wrote stories when they could not find the time for a novel and needed an immediate source of income'.[64] Because of their traditional domestic role, many women have little leisure time at home, especially if they have children. For the Catalan writer, Carme Riera, time is the main constraint and hence a major reason for writing short stories.[65]

'Submerged groups' have a tendency to lack self-confidence and short-story writing is nothing if not a modest genre. Traditionally it has received little attention from critics, who have tended to see it as a minor genre – one in which a writer serves an apprenticeship before going on to write something 'serious', such as a novel or a play. A good example is Edna O'Brien. She is known as a novelist, whereas most of her production as a mature writer in fact has been in the short-story form. In Catalonia, Caterina Albert is best known as a novelist, even though she has produced hundreds of short stories. The marginal aspect of the genre may even suit women writers. For a variety of social reasons, women have been less drawn to following careers and have been less motivated by material success. Lack of confidence and feelings of embarrassment have also been barriers. Moments after the Catalan writer Monsterrat Roig received the national prize for a collection of her stories, *Molta roba i poc sabó*, she said: '*Aquest darrer recull, de fet, és una novel.la, però es veu que tinc una certa por psíquica a enfrontar-me amb l'estructura novel.lística*' (This last collection is actually a novel but it seems that I have some psychological fear in dealing with the structure of the novel).[66]

Writing for magazines and papers is less problematical. According to Madden-Simpson: 'Irish women have collectively, and until very recently, found it difficult either to take the business of writing seriously or to be seen to take it seriously'.[67] A Catalan writer, Carme Riera, confesses that she started writing short stories because she never thought she was capable of anything more ambitious in the field of writing.[68]

The form of the short story also allows authors to avoid unconfortable feelings. In many female short stories written before the 1980s, sex is rarely present, at least explicitly. A lack of sexual fulfilment feeds into a lack of self-confidence. When sex is described, it is often presented as unpleasant or unfulfilling for women. Helen's view in Mary Beckett's 'The Master and the Bombs' is fairly typical: 'I satisfy his appetites'.[69] Eilís Ní Dhuibhne describes this traditional absence of sexuality in Irish culture in a humorous way:

> It never struck me, however, that there was any sexual relationship between my parents. The only time they touched one another, as far as I saw, was when my mother pecked my father on the cheek as she said goodbye to him in the morning. And that was more a ritual than a display of affection.[70]

On similar lines, writing about Irish fiction in general, and about James Joyce's 'The Dead' in particular, Colm Tóibín argues that 'if you wrote short stories you didn't have to mention sex'.[71] In short fiction, 'uncomfortable' or 'unresolved' issues can easily be avoided.

'Submerged groups' feel lonely, in the view of Frank O'Connor. Similarly the short-story theorist, Charles E. May, believes that characters in short stories are normally alone: 'We are presented with characters in their essential aloneness, or in their taken-for-granted social world. The short story, more than the novel, presents the world as I-thou rather than I-it.'[72] Again, it might be argued, this tends to suit women writers because solitude is a major theme in their writing. Also a large part of their writing focuses on women's relations with people rather than things. Those relations, though, are often troublesome or disappointing and lead to a deep, unavoidable loneliness. For example, a need for protection leads O'Brien's heroines to fall for father figures. But giving themselves leaves these women lonely and unfulfilled.

Perhaps because of its more recent origins, as compared to poetry, the novel or the play, the genre of the short story offers, or has offered, more possibilities for an emerging women's writing. It is more conducive to experimentation with language than is the novel. It is a malleable genre, open to what Julia Kristeva calls 'the semiotic language'. A similar point is made by Nadine Gordimer: 'the short story always has been more flexible and open to experiment than the novel. Short-story writers always have been subject at the same time to both a stricter technical discipline and a wider freedom than the novelist.'[73] That openness gives freedom to the artist and, consequently, more possibilities to indulge in fantasy: 'Fantasy in the hands of short-story writers is so much more successful than when in the hands of novelists because it is necessary for it to hold good only for the brief illumination of the situation it dominates.'[74] The Uruguayan writer Cristina Peri Rossi says that, even if she uses different genres, the short story is her favourite because it is the one which allows, as well as poetry, a high degree of experimentation and innovation. According to Peri Rossi, it is the most modern genre of today's narrative forms, especially after Edgar Alan Poe, and she thinks that the reader of stories and poetry is more demanding than the reader of novels.[75]

This deeper capacity to express may also be linked to the fact that the short story is a genre inspired more by emotions and the unconscious than the world of rational consciousness. According to Charles E. May, the short story derives from '"an experience" directly and emotionally created and encountered', whereas the novel derives from '"experience" conceptually created and considered'.[76] To May, the novel is, in a way, elaborated along more rational lines because it has to do with a more expansive construction, with experience in general, whereas the short story normally concentrates on one particular experience. That gives space for the short story to delve deeper into the internal world while the novel navigates the external. Thus the short story is bound to meditate upon the primitive, anti-social world of the unconscious.[77] It engages with dreams, whereas the novel is closer to the social world. Charles E. May goes on to relate the short story to the mythic and the spiritual, the intuitive and the lyrical, whereas the novel is related to social and public reality, the conceptual philosophical framework. To an extent, the short story wants to 'defamiliarize' the everyday whereas the novel wants to reaffirm everyday reality. As women have had little place in public life, a tendency to write about the private and the unconscious, in place of the public and the rational, becomes more understandable.

Women writers want to create a new style in literature. That could explain their interest in the present moment rather than studying and reflecting on the past. Due to its brevity, the short story is an appropriate genre to depict a short moment in a life. According to Nadine Gordimer:

> Short story writers see by the light of the flash; theirs is the art of the only thing one can be sure of – the present moment . . . A discrete moment of truth is aimed at – not *the* moment of truth, because the short story does not deal in cumulatives.[78]

In a collection of short stories, the writer has freedom to offer a plurality of viewpoints. This diversity may conceivably be of particular value to women who seem to want to depict the plurality of human subjectivity. According to Wendy Hollway: 'My position in relation to men demonstrates the non-unitary nature of my gendered subjectivity. I aspired to similarity in some spheres because of the value attached. At the same time I preserved my difference.'[79]

The short story has sometimes been used to react ideologically and to embody subversive messages. Thus, as we have seen before, a number of Irish writers, among them Líam O'Flaherty, Frank O'Connor, Mary Lavin and Seán O'Faoláin, developed a strong reaction against the ruling ideology of the new Irish state. The fusion of Catholic and nationalist ideas and ideals was seen as oppressive. They considered that Gaelic Ireland had died in the eighteenth century and articulated a need to open up to Europe rather than remain fixated on the past. In more recent times, Northern Irish writers, though the medium of the short story, have complained about 'the ideology of violence' and dream of a tolerant and open society.

In a similar way, contemporary women writers have been known to use the short story as a means of reacting against a patriarchal ideology. For example, during the dictatorship, Carme Riera published one of her most widely read stories, which is about a lesbian couple: 'Te deix, amor, la mar com a penyora' (I Give You, my Love, the Sea as a Token). Female stories often embody a strong criticism of marriage and the situation of women in general. Mary Louise Pratt makes the more general point: "Just as it is used for formal experimentation, the short story is often the genre used to introduce new (and possibly stigmatised) subject matters into the literary arena'.[80] It is, therefore, both innovative and challenging:

> In other parts of the world we similarly find the short story being used to introduce new regions or groups into an established national literature, or into an emerging national literature in the process of decolonisation. In France, Maupassant through the short story breaks down taboos on matters of sexuality and class. In the establishment of a modern national literature in Ireland, the short story emerges as the central prose fiction genre, through which Joyce, O'Flaherty, O'Faoláin, O'Connor, Moore, Lavin and so many others first document modern Irish life.[81]

Short fiction and poetry are sometimes linked. Grace Paley observes that the two genres are brief, concentrated and economical. Yet some female authors abandon poetry and turn to short stories. According to Paley, in her experience the short story furnishes a more congenial and effective medium for exploring relationships:

> First of all, I began to think of certain subject matter, women's lives specifically, and what was happening around me. I was in my thirties, which I guess is the time people start to notice these things, women's and men's lives and what their relationship is. I knew lots of women with small kids, and I was developing very close relationships with a variety of women. All sorts of things began to worry me, and I began to think about them a lot. I couldn't deal with any of this subject matter in poetry; I just didn't know how. I didn't have the technique. Other people can, but I didn't want to write poems saying 'I feel this' and 'I feel that'. That was the last thing I wanted to do.[82]

Before leaving this section on women and short-story writing, there is a further point I would like to make. Perhaps the classification and hierarchisation of genres responds to a masculine order. It might be that women are less interested in those divisions and prefer creating texts which sometimes are like poems, sometimes like short stories and sometimes like critical essays. Women writers might be less concerned in forms and shapes than in meanings and concepts.

CONCLUSION

A variety of explanations have been offered for the prominence of short-story writing in Catalonia and Ireland. No doubt there are reasons which are specific to one country or the other,[83] but the interesting point is that a fair degree of overlap in terms of explanatory schemes seems to emerge. Thus a partly economic interpretation seems relevant to both societies, though it probably carries more weight in the Catalan case. Writing in Catalan has always gone against the flow in the sense that resources to write in a minority language have been meagre, and incomes in the Iberian peninsula over much of this century have been below Western European levels. It was simply cheaper to publish short stories than novels. Being a full-time professional writer in Catalan literature was an option for very few indeed.

Ideological forms have also been at play. Writing in Ireland and Catalonia in this century was often to sail against the current because of the strong conservative ideology and censorship which flowed through both societies. In this respect, the genre attracted marginal individuals and groups, including women.

In his introduction to *The Lonely Voice*, Frank O'Connor mentions that in the short story there is 'an intense awareness of human loneliness'.[84] Here also is the solitude of a colonised society which is not 'normal'. Colm Tóibín has developed this point further, arguing that, lacking a coherent and continuous history, postcolonial societies tend to produce a series of short stories 'full of moments of great bravery and daring, immense tragedy with blood everywhere and tears in every eye'.[85] For these reasons the genre of the short story has flourished in these two European societies.

In Ireland and Catalonia the impulses of romantic ideology reinforced a sense of nationalism. In both societies the land was vital to romantic and nationalist conceptions of the world. In Catalonia this phenomenon was known as 'ruralism'. In Terence Brown's words, land is associated with purity, suggestive of an ancient civilisation, uncontaminated by commercialism and progress.[86] It involved a new emphasis on the importance of nature for humankind and a view of life on the land as the most authentic expression of moral and good living. It also brought the revalidation of the oral tale. As noted earlier, the idealisation of the land was challenged in the Catalan case, but not the Irish one. Catalan Neo-Classical writers were fiercely critical of many of these assumptions and aspired to create an urban society – industrialised, modern and international. The values and alleged virtues of rural society would find little place in this New Jerusalem. This might help explain, incidentally, the apparently higher status accorded to the short story in Ireland as compared to Catalonia. In Ireland the continuing importance of the rural, both at a structural level (in the sense that much of Ireland remained dependent on agriculture and unindustrialised until after the 1950s) and at an ideological level (idealised images of life in the countryside persisted) may well account for the stronger influence of the oral tale. In other words, many Irish writers remained in direct contact with rural life or were, at most, one remove from it. In terms of postcolonial discourse, the emphasis on the land can also be seen as a reaction to a foreign culture which had 'subdued' the country, through banning the culture in the Catalan case and through expropriating the land in the Irish one.

Broadly speaking, the short story has occupied a marginal role as far as literary criticism has been concerned. Still, the genre has attracted female writers who, as a 'submerged group', lack tradition, resources and the confidence to practise other forms. These features, in turn, link back to the position of women in society: that of producers of (relatively) lowly-valued outputs in the marketplace and as reproducers within the structure of the family and household. The openness and flexibility of the genre fit well with the postcolonial text, fulfilling two of the functions of female writing today – on the one hand, delineating and challenging the oppression of women, and on the other creating new literary languages and spaces.

Going back to the question broached in the title, it would be an overstatement to say that postcolonial status and the propensity to use the short-story genre are intimately related. Still, there are some reasons to suspect that subservient or marginalised groups are disproportionately attracted to a genre which offers more freedom and space than others. It may not be simply coincidence that each shares a marginal status. Some of the issues are intrinsically elusive, such as the relationship between genre and gender or the implications of the postcolonial condition for the choice of genre, but are no less worthwhile pursuing for all that.

CHAPTER TWO

'Compulsory marriage': a colonising device?

> – Les dones s'han de casar aviat.
> – Les dones . . . I per què els homes no?
> – Els homes no necessiten casar-se.
>
> (– Women have to marry soon.
> – Women . . . And why not men?
> – Men don't need to marry.)
>
> *Maria Aurèlia Capmany*[1]

> And I wondered . . . why did people want to be in twos?
> What was wrong with threes, or fours?
>
> *Katy Hayes*[2]

INTRODUCTION

IF IN postcolonial literature the theme of the nation and questions of national identity constantly appear as important but problematic and unresolved issues, in women's literature that space is monopolised by marriage and relationships.[3] Little wonder, as women's lives, to a much greater extent than in the case of men, have revolved around and within this social institution. Women have been socialised to put marriage and family first, with participation in the workforce and in public life at best secondary and at worst undesirable. The term 'compulsory marriage'[4] refers to the necessity, almost the obligation, on women to get into the system of marriage.[5] Even if times are changing and marriage is now in crisis, there is still the force of tradition which impels women to become wives[6] and to regard other activities and interests as of secondary significance.

Marriage has been effectively compulsory for centuries. Women's education was geared to getting married and not to further study or work. In one of Maria Aurèlia Capmany's novels, the uncle of a girl says to her parents: *'Per què la fas estudiar? Casar-la has de fer.'* (Why do you make her study? What you should be doing is getting her married.)[7] At the beginning of the twentieth century, Dolors Montserdà, who defined herself as feminist and a Catholic, argued that women should be submissive towards their husbands when they got married. According to her, submission is an impulse of a woman's heart which she must always obey.[8] At that time, the husband had control of his wife's income, and, in the case of adultery, the man who killed his wife was only supposed to abandon the house for some months whereas the wife's punishment after killing her husband was a life sentence. More generally, women in Ireland were subservient to masculine authority in the household and in the public sphere.

Despite the persuasiveness of the institution of marriage in the two societies, what is striking is the dark portrayal of marriage in so many contemporary Irish and Catalan short stories by women writers. This forms part of the corpus of commonalties which span the two literatures. The analysis of the texts is conducted with reference to feminist theorising, drawing in particular on French feminist thought. Postcolonial theorising is a further resource. In terms of the latter, 'compulsory marriage' might be viewed as a colonising device in relation to women. The metaphor seems appropriate; the notion of women as a colonised group is in common currency in some feminist writings, though as with all arguments by analogy it should not be pressed too far.[9]

In order to analyse marriage in literature, it is helpful to have a brief look at its historic origins. The French historian Georges Duby has observed that during the eleventh and twelfth centuries in Europe, Church law on marriage was formally defined, with a view to its universal application throughout the church.[10] Rituals were laid down which last to this day. For example, marriage was celebrated publicly.[11] For Duby, as for other social historians, marriage is a fundamental feature of the social structure. According to him, it was established to distribute women among men in order to regulate men's competition for women and to control procreation. Marriage and the family have profound economic significance as they give rise to structures which are effective means of accumulating wealth. Through the provision of offspring, men are guaranteed a form of immortality. Marriage ensured clear lines of paternity and established a distinction between legal and illegal relationships. Children inherited and had ancestors, surnames, rights. Marriage was based on monogamy and repression of sexual pleasure in favour of sex for procreation.[12] However, in practice this control over sexuality was mainly over women. Men were quite free to have concubines whereas extramarital relationships were strongly penalised for women. While these legal shackles have been progressively broken in Western society, the socio-economic system continues to act to restrain women. Drawing on Marx, Luce Irigaray observes that man subordinates the natural world to the service of his own needs. Because of her reproductive function, woman has been seen as an extension of nature. So women, in the same way as land or other natural resources, become part of the same process of exploitation. For a particular man, a woman has 'use value'; between men she has an 'exchange value' like cows, cars or other commodities in economic exchange. In Irigaray's words: 'Woman is never anything but the locus of a more or less competitive exchange between two men, including the competition for the possession of mother earth'.[13] Thus, the father gives his daughter to his prospective son-in-law.

As a result of an ideology based on making marriage 'compulsory' for reproduction and making fatherhood unique, two contrasting stereotypes of women were produced. On the one hand, 'the good woman', the obedient wife, who conforms and submits; on the other, there is 'the bad woman', the socially unacceptable, the prostitute. While the image of the prostitute has traditionally been stigmatised, by contrast the image of 'Don Juan' has been deemed worthy of admiration. For example, Concepció Gil points out that in early-modern Catalonia, men's adultery was tolerated much more readily than women's. Adulterous women were considered prostitutes whereas men could have concubines, and having sexual encounters with prostitutes was not considered a sin.[14] Wife versus prostitute is one of the binary oppositions in a patriarchal society whereas there is no masculine equivalent of this dichotomy. Less obviously, both positions locate women at the social margins.

Going back to Duby, marriage rituals were originally constituted by copying the hierarchical relation between serf and feudal lord in which the former accepted being dependent in favour of protection.[15] Whereas this relationship has gone through revolutionary changes, man-woman relationships by comparison seem relatively frozen in time. The unbalanced relationship within marriage, in terms of postcolonial imagery, might be likened to that between coloniser and colonised. The coloniser is also motivated by economic reasons. Like the husband, he wants to impose his order and has no inhibitions in renaming his new possessions. Moreover, Christian philosophy lies at the core of marriage in Europe and this set of doctrines has played a major role in colonisation also. In many cases, colonisation has gone hand-in-hand with the imposition of the Christian religion. This was not the case in relation to Catalonia, which was Catholic, as was Spain, but it is certainly true of Ireland, whose indigenous peoples faced severe penalties in maintaining their Catholicism in the face of a colonisation process that derived some of its energy from Protestant zealotry.

It would of course be wrong to give the impression that marriage, and relations within marriage, have not changed over time. Processes of globalisation and other forms of social change (both internal to and external to Irish and Catalan societies) have disturbed and recast traditional expectations and practices. Some of this changing reality can be gleaned from very recent women's writing, as we shall see towards the end of this chapter.

Marriage, relationships and their associated costs and satisfactions, are at the heart of much women's writing. As Ann Owens Weekes suggests in her study of Irish women's writing: 'Awareness . . . of both the value and the cost of human relationships forms a constant undercurrent in Irish women's writings, the emphasis shifting from cost to value'.[16] Much the same sentiments in relation to Catalan women's writing are expressed by another literary critic, Anne Charlon.[17] It is not surprising women write about these issues if we consider that women's functions have been relegated, through marriage and other social conventions, to loving and caring rather than having active voices and roles in public and professional spaces. As a result, in their writing, the emphasis is mainly on exploring their emotions, especially in relation to love.

In many of the short stories discussed here, women come across as frustrated and seemingly cannot fulfil themselves within the confines of marriage. These short stories show how women reject the assumption that marriage is the only way for them. The outcome of those asymmetric relationships is that both partners, but the woman in particular, easily find themselves trapped in unhappy situations which generate tension, even hate. Physical and psychological violence often follow. Thus, one of the most valued collections of Catalan short stories, Caterina Albert's *Drames Rurals*, written as early as 1902, features eight married couples. Five of these marriages end up in killings, death or wives who become insane.[18] The irony is that marriage, which is generally celebrated in male-authored romantic literature as a source of unending bliss, is productive of the opposite condition. In effect, the authors, through their literary creations, are developing a radical critique of marriage which plays up the contradictions, the cruelty and the unfulfilling nature of the institution. With barely a change of terms, one might be describing the destructive nature of the relationship between the coloniser and the colonised. Both situations leave the 'victim' feeling trapped in a situation over which she has little control. In women's writing there is a strong desire for freedom.

In Ireland, the female critique of marriage is not only common among contemporary female writers but also has deeper historical roots. Reviewing a variety of treatments of marriage in Irish literature, Anne Owen Weekes observes:

> Maturity for (Jennifer) Johnston's heroines seems to entail the independence of living alone – Nancy gives up her dream of marrying Harry; Constance and Helen refuse to live with their lovers. Similarly, Maria Edgeworth, in the one text she wrote to entertain rather than instruct in acceptable behaviour, releases her female characters from marriage. Although Charlotte desires to marry Roddy in *The Real Charlotte*, marriage is presented throughout the text not as source of companionship and love, but as solitary confinement. Elizabeth Bowen's Lois, having attained some level of maturity, wishes to cultivate her own talents, not to marry. Aroon St Charles expresses her desire to be married, but her text suggests that her traditional wish masks her real desire for economic independence.[19]

This is true not only of Anglo-Irish writers, but of Gaelic-Irish writers of Catholic descent such as Kate O'Brien, who also portrays women as severely restricted within marriage.[20] In Catalonia, Anne Charlon points out that, at the beginning of the century, most Catalan women writers expressed such resentment towards men that celibacy was presented as a better option than marriage.[21]

Despite such subversive messages and the gradual liberalisation within Catalan and Irish societies in recent decades, the hegemonic grip of traditional conceptions of marriage remain firmly in place. The patriarchal family, while by no means the only family form, is still the typical or modal arrangement. An attack on this structure, as divorce was portrayed, is viewed as threatening a descent into 'anarchy'.[22] Similarly, it has been argued that the alternative to the 'civilising' mission of the colonial power was a state of barbarism. Each power structure has its own particular set of rationalisations for its behaviour. As writers in the political economy tradition would argue, colonised societies are incapable of achieving their full potential by virtue of their subordination to a colonial power.[23] Consequently, much postcolonial literature is about subversion:

> A characteristic of dominated literatures is an inevitable tendency towards subversion, and a study of the subversive strategies employed by postcolonial writers would reveal both the configurations of domination and the imaginative and creative responses to this condition.[24]

In women's fiction, there is often the intention to find different alternatives to a reality which women reject. The cry of freedom is a recurrent

element, echoing the aspiration for freedom of pre-independence colonial
countries. Indeed postcolonial theory calls the text 'a site of struggle'
precisely to underline that wish to change reality. Among women writers,
there is a desire to find love which implies freedom and not possession or
subordination. Some suggest that love is free and cannot be reduced to
monogamy (one relationship for life), fidelity and all the rules and
implications of marriage. Mercè Rodoreda believes that the nature of love
and desire are always linked to the unattainable, which means they cannot
be achieved within marriage. In 'El parc de les magnolies' (Magnolia Park),
she says: *'L'amor és com les magnòlies: molta olor mentre són a la branca, però
si les culls se't tornen negres el temps de bufar un misto. L'amor, com més lluny
més bonic'* (Love is like magnolias: very fragant when they are in the
branch, but if you pick them, they become black in no time. The farther
away love is, the better.)[25] In another story Rodoreda says:

> *El cinturó de castedat era una defensa innocent perque aquesta cosa misteriosa que
> tot d'una s'estableix entre un home i una dona . . . imperceptible pero aquí.
> Impalpable com polsim d'ala de papallona*

> (The chastity belt was a naive defence because this mysterious thing which
> suddenly happens between a man and a woman . . . imperceptible but here.
> Impalpable like the powder of a butterfly wing.)[26]

Another Catalan writer, Maria-Josep Ragué-Àrias, relates freedom with
love, which are two notions often linked in women's writing: *'l'amor no té
braços quan vol dir llibertat'* (love has no arms when it means freedom).[27]

In fact, in terms of the stories discussed here, it seems that these are the
experiences of love and freedom women feel it is most necessary to write
about. Thus in Edna O'Brien's 'The Love Object', which is a story about
the relationship between a single woman and a married man, the illicit
character of the liaison heightens its appeal. Indeed, freedom is a constant
element in women's writing.

To summarise the argument so far, 'compulsory marriage' colonises
women and it does so mainly in two ways: economically/socially and
emotionally/sexually. Firstly, I will discuss the economic and social
colonisation of women in marriage, as reflected in many of the stories.
Then I will turn to the theme of emotional and sexual colonisation. In the
third section I will explore loneliness, unhappiness and violence. Finally, I
will take up some alternative possibilities to conventional marriage as
appear in the newer writings on women and relationships.

ECONOMIC AND SOCIAL COLONISATION OF
WOMEN IN MARRIAGE

Since its origins, marriage has been intimately linked to economy. In modern times, in the Western world, it has been hidden behind a superficial veil called 'romantic love' but still the economic component is important. Catalan women were expected to improve their social and economical status by getting married. This is still the case today.[28] Among the wealthy classes, an attractive woman is seen as an external sign of wealth. There is a term used in everyday language, '*un bon parti*', meaning 'a good catch'. This notion, which is also current in Irish society, links marriage and economics. In a similar way, economy and gain are also at the core of the colonial enterprise. In both peasant and industrial society prior to this century, women were economically dependent on men – either their fathers or their husbands. They did not inherit apart from in exceptional circumstances, and had access to money only through men. True enough, there might have been a period of partial economic independence between adolescence and marriage when women worked as servants or factory girls, but much, indeed most, of their adult lives were spent in an economically dependent relationship within marriage.[29]

The inferior status of women within the United Kingdom was, at one time, legally enshrined in the workings of the state. These legal restrictions weakened the position of women and, as Owens Weekes explains, made them more dependent on men:

> Studying the subjection of women in the second half of the nineteenth century, Harriet and John Stuart Mill reasoned that marriage and mothering could hardly be as natural as Englishmen proclaimed, for if they were, then laws denying women other opportunities and enforcing their economic, legal and social dependence in marriage would not be necessary. Indeed, the Mills continued, the only rational defence for these laws was the belief that 'the alleged natural vocation of women was of all things the most repugnant to their nature'. Hence men denied women opportunity, they suggested, fearing that if allowed alternatives, women would demand marriages of equality rather than of dependence. The laws of England, in order to support women's 'natural vocation', had rendered them less free economically and legally than the slaves of ancient Rome.[30]

Historically, then, women were often economically poor within marriage, and sometimes made poorer still by virtue of being married. They were not encouraged to study or prepare themselves for competition. If they had a job, they frequently left it soon after marriage or worked part-time and came to depend financially on their husbands. Women were expected to find a husband who could support them instead of being self-sufficient economically. Nowadays, they might have better jobs but often these are less well-paid or less socially valued than those of men. This leaves women in a vulnerable situation of dependency which, in practice, results in varieties of abuse with violence as the most extreme. Abused wives, turned almost into powerless daughters, lose interest in self-improvement or other alternatives and come to rely, almost exclusively, on their husbands and children. This in turn undermines their confidence still further. In some of Caterina Albert's stories, centring on poor families, women have to work very hard in the house and are considered little more than free servants. That is the case in a story called 'Substitució' (Substitution) by Caterina Albert, where there is talk among the members of a family to find a wife for the heir capable of doing the work of the house, this being the main priority.[31] As usual in Albert's stories, this is set in a rural enviroment at the beginning of the twentieth century.

In Franco's Catalonia and in de Valera's Ireland, the destiny of women was to get married, raise a large family and not take employment outside the home. Divorce was forbidden, not only by the Church, but by the state in both societies.[32] Anne Charlon delineates the intensification of female repression under Franco's regime:

> *La dona casada va tornar a trobar-se en situació de menor d'edat sotmesa al seu marit, ni tan sols podia fer compres importants . . . Les dones casades no podien treballar en cap funció pública i tenien prohibit l'accés a moltes altres professions . . . La dona ideal, en la ideologia franquista, era esposa i mare. També calia que fos cristiana, casta i pura.*

> (The married woman went back to find herself in the situation of a minor, submitted to her husband, she could not even make expensive purchases . . . Married women could not be civil servants and were forbidden access to many other professions. The ideal woman, in Francoist ideology, was wife and mother. Also she should be Christian, chaste and pure.)[33]

From a feminist view, we could say that socially enforced efforts to find a wealthy husband involved a strong, albeit hidden, element of prostitution. Thus, the Christian duality of wife versus prostitute breaks down when it is acknowledged that, in trying to improve one's social and economical position, marriage becomes a kind of legalised prostitution. In other words, we could say that 'compulsory marriage' makes it difficult for women to avoid prostitution – being in or out of marriage makes only a difference of degree.

It might be objected that marriage is an option women choose freely, whereas colonisation is obviously an imposition through violence. But in practice it has never been just an option. There has been tremendous social pressure on women to get married and, if possible, to choose a better-off partner. There are several pejorative words for women who remain single: for example, the word 'spinster' has different connotations from those of 'bachelor'. This is changing fast as women are entering the paid labour force in large numbers and have different partners in their lives. Still, even in stories written in the 1990s, we find examples of women feeling pressurised to conform to traditional family roles and norms. For example, in '*Amor i cendres*' (Love and Ashes) by Montserrat Roig, Maria thinks her husband does not want to kiss her because her body is smelly. She believes it probably became smelly the day the doctor said she was not able to have children.[34] The smell symbolises a woman who is sterile. In 'Wedding Bells' by Katy Hayes, Geraldine says: 'Third level education was seen as a waste of money for me, because I'd give it all up and have babies.' But Katy Hayes 'fights back': 'The birth accident of my gender rendered me compromised to such an extent that I refused to compromise on any other issue. I only barely accepted my girlness, and never wore dresses.'[35]

In this context, we could relate the opposition women experience to that which colonised countries suffer when they fight for independence. The creation of the Irish Free State was preceded by strong resistance from the British government to the Irish independence movement. The wish for independence by the Catalan people became one of the reasons why the Francoist rebellion took place. The expansion of women's freedoms has also been in the teeth of opposition from entrenched interest groups. Writing earlier in time than Montserrat Roig and Katy Hayes, Mary Beckett and Caterina Albert have a particular interest in portraying different kinds of troubled marriages. In their stories we find very young women who have been brought up with the single ambition of getting a husband in order to fulfil their lives, to the exclusion of friendship, professional careers or creative and artistic activities. In Edna O'Brien's story, 'Sister Imelda' (1982), the central character resents this fate of 'compulsory marriage and motherhood':

> We never swam or sunbathed, we never did anything that was good for us. Life was geared to work and to meeting men and yet one knew that mating could only but lead to one's being a mother and hawking obstreperous children out to the seaside on Sunday. 'They know not what they do' could surely be said of us.[36]

Mary in Beckett's 'The Master and The Bombs' (1980), which is set in Northern Ireland, does not love her husband and does not even know why she married him. Mary started talking to him because he was a teacher.[37] Later we learn she herself had wanted to be a teacher. But as a girl she was brought up to catch a husband and was deprived of the opportunity of developing professional skills. Possibly she was projecting her wish to become a teacher onto the man she chose. This bears some resemblance to Hilary in 'Heaven', by the same author, who says: 'She had seized on the prospect of marriage with him as the only way to a real life – her old life had no sense or meaning'.[38] In 'A Farm of Land',[39] also by Beckett, a father wants his daughter to marry the neighbour in order to get land. In this case, the marriage alliance is directly linked to economics. This theme is common also in Caterina Albert's stories set in a rural Catalan context. Here we have almost pure examples of Irigaray's concept of men treating women as exchange objects.[40]

Indeed, in the work of Caterina Albert we discover even more troubled depictions of marriage. Catalan women's writing seems to depict an even more oppressive situation for women than in its Irish fictional counterparts. In 'La Pepa',[41] which is set in rural Catalonia and written in 1950, marriage is preceded by rape. Here a wealthy and attractive woman, Pepa, is married to a peasant and there is only hate between them. They sleep in separate rooms. When she is asked, she explains that when she was single her present husband was one of the family servants. One day he revealed his desire for her and she refused his advances. Though she continued to reject him, this served to inflame his desire further. Then one day, seeing his opportunity, he raped her. After the rape Pepa felt guilty about it and she felt obliged to marry him because she had been 'dishonoured'. She could not even explain to her mother why she married him. This was to avoid suffering on her mother's part, though she did apologise to her for her choice of partner. Her mother died shortly thereafter, compounding her woes. Pepa had married because the overriding imperative was to hide the shameful act and to save appearances. Rape seems to be a common feature in Catalan stories. Mercè Rodoreda's 'En el Tren' has another example. Being rejected, men feel the need to rape, which is one of the consequences of regarding women as objects and the crude use of violence to 'conquer', to obtain the desired. Through this heartrending account Caterina Albert appears to be saying that marriage is founded on appearances, power and violence, and at heart is false and unfulfilling for women. Women are the ones who end up being ashamed, even if they were not responsible for the shameful act. Other stories about forced marriages include Mary Beckett's 'Theresa',[42] where a girl has to marry a man she does not like because she has become pregnant. A single mother represents a serious threat to the economy of marriage. Núria Pompeia's 'Els Aparadors' (Shop Windows) depicts a nameless woman who chooses a much poorer man as a husband and as a result her horrified parents and her brothers declare she is dead as far as they concerned.[43] They no longer talk to her and she is disinherited. Worse still, her husband later abandons her and she has to support their children herself.

In terms of wealth, women are often disadvantaged relative to men. A good example of this is in one of Caterina Albert's rural stories, 'The Daughter-in-law'. While making bread in the family business, the young woman, Beleta, discovers her father-in-law's secret – a large amount of money. When the man dies, she shows the money to her mother-in-law who immediately recognises it as her own. It is her dowry. Her husband took it from her on the wedding day, saying later that he had lost it in a business deal. She was of course the poorer for all this. Later on, Beleta discovers something else. Her own husband also lies to her. Not only has he an affair with another woman but Beleta learns he never really loved her. Moreover, he is siphoning off money from their household to give to his lover.

Lying is intrinsic to marriages of this kind. The coloniser/husband takes advantage of his position of power and tries to enrich himself by conquering territories and/or women, and one of the resources at his disposal is lying. The coloniser rationalises his actions by claiming the colonised will also benefit. Women are assured that marriage is to their benefit also, both materially and psychologically. Their masters will protect them from outside aggressors and provide them with security. But the reality can be very different. We know from sociological studies that most violence against women is perpetrated within the household.

One avenue to economic independence for women, perverse as it may seem, is through widowhood. According to Concepció Gil, in Catalan history widows were the women who achieved a highest degree of independence.[44] The protagonist in 'L'Airet del Matí, a Barcelona' (The Morning Breeze in Barcelona) has just become a widow and she says: '*El primer dia que vaig sortir al carrer a les set del matí, va ser el dia mes feliç de la meva vida.*'[45] (The first day I went out at seven in the morning was the happiest day of my life). As in other stories, an air of freedom, expressed through the freshness of the morning breeze, accompanies her new-found independence. She exults:

Em sento de vint anys. Vaig a treballar. Jo. Com un home, com una personal qualsevol, que no ha de restar a casa rumiant les malures. Sóc jo qui espera l'autobús . . . Ningú no m'ha de demanar comptes, ara.

(I feel I am twenty. I go to work. I. Like a man, like anyone who does not
have to be at home having bad thoughts. It is I who waits for the bus . . .
Nobody is going to call me to account.)[46]

There are parallels in Irish literature where issues of economic independence are also to the fore. In Eilís Ní Dhuibhne's 'Lili Marlene',
another widow, Lili, says:

> I loved all the work, actually. I just loved working, and feeling that I was
> making something . . . Also, I liked feeling that I was making money. Every
> minute I spent working in that hotel was different from the time I spent
> working at home, because every minute was money in my pocket. That
> gave my time a new meaning, and it made me feel valuable, precious.[47]

An independent widow is a woman without a man to control her and her
sexuality. In that sense she is threatening to the social order of the local
community. In 'The Widow',[48] written by Edna O'Brien in 1990, Bridget
becomes an independent woman following her husband's death. This
sense of independence, even contentment, deeply annoys the people of
the village. They come to criticise her for this reason, going out of their
way to find defects in her personality and behaviour. A particular focus of
malice is the fact that she likes drinking: 'The news of her drinking soon
spread, and the verdict was that she could bend the elbow with any
man'.[49] Here the word 'verdict' emphasises the collective nature of this
hostility. The fact that the widow has male boarders in her house leaves
her open to the suggestion of being a sort of prostitute: 'Her house was
sarcastically called the Pleasure Dome, and sometimes, more maliciously,
she was coupled with the song "Biddy the Whore, who lived in a hotel
without any door"'.[50] It is worth noting here how people in the village
come to associate a woman possibly enjoying sexuality with being a
prostitute. But the worst comes when she starts going out with one of the
boarders. The people simply protest:

> After all, she was a widow, and she was a woman in her forties, who ought
> to know better. Neighbours began to watch more carefully, especially at
> night, to see how many lights went on in the upstairs rooms – to see if they
> had separate bedrooms or were living in mortal sin.[51]

In this particular story it is easy to see how a strongly conservative and
Catholic society had power over people's lives and minds and over
women's lives in particular. Unsettled by apparent happiness outside
conventional modes of behaviour, people in the local community eagerly

await their downfall: 'Her happiness was too much for people to take; they called her a hussy, they predicted another breach of promise, they waited for the downfall'.[52] The priest, however, does not protest because Bridget's fiancé had given him a 'substantial offering for Masses',[53] which reflects the hypocrisy of the Church. The level of malice, in the end, reaches the point where people accuse her of having killed her own husband. In a tragic, almost inevitable ending, her life having been made almost unbearable, Bridget dies in a car accident after drinking too much.

In Carme Riera's 'Es Nus, es Buit',[54] (The Lump, the Emptiness) Bel, a hard working older woman, is constantly harassed by her husband and when he dies, amazingly, it takes her a few weeks to get used to the absence of male aggression. When she does so, she begins to savour her new life on her own. This does not last long. She is treated by her male relatives as an encumbrance, something left over from her husband's life. Bel's nephews arrange to put her in an old people's home even though she wishes to stay in her late husband's house. Consigned to the old people's home, she feels unwell. She imagines she has a lump in her stomach and there is a great emptiness within.[55]

A number of women authors writing before the 1980s take up the theme of how social pressure prevented women from taking up paths other than those leading to marriage. They wonder about why options such as single motherhood were so heavily punished by society and in what particularly violent ways that punishment was meted out. Clearly, sexual life outside marriage and single motherhood both strongly challenged traditional views of marriage. For instance, in Caterina Albert's 'La jove' (The Daughter-in-law),[56] mentioned earlier, a single girl becomes pregnant. Her mother is terribly worried about it and warns her that if the girl's brother knows about it he will kill her. As her brother, he has no reason to be jealous, but as a male member of the family, he is supposed to act to control such behaviour and act to enforce the patriarchal order.

An extreme example is furnished as one of Mercè Rodoreda's more melodramatic stories. 'Divendres 8 de juny' (Friday 8th June)[57] describes how a nameless girl, in the extremes of poverty and despair, throws her baby and herself into the river. The protagonist of the story did not have work, or even a house in which to live. The baby is the result of a rape by two men who also tried to kill her. But violence from men did not finish there. After the rape, she had gone to the police station but she was afraid to accuse the two men, as they were well known to her. While in the station, she was harassed by the policeman who kept saying: 'Quina pinta, quina pinta mes galdosa' (What a good-looker).[58] In despair, she sees death as the only escape.

Edna O'Brien details a comparable situation in 'Savages'. Mabel is a single girl, just back from Australia, having spent ten years there. There is some suspicion in the village that she may be pregnant. A few women cruelly set a trap for her:

> The plan was that they would invite Mabel to tea, flatter her by telling her how thin she looked, and then having put her off guard, Rita was to steal up on her from behind and put a measuring tape around her waist. It turned out that Mabel was huge and by nightfall the conclusion was that Mabel was indeed having a baby. After that she was shunned at Mass, shunned on her way down from Mass, and avoided when she went into the shops.[59]

To compound these difficulties, she is rejected at home as well, to the extent that her father threatens to kill her. Any relationship outside marriage, be it heterosexual or homosexual, attracts censure and this is especially so for women. In Carme Riera's 'Unes flors' (Some Flowers), a man leaves his wife and takes their daughter with him, just because he thinks his wife is unfaithful. It later turns out he has been wrong. The wife is merely told she was lucky: after all, she could have been put into prison. In Franco's time, adultery was strongly penalised. Unorthodox behaviour is heavily penalised in another of O'Brien's story, 'Dramas'.[60] A newcomer tries to settle in a village in rural Ireland. When people in the village discover he is homosexual, the communal urge is to kill him.

Moral or religious reasons give grounds for stigmatising single parenthood, but Caterina Albert points to more material reasons why single motherhood arouses such strong criticism from society. In a story written as early as 1950, Albert's 'Diàleg prismàtic' (Prismatic Dialogue), the question posed is about parenthood. In this story, two men talk about women and one says: 'Si se'ls dona llibertat, com tindrem seguretat de la nostra nissaga?' (If they are given freedom, how are we going to be sure about our lineage?).[61] Clearly this is of concern to fathers, especially those with property. The practice, which still persists to this day, of placing the father's surname on the children of the union, testifies to these sensitivities. Though it is often left unremarked, a woman loses part of her social identity when she adopts her husband's surname. Again there is an analogy here with colonial expansion, where the colonising power marks out new territories in its own image, naming and renaming settlements, places and other features of the landscape. Hence New England, New Amsterdam and New France; so also San Francisco, Salisbury and Santiago.

EMOTIONAL AND SEXUAL COLONISATION OF
WOMEN IN MARRIAGE

In 'Cendres' (Ashes), a story written in 1950, Caterina Albert illustrates how men may act as colonisers in marriage. In this story Marianita and Eusebi meet again after many years spent apart. He had emigrated to Argentina, but before that they had started a relationship which he then broke off. She had never known why. Reaching back in time, he now tries to explain why, despite loving her, he had decided not to marry her. With her he did not have the feeling that he 'possessed' her totally. She was too strong a personality for him. The text is quite explicit, locating the psychology of the masculine coloniser in nature itself. Not being in command leads to man's self-extinguishment:

> *per imperatiu de la naturalesa, l'home té sempre l'instint de manar, i si no pot manar, més o menys despòticament, sobre tot lo que el rodeja, se'n faci cabal o no, no es feliç . . . Tot el foc intern se li apaga . . . tot se li queda reduit a cendres . . . que es van refredant gradualment.*

> (By nature, the man always has the instinct to be in command and if he cannot be in command, more or less despotically, over everything which is around him, whether he is obeyed or not, he is not happy . . . All his internal fire dies down . . . everything becomes reduced to ashes . . . which cool down gradually.)[62]

Eusebi had married Marianita's cousin instead, who was her opposite: innocent, naïve, very young. He goes on to describe what kind of man he is in relation to the young woman:

> *la més lògica temptació per a un mascle dominador, per a un home de presa . . . per a un qui vulga centrar-ho tot en ell, regnar en tot amb autoritat pacífica i indiscutida, sense resistències ni retops destorbadors; que vol que la muller no pensi ni senti per compte propi, sinó d'acord amb el pensament i amb els sentiments d'ell.*

> (the most logical temptation for a dominant male, for a man of prey . . . for somebody who wants to be the centre of everything, to reign over everything, with peaceful and unquestionable authority, without resistance, who wants his wife not to feel or think for herself but according to his feelings.)[63]

In a significant exchange Marianita asks him if he has been happy with the outcome. On balance, Eusebi is not so sure dominating his wife has, in fact, brought much happiness to him. Their sexual relationship became monotonous, predictable, boring. In this case, a traditional-type marriage has proved harmful also for the man:

potser la personalitat que a tu et sobrava li mancava a ella una mica massa . . . Ella no era pròpiament ella, sino un reflex meu, tal com un dia jo havia anhelat . . . et confessaré que a causa de l'absoluta identificació de l'un a l'altre, potser les nostres relacions íntimes sobrenadaren, en general, en una mena de llac de plàcida monotonia.

(Perhaps the extra personality you had was lacking in her too much . . . She was not herself but my reflex in the way I had longed for . . . I'll confess that, because of the absolute identification with each other, maybe our intimate relationship floated in a kind of lake of calm monotony.)[64]

Unexpectedly, at the end of the story, Marianita turns the tables by proving to Eusebi that his wife was more complex than he imagined. She shows him love letters his wife wrote to another man. Her intention is to punish his male vanity, the coloniser's male vanity.

Underneath the mask of deference and submission the colonised entertained powerful contrary emotions and feelings. In 'Cendres' female subjectivity is represented as being very different from male subjectivity. The point is more heavily underlined in Núria Pompeia's 'L'ordre i el matrimoni' (The Order and Marriage). The nameless protagonist is analysing the failure of her marriage. According to her, men are less objective, more unidirectional and more selfish. By contrast, women have a more extensive range of interests and concerns, being engaged with friends and relatives and less preoccupied with the ego. But in the end she feels hollowed out, emotionally as well as physically: '*tinc la sensació que m'esteu engolint mica a mica, tots plegats – tu, la casa, els fills – des de fa molt de temps i que ara ja heu arribat als ossos*', (I have the feeling that you, the house and the children have been gobbling me up, little by little, for a long time now and you have already got to my bones).[65] She feels she is the only member in the family who has been cheated, who has empty hands which are open to receive a blow and to beg, to ask for affection. She thinks it is not her husband's fault but in the nature of traditional marriage which creates so much stress for the woman who has to stay at home and sacrifice her life for the other members of the family. She is living for others but, at the same time, her work is not socially recognised nor is she paid. Her work is invisible. She uses an old Catalan saying: 'Qui paga, mana' (The one who pays is the one who commands). It is true that at the end of the twentieth century more women are economically independent. Yet many are still dependent on their husbands which, in practice, means some will put up with abuse. The subservient position makes them vulnerable emotionally as well as feeling disadvantaged compared to men.

If one of the most powerful tools of colonisation is control of language, perhaps the most powerful tool of patriarchy is the control of women's sexuality. Though waning in recent decades, the control of women's sexuality has been paramount, disempowering women because sexuality, like language, is the most intimate sign of personal identity. In some African countries, this control over women's sexuality is extreme, with the amputation of women's genital organs, but in the Western world it is also subjected to patriarchy, although in a much more indirect way.

In the short stories produced before the 1980s, sex is rarely present, at least explicitly. When sex is described, it is often presented as unpleasant or unfulfilling for women. French feminists argue that sex in Western culture is constructed to satisfy male desire. There is an emphasis on male erection and on penetration. The stress on penetration is seen in feminist discourse as a way to colonise women. The urge to penetrate, to possess, may be compared with the desire to possess and dominate another country. Masculine sexuality is conceived as foreign to women's sexuality, a sexuality which has not been allowed to develop properly. Women even feel guilty of their own desire, as Hélène Cixous points out. According to her, this is what explains female rape fantasies, for example, and it also explains women feeling guilty about their desire to obtain mastery over language.[66] Women do not normally use the word 'possession' in love language. More specifically, Irigaray says that a man needs an object to enjoy sexuality but a woman does not.[67] Unlike him, she derives pleasure from her own sexual organs and her body in general. Penetration is a secondary consideration. The images of mother, virgin and prostitute in patriarchal societies are social roles imposed on women to deprive them of sexual pleasure. Those categories disempower women. That is the reason why frigidity is said to be so high among Western women.[68] Perhaps, one might speculate, frigidity is a consequence of being a 'colonised gender'. As usual, language is revealing in this matter. The word 'impotence' has a Latin origin which means 'lack of power'. That means that male sexuality has to do with power. However, etymologically, the term 'frigidity' has to do with 'coldness' which is more linked to 'death' or the 'lack of warmth' than to anything related to power. Once more we can suggest that male-centred constructions of reality are harmful for women's lives and in this case for women's sexuality.

Sexuality is useful in explaining the link between femaleness and colonisation. If sexuality is intimately related to the unconscious, then the root of woman's being is colonised. Irigaray goes further and says that, even if women feel pleasure in traditional sex, it is 'a masochistic prostitution of her body to a desire that is not really her own, and it leaves her in a familiar state of dependency upon man'.[69] The consequence is that women feel confused: 'she does not know, or no longer knows, what she wants'.[70] This feeling of confusion often finds common expression in female writing. The young and nameless protagonist in Carme Riera's 'Un capvespre' (An Evening), has the opportunity to make love with her partner, Sergi, for the first time because somebody has lent them a flat. However, she cannot do it. She feels as if she is in prison and Sergi is her warder. She is envious of the people she hears in the street. Her only desire is to leave the room and be free.[71] In Rodoreda's 'Pluja' (Rain),[72] the woman waits for an hour in her flat for the man to come but, all of a sudden, she leaves the flat leaving a note to him saying she does not want to see him anymore. So does Miss Hawkings in 'Christmas Roses'.[73]

Sometimes the sense of alienation from sex takes extreme form. In a wedding-night scene from the story 'La sang del castell' (Blood in the Castle), the protagonist describes the man-woman encounter in martial terms.

> Enric has penetrated me with his sword, I have felt whipped by his aggressive and triumphant desire, he has broken me after breaking my bride tulles violently, he has cried 'you are mine!' and he has not heard my fearful scream. 'Mine, mine', he cried whereas he was jumping and jumping again and again on the top of me, breaking my fragile and tender dream.[74]

Her dream was about princes and castles and mermaids but the reality turns up to be totally different. Charlon says that women's disappointment after the first sexual encounter is a recurring theme in Catalan women's fiction.[75]

A lack of sexual fulfilment is also evident in the literature, though perhaps not to the same degree. In Julia O'Faolain's 'Man in the Cellar', after love-making Una's husband, Carlo, feels bad and withdraws. He does not 'need' her for another while. As she ironically explains:

> After making love . . . Carlo tended to become testy, even truculent. He may have felt he needn't be pleasant any longer since he wouldn't need me again that day or he may have held some sort of grudge against me: a sense perhaps of loss.[76]

Una leaves her husband but, in general, though unhappy, the wife in many of the stories is unable to leave her husband, not only because of fear of the economic and social consequences, but also because of emotional ties which bind her to her unhappy fate. She has been emotionally colonised. Those ties are not normally primarily sexual, this being often the least satisfying aspect of marriage, but emotional. The woman's life has been concentrated on her husband and their children. There is not much else. If one adopts Irigaray's perspective, then many women in marriage rapidly lose confidence and are little more than the objects of male power and male sexuality.

There is no doubt younger women writers want to create a totally different sense of sexuality which has more to do with themselves, their bodies and a sense of freedom. The Irish writer Angela Bourke exclaims in 'Mayonnaise to the Hills':

> I just feel so alive when I come down here. I walk along the road and smell the turf smoke and the salty air and I want to open my mouth and my nose wider and wider to take it in. And then at night the sky is so clean. You feel if you could open wide enough you could swallow the stars. That's what sex is about after all, isn't it?[77]

Failure in sex, for a variety of reasons, is a common theme in postcolonial Irish writing. Patrick Kavanagh, in his long poem 'The Great Hunger', associates images of the famine of the 1840s with sexual starvation in the Irish countryside in the mid-twentieth century. (In Kavanagh's lifetime the Irish Free State had the highest level of permanent celibacy in the world.) At the end of James Joyce's short story, 'The Dead', the natural outcome in terms of the storyline might seem to be making love. Joyce avoids this climax. Gretta falls asleep and her husband, Gabriel, is left alone looking out at the snow. According to Colm Tóibín, the snow symbolises sex, the unmentionable in Catholic Irish society. For Tóibín: 'Snow was general all over Irish fiction' and the writers discovered that 'if you wrote short stories you didn't have to mention sex'.[78]

Failure in sex is also common enough in writings in postcolonial Catalonia. According to the Catalan writer Montserrat Roig, Catalonia is sexually a very frustrated country, much more so than other parts of Spain. Roig claims that the language of love, for example, is poorly developed. Catalan women experience sexuality with guilt and feelings of sin; they constantly repress themselves sexually. Roig goes on to say that, in general, 'el hombre catalán es muy inhibido; en la cama es bastante infantil' (the Catalan man is very inhibited; in bed, he is very childish).[79] In her survey of Catalan women's literature, written between 1960 and 1980, Anne Charlon discovers little sensitivity to women's needs and feelings:

> *l'home, en la relació sexual busca el plaer personal i poques vegades es preocupa dels desigs i dels plaers de la seva companya. En molts casos la relació sexual és imposada i dolorosa*

(in sexuality, man seeks his personal pleasure and rarely is he concerned with his partner's wishes and pleasure. In many cases, the sexual relationship is imposed and full of tears.)[80]

Going back to fiction, most of Mary Beckett's stories unfold in a household setting where tired, fed-up wives with numerous children have dreadful husbands and feel emotionally isolated and frustrated in an atmosphere which is everything but sexual. Her story 'The Master and the Bombs' is a good example of the universe in which her short stories develop. In this case, Helen is an unhappy wife. Her husband is the master of the primary school and in five years they have had four children. Presumably they have been following Catholic directions regarding birth control. Helen received little affection because her mother died when she was a child. Her father, the first male figure in her life, was distant. Egotistical, busy with life outside the home, he had little time or inclination to give affection to his daughter. Women are the ones who are supposed to have an affectionate and relational function. Men do not have to worry about that difficult sphere, even if there is no woman in the family. Coming out of such a damaging childhood, Helen thought the only solution she had, the only way to be happy and fulfilled, was by having children, substituting love for her children for the love her mother and father, for different reasons, had not been able to give her. Moreover, in Irish Catholic society motherhood was presented as being necessary to achieve womanhood. In order to achieve womanhood, women needed to have children – that is their main function in life, yet women writers are strongly critical about it. Julia O'Faolain makes this point in one of her stories: 'A woman's first obligation is to her family. No matter what her husband does, she must strive to keep it together.'[81] Going back to Beckett's story, when Helen was pregnant, she was extremely happy in herself but the communication with her husband, even in those moments, was non-existent to the point of hate. Her enjoyment of pregnancy has resonances with the concept 'joissance' of French feminism which is a way to protect herself from caring too much about others:

> It was a different world I discovered. I was placid, I was contented. Nothing penetrated me. I stopped aching for the people who were poor or lost or cold. I read books and couldn't remember a word of them. I sat in company with my hands in my lap not offering a word to the conversation. At Christmas I was so besotted that instead of talking to Christ in the stable I talked to him as if He were the child moving in my own womb. I would have shared all this with Matthew, but he didn't seem to want to hear, nor to feel the child kicking nor to be seen out with me.[82]

Being pregnant, she was both happy and self-contained. She did not need anything or anybody. A sense of communion with her baby gave her an intense feeling of happiness to the point that gave meaning to her life. Inevitably, the feeling was temporary; children grow up. Childbearing is only one phase in the life cycle, and hence only a temporary release from emotional emptiness.

Not only does Matthew not love her, he is selfish and does little or nothing in the house and never helps with the children. That is the wife's job. On holidays, he is content to read the newspaper, excluding others: 'He'd continue reading the paper but I'd say he wasn't reading it; there never was enough in any paper to give such long reading. He must have been sitting there hating me much more than I hated him because I was busy and I had the baby'.[83] Helen does not seem to be terribly worried about him hating her, but she is aware of it. She recognises both are unhappy and trying to escape. In her case, it is by having children. In his, it is by the more extreme expedient of going to prison. 'The master', as people call him, volunteers to go to prison. He had been suspected of terrorism and he bonds himself in. He cannot stand his family any longer. She has similar feelings of rejection: 'when he arrives home tired, I feel revulsion. I have to go to another room'.[84]

Marriage was not good for either of them. But if we compare the two outcomes, the difference is that maternity, because it is a female experience, is not recognised sufficiently in a patriarchal society, whereas masculine activities are usually more highly valued, even if they have to do with terrorism. After all, 'he can be a hero when he comes back'.[85]

We have seen in Mary Beckett's 'The Master and the Bombs' that motherhood is only a temporary solution for women. In these stories there is a deep desire for freedom, as a result of feeling trapped within marriage. 'The Excursion',[86] again by Beckett, offers a further perspective on marriage, frustration and violence. This is the story of a submissive Belfast wife who, at the end, finally explodes. Her local community committee has organised a trip to Dublin. She would love to go but she knows her husband will not allow her. He is more of a domineering father figure than a companion. Like a child, she is afraid even to ask him: 'Presently she got up and began to clear away the tea things with slow, ponderous movements, as if she had used all her energy in making up her mind to ask James about the excursion'.[87] In fact, she is normally afraid to ask him for permission: 'But she never was able to ask James for anything without nerving herself for hours beforehand. And each year it was getting harder and harder to talk to him at all'.[88] Lack of communication has become endemic within the married relationship. When her husband arrives, he lets her know that he is the one who is going. She is not. She regrets having dreamt about the trip: 'All those dreams that she had were nonsense – wasting her time imagining foolishness like that. Why should she have a whole day to enjoy herself?'[89] Her long experience of submitting makes her used to the disappointment – it even allows her enjoy it. There are elements of masochism in the acquiescence.

When her husband gets back home from the excursion, he is so drunk that he cannot walk and some men have to carry him. They tell her he spent the whole day drinking in a pub beside the station, not seeing anything of the city. Anger wells up within her because he has not even used the opportunity to enjoy the day:

> There would be no conversation to be made out of that. What right had he to take the day and waste it when she could have made such good use of it? He staggered towards the fireplace, groping blindly for the mantelpiece. She watched him, tight-lipped, and then a wild urge made her push him furiously in front of the fire. He threw up his hand, grabbing at the mantelpiece as he fell, and pulled himself into the chair.[90]

Another case of emotional disappointment in marriage is Rodoreda's 'Abans de morir' (Before Dying).[91] In this story, Marta marries a man who had been chasing her. Marius is arrogant: instead of asking her to marry him, one day he introduces her as his fiancée. He is very sure of himself, maybe too sure. He does not bother to ask her to marry him, rather he lets her know. At the time she is impressed by a confidence she lacks. Once she is married she realises that her husband is still in love with his former lover. He married her to use her. Like the colonisers use their colonies, husbands use their wives for instrumental reasons. Marius does not want to talk about his lover and does not want to change the situation. Understandably, she feels imprisoned and cannot find a way out. Before marrying, she used to paint but as a married woman she becomes totally isolated and has no other activity than looking after her husband and the house. As a result, she feels lonely and empty to the extent of wanting to kill herself. At least, in this way, she reasons, her husband will feel guilty for the rest of his life. Committing suicide is the only way she can hurt him. She does take her own life. On her wedding day, Marta had caught a ghostly image of herself in the mirror, dying. Now, holding her wedding dress, once more she looks at herself in the mirror and again she sees a ghost. Rodoreda uses the image of impending death to express how women are emotionally destroyed through marriage.

The limiting effects of traditional marriage, but with suggestions of a consciousness of the nature of the problem, are apparent in Boylan's ironically titled 'Bad Woman'. About Jude, the protagonist and the story, the narrator says:

> There was nothing special about her marriage. They got married, had children and those grew up. Because so little happened to her, she was like a grate that has never been properly cleaned, and over the years the flame burned lower and now there was only a dull glow.[92]

As a result, she concludes she needs a new life. But escape from marriage is not necessarily easy. In 'Amor de mare' (Mother's Love), written as late as 1997, Isabel-Clara Simó explains a much more dramatic case in which a woman is beaten by her husband who does not give her enough money for the family. When she does finally divorce him she is not accepted socially as an independent person.

LONELINESS, UNHAPPINESS, VIOLENCE AND EXILE

In many women's stories we find one's love for life is often the source of unhappiness and solitude. Married life turns into boredom and monotony for women. The ending of O'Brien's magnificent story 'The Connor Girls', written in 1982, is poignant. It shows how marriage changes women utterly. On her first trip home to the West of Ireland, her husband, 'who was not of our religion',[93] shows no appreciation or respect for her origin. She says: 'at that moment I realised that by choosing his world I had said goodbye to my own and to those in it. By such choices we gradually become exiles, until at last we are quite alone.'[94] For O'Brien, 'choosing his world' (marriage), means 'goodbye to my own' (abandoning herself). O'Brien is not a young writer – she was born in 1932 – but the story might have been written by the new generation of Irish women writers. It refers to a key issue. Women lose much of their identity, in the same way as they lose their surname, when they get married.

Loneliness is a common feeling among women who fall in love and give themselves completely and this is a recurrent feeling in the literature they produce. For Edna O'Brien love is a transcendent experience,[95] a substitute for religion. Simone de Beauvoir established this analogy between love and religion in *The Second Sex*. She said that women give themselves totally to their 'masters' as a way of escape whereas men want to take possession of women in order to remain 'sovereign subjects'.[96] As we shall see later, women now tend to confront their situation rather than invoke defence mechanisms to avoid uncomfortable realities.

It has been observed that, following colonisation, people experience feelings of emptiness, confusion, lack of confidence and solitude. It is remarkable how closely these feelings parallel those experienced by some women in marriage, both in their fictional representation and in real life. Intellectuals in postcolonial societies have an urgent need to define themselves 'both against the identity given them by their colonial past and against international postmodernism'.[97] The nameless protagonist in 'Alfonso' by Isabel-Clara Simó, written in 1995, undergoes just such a 'crisis of identity'. After her wealthy and successful husband dies, she can't stop questioning herself about what she has been and the meaning of her life of subservience to him, and she questions if she had loved him. She wonders if she has been only the parasite of a man. She concludes by asking herself: 'Què sóc jo, doncs'[98] (What am I, then?). Those crises of identity can lead to exile. Some women and some postcolonial peoples find they have to leave their countries of origin as a result of political or social pressures. Among the women writers who have left their countries, either temporarily or permanently, we may count Mercè Rodoreda, Edna O'Brien, Montserrat Roig, Julia O'Faolain and Helena Valentí.

The unbalanced emotional relationship between wives and husbands can, tragically, evolve into violence. The degree of domestic violence, both physical and psychological, in women's short-story writing is alarming in both literatures but especially in Catalonia. In the curiously entitled 'A Sense of Humour', Mary Dorcey delineates the condition of one battered woman. Kate is frequently beaten by her husband and she accepts it but worries about her children being beaten too:

> 'After that, it happened again. Always after the pub. Shouting and yelling, beating me about the head and chest. One time my face was so bruised and swollen I could not leave the house for days. I did not mind for myself. I could have put up with it, it was only when he started on the children I had to do something . . . Once I tried to escape. He caught me and threw me down the stairs. I had a broken arm that time.'[99]

Enduring that kind of violence and even accepting a rationale for it may be a psychological disorder which is common among housewives. Kate adds:

> She had told no one . . . In the end she did not even try to escape. She knew she deserved it. He would not beat her and abuse her unless she did, unless she was all the things he called her. The pain was final then. She knew that she was stupid, vicious, ugly; everything he named her and when she slept

with him again it made her the whore he said she was. But only he could absolve her because only he knew how base she was. That knowledge was what had kept her with him so long.[100]

This kind of violence in which women find themselves is probably the extreme result of having lost their personal sense of identity after 'compulsory marriage'. Wives believe themselves to be mere objects, mere appendages of their lords and masters. It also shows how human beings can come to accept and treat as normal extreme forms of abuse and degradation. Kate, despite or because of her suffering, internalises images of herself as worthless and as a prostitute.

Northern Ireland is not an exception in relation to domestic violence. Indeed, it may have been intensified by the long years of political violence. Women complained about political violence, but not, paradoxically, about violence at home. Monica McWilliams points out: 'women protested vociferously against the violence of the British Army throughout the 1970s . . . but they were less likely to protest against the violence of their male partners in their own homes'.[101]

Take the short story 'A Social Call' by Brenda Murphy. Bernie has just had her fourth child. The fact that she married only four years before reflects her powerlessness in terms of controlling her own fertility. When she discovers that her husband has weapons, she does not want him to leave the house. He beats her in front of the children: 'Bernie was lying on the floor, hands up over her face, knees drawn up close to her belly. He was standing over her, legs apart. He lifted his boot to kick her'.[102] When Bernie's friend tries to help her, the man says: 'Now you listen, you interfering wee whore. This is my house; that is my wife. Keep your fucking nose out of my business or I'll break it for you.'[103] At the end of the story, the husband is shown conducting a 'punishment' shooting. A sixteen-year-old is shot in both knees because of anti-social behaviour. Anti-social behaviour, it seems, only happens outside the home.

Also from the north, Fiona Barr explores male violence in the story 'Excursion'. Angela is afraid her husband will be drunk when he gets back home, which means he will give her a beating. He does:

> As she tried to move round him to avoid his threat, he swung at her suddenly and punched her face. 'You're no better than a whore,' and he pushed her to the ground. By now she was crying. She tried to crawl back to the front door, but he had caught her by the hair and dragged her towards the wall. The children began screaming though they dared not help her. He pushed her face to the floor and started to bang it hard against the

carpet. Carpet, wall, carpet, wall. 'You old whore, you're a dirty bitch,' he roared at her, finding strength in his fury . . . 'I'll fix your face for you. They'll not know you tomorrow. I'll fix it right and good. Lifting her battered face to him, he whacked it with his hand, dropped her like a rag doll and staggered to the bathroom.[104]

These scenes of violence are frequent. Once a person takes power over another (husband-wife, coloniser-colonised), there is no resolution, no means of control. A partial explanation might be that within the territory of the marriage and the home men regress, becoming child-tyrants again. Certainly there are a number of references to men as 'childish', wanting always to win. Thus Jonathan in 'Losing' who 'couldn't bear to lose'[105] or the more extreme case in which a man commits murder and, at the end of the story, explains why: 'Io tenia rao. El mavia rrubat 3 sac de garofes i io ma vai rebengar.' (I was right. He had stolen three bags of vetches and I took revenge).[106] Women are resisting now. So did postcolonial countries.

Also noteworthy is the association between abuse and seeing wives as prostitutes, even though the women are marriage partners. This reinforces the argument that marriage does not really 'save' women from being the objects of men's attentions. Rather the opposite. To take a more extreme example, Carme Riera gives another example in 'Melodrama Alcoia'.[107] Conxita is married to a man, Jacint, who does not earn much but he still does not want his wife to work outside the home. Eventually she feels obliged to prostitute herself to be able to support her children. When her husband discovers what is going on, he calls her a whore and he kills her. The husband's violence is a complex phenomenon but it is certainly linked to male pride and the asymmetric power relationship within marriage. A similar kind of jealousy ending up in murder also occurs in Mercè Rodoreda's 'En el tren' (On the Train).[108]

Caterina Albert is a writer who is drawn almost obsessively to violence. In 1898, at a very early age, she published a play about a young woman who feels obliged to kill her own child. The same happens in Rodoreda's 'Divendres 8 de juny' (Friday 8 June)[109] where the mother also kills herself and her baby daughter. Albert tried to explain, possibly justify, this fascination with the violent side of humanity in her introduction to *Ombrívoles* (Sombre Stories) (1904).[110] There she observes this orientation is a technique which aids her writing. Depicting violence is not a result of pessimism; rather, she had to choose a side and she chooses what she calls 'the fourth side', the one of 'the shadow'. Her argument homes in on essence: the fourth side does not contain superficialities or details; it is authentic because it comes directly from the unconscious. A more

mundane explanation might be that violence makes the text more powerful and, in a sense, more masculine. Making the text more masculine may
have helped this author at a time when women's writing was undervalued.
But there is no doubt she uses violence to denounce injustice, particularly
that produced by gender asymmetry.

Two examples of violence are the stories 'Fideuet' and 'Xona', where
women are described as sensible and hardworking whereas men are
portrayed as incompetent and lazy. Institutionalised relationships of power
and inequality, particularly within marriage, structure personal experiences
of unhappiness and violence. One also has a sense of these patterns of
inequality being reproduced in time. In 'La Xona', even the little boy
settles into the mould of male irresponsibility while the poor baby girl, as
if her fate had already been sealed, loses both her hands.

Violence by married men is more frequent, at least at the level of
representation in short stories, in the case of Catalonia as compared to
Ireland. This possibly reflects the social reality, although it is hard to be
sure. It is also noticeable, again at the level of representation, that the
violence portrayed in Catalan stories is of a more extreme kind. We have
seen some examples of this already. One might add that of Albert's 'El
Met de les Conques' (Met from Les Conques) . In the story Met recalls an
incident he saw in the country. In this scene, a peasant beats his wife until
she bends over and agrees to work like an animal, placed alongside the
horse to pull the plough.[111] She becomes, literally, a beast of burden. In a
similar way one might speak of the coloniser reducing indigenous people
to beasts of burden.

These writers' stories about unfulfilling marriages also include women
going mad and even trying to kill their husbands. Yet, women only use
violence after madness or in extreme cases as a desperate response to long-
running abuse. A good example is Caterina Albert's 'Després de l'amor'
(After love).[112] Sandra M. Gilbert and Susan Gubar in *The Madwoman in
the Attic*[113] discuss the figure of the madwoman as 'the author's double, an
image of her own anxiety and rage'.[114] These destructive emotions arise
from the need to accept the strictures of patriarchal society and also the
need to reject them. According to Gilbert and Gubar, the imposed image
of the woman as passive leads her to become void and self-less.[115] Being
delicate, fragile, beautiful makes her an *objet d'art*. The imagery of
enclosure reflects the woman writer's own discomfort – her sense of
powerlessness. That is why many female authors write about houses.[116]
Women escape through madness; 'the mad double' is the author's desire
to escape male houses and male texts. It is also an escape from the rage

which has been repressed. Thus, exile and madness were, until recently, alternatives to marriage.

The woman in 'Després de l'amor' has been imprisoned by her beauty, her wealth and her upbringing until the idea of romantic love culminating in 'compulsory marriage'. She has never enjoyed real freedom. The point is that female beauty makes women objects for men to enjoy. At the end of the story, the narrator thinks it is sad that such beauty should be imprisoned in a frame, which is an allusion both to her seclusion and her restricted life.

The story 'Heaven',[117] by Mary Beckett, also portrays a woman with urges to kill her husband. 'Heaven' refers to the happiness she has when she is at home on her own. She confesses to the local priest: 'I have feelings of hatred for my husband, murderous feelings. I am afraid I will do him an injury – I have carving knives and heavy casseroles in the kitchen.'[118]

Having explored the dark side of marriage as seen through the imagination of women writers, we will now consider some representative new responses and alternatives.

NEW GENERATIONS: THE WOMAN WARRIOR

In 'The Search for the Lost Husband', Eilís Ní Dhuibhne reveals not only the subjugation of women to men we have seen in many stories, but something new – a radical alternative. A full rejection of the institution of marriage takes place. While ironically the story is written in a traditional fairy tale mode, it is also innovative in terms of presentation. A little chapter of the tale appears just before each of the more conventional stories in the collection. Thus 'The Search for the Lost Husband' runs through the whole book. In the story itself, a white kid goat suddenly appears in a remote farmyard and returns day after day to visit the farmer's daughter until she falls in love with him. When that happens the goat leaves and she sets off to find him. Her life with him is a torment because every time she has a baby (the goat is a man at night), the baby is taken away from her and she cannot make any protest otherwise the white goat will leave her. After a long process of torture, at the end of the story she has the opportunity to marry him and have her children back again. Unexpectedly, she does not want this anymore. She explains why: 'Passion is so time consuming, and it makes me so unhappy'. She gives out to him: 'You were the one who came to my doorstep, day after day, fawning all over me until I fell in love with you. And as soon as that happened, off you went.' She rejects her lover, despite being 'in love'. She wants something more, and is setting out actively to achieve it:

Goodbye to you now. I'm going home to my father and my mother, and I'm bringing my dear little children with me. And we'll have a bit of fun, playing together and laughing, and I'll love them more than I ever loved you or anybody else. And maybe I will find another husband, who will be kind to me and my children, and who will look after all of us and not lead us around in circles. Because it's time for me to try another kind of love. I'm tired of all that fairytale stuff.[119]

Women writers in the closing decades of the last century are clearly rejecting older, repressive models of behaviour and, at the same time, trying to find new ways in which they can represent fulfilment. A similar example is 'Man in the Cellar',[120] written earlier in 1974, which expresses woman's rebellion against marriage. Julia O'Faolain explores a wife's subjugation in marriage and eventual rebellion. This story could be considered as belonging to a transition period between earlier depictions of the condition of women as passive victims of male power and more recent celebrations, prominent since the 1980s, of women as empowered beings. These are women who 'write back', in more ways than one, sometimes with black humour. Humour is used more in Irish stories than in the Catalan ones and this is a good example. Una is so angered by her husband that she ties him up and imprisons him for a month in the cellar. The action happens in Italy. Una is English and he is Italian. The story takes the form of a letter which Una addresses to her mother-in-law. She starts in this way:

Carlo (yours and mine) is at this moment chained to a bedstead in the lower cellar of our house. He can only move about half a metre. His shouts cannot be heard outside the house and nobody can get into it. The doors and shutters are locked. The keys are in a bucket at the bottom of the backyard well. All you have to do when you get there is turn the crank and pull it up. Inside, on a key-ring, are the keys to the front and cellar doors and a smaller one for the padlocks which fasten Carlo's chains.[121]

From the outset, the tone of the narrative is ironic. After a month, Una has decided to leave him and sends instructions to her mother-in-law to rescue him. There are all sorts of incidental details, some hilarious, about the wife's arrangements in kidnapping her husband, such as sending a forged letter to his office saying that he has resigned. She believes her mother-in-law is guilty of many of her husband's defects, in particular his inability to control his temper, and also his dependence on her. He, however, strongly defends his mother: 'Don't say a word against la mamma', he cries, 'she is a saint'.[122]

But this submission can eventually lead to aggression. Una has been beaten: 'You've seen me with a black eye', she appeals to her mother-in-law.

'It wasn't the only one I got. I had to go to a doctor with a dislocated neck, and again with my nose.'[123] There is a clear connection between gender and violence. The traditional construction of gender roles facilitates violence: the husband argues that, although he beat her, it is her own fault. 'The truth of it is you're a masochist. You like me to hit you. What's more, you know it gives you an advantage by making me feel bad.' According to Carlo, her trouble is that 'you're not sure of yourself as a woman. You're afraid to let yourself be womanly.'[124] For Carlo and his mother, being a woman means being submissive, even to the extreme of accepting violence. It is male culture which defines what being truly 'womanly' means.

The situation of women changed in important respects during the last twenty years of the twentieth century. The traditional family changed into more diverse forms with homosexual couples, single parents, gay relationships and temporary relationships. Young generations of European women have been entering and remaining in the labour market in ever increasing numbers. They are doing so in the less well-paid areas but it is, nonetheless, an important step. However, there is still a long way to go because the atmosphere in which they have been brought up is one of women as second-class citizens and that is difficult to change. For example, writing in 1995 Katy Hayes says: 'I was never encouraged at school, because too much education would make me into a bad wife. Third level education was seen as a waste of money for me, because I'd give it all up and have babies.'[125] Needless to say, competing in the market place with men who come from a different experience in their education is not easy. No matter if women work out of the house and are more independent, resentments linger about how they have been brought up and the gender models they have experienced as children.

Moreover, there is still strong pressure from within families inhibiting young women from liberating themselves and finding their own ways. This is well illustrated by Katy Hayes in 'Wedding Bells'. In this case, Orla and Kevin decide to get married in a registry office. The families cannot accept this. Kevin's mother says: 'Not only will I not come to this affair, but neither of you need darken my door if you go ahead with this travesty. What will I say to everybody? My son and his harlot in a registry office?'[126] More authoritarian, Orla's father will not give his permission to her to go ahead with the civil wedding and when he realises that Orla is unfazed by this, he cuts her out of his will.[127] The two families are mortified at the prospect of an unconventional marriage ceremony and the damage it will do to their social standing. Kevin's mother does not hesitate to call the young woman a prostitute. As we saw at the beginning of the chapter, women are easily presented as being close to the 'borderline' of being a prostitute.

Some women, only a minority of whom are actively engaged in feminist politics, aspire to liberate themselves and, in the process, change society. This tendency to open up new possibilities and alternatives for women is strongly represented in contemporary women's writing. But it has been an uphill struggle. Women have had no alternative but to become warriors. In 'Wedding Bells', Orla says: 'If I hadn't fought for it, I would have never been given steak for dinner'.[128]

Two of the possibilities available for women are personal self-discovery and friendship between women. Again, we could find parallels in postcolonial theory: the revival periods in Ireland and Catalonia were, in fact, periods of self-discovery. Moreover, in that process of self-discovery and inventing themselves, there was contact between the two countries. In Catalonia, the Irish way was very much admired and imitated. For example, a Catalan poet and politician, Ventura Gassol, wrote a nationalist poem, 'Glossa' (Gloss)[129] in 1923, in memory of Cork's mayor, Terence Mc Swiney, who died on hunger strike.

Caterina Albert and Kate O'Brien offer the lesbian alternative, but, as writers from an earlier generation, only discreetly. In fact, the only authentic love relationship in Caterina Albert's stories happens to be between two women in one of her first short stories, 'Carnestoltes' (Carnival),[130] written in 1907. The title is not an accident. During carnival time people dress up and conceal or invent sexual roles. In this story, an old and single aristocrat, Marquise Artigues, realises she is in love with her servant and she meditates: '*Estimava! Estimava amplament, fortament. A qui? . . . Que li importava el qui . . . A una criatura humana, a un altre esser com ella*'. (She loved! She loved widely, deeply. Whom? . . . What did it matter whom . . . A human creature, another being like her)[131]

Later, there are other examples of lesbian love. In Ireland, Mary Dorcey has several examples of lesbian love in stories such as 'A Country Dance' and 'A Noise from the Woodshed'. In the former, Maeve and Molly do not have any problem in showing their love for each other, but some men in the dance hall call them names and even try to beat them: 'Fucking lesbians'[132] they say. For Dorcey, the advantage of love between women is that it is love between equals and avoids the heterosexual hierarchy. As she presents it:

> Adorning their bodies . . . took on new meaning because neither of them was a man. Helen did not need to flatter, she did not need to patronise or idolise, she did not need to conquer or submit, and her desire would never

be exploitative because she was a woman dealing with a woman! Neither of them had institutionalised power behind them.[133]

Dorcey's view seems to be that happiness in heterosexual relationships is almost a utopia because of the rigidity of the roles inherited from a distant and different past. By contrast, homosexual relationships are young and recently negotiated and thereby avoid old assumptions about gender roles. For example, 'de-objectifying' women's bodies is fundamental for them to express themselves sexually.

Lesbian experiences do not occur only in stories written by declared lesbian writers. We find other examples of explicit love experiences between women. The setting of Edna O'Brien's 'Sister Imelda',[134] written in 1982, is a repressive Catholic boarding school where children were 'forbidden to bathe because baths were immoral'[135] and where 'letters were always censored'.[136] In a single-sex school it seems natural enough that a young girl falls for a nun who seems to return the feelings of love:

> The first morning when she came into our classroom and modestly introduced herself I had no idea how terribly she would infiltrate my life, how in time she would be not just one of those teachers or nuns, but rather a special one almost like a ghost who passed the boundaries of common exchange and who crept inside one, devouring so much of one's thoughts, so much of one's passion, invading the place that was called one's heart.[137]

This bears comparison with Carme Riera's discussion of a love relationship which develops between a female teacher and a girl student. The story is set during the period of Franco's dictatorship, when even a hint of lesbian feelings was beyond the pale. At the very end of 'Te deix, amor, la mar com a penyora' (I Leave You, My Love, the Sea as a Token),[138] we discover the girl is pregnant. But the subversive twist is that the baby will bear her lover's name – that is the other woman's name.

Catalan women authors indeed write back, sometimes in unexpected and complex ways. There is a story by Maria-Josep Rague-Àrias in which there is also a surprising element at the end, but in reverse.[139] A woman makes love with a person who is described as a woman. However, at the end, we learn he is a man, implying that a heterosexual relationship could be as good as a lesbian one, if it were not for the patriarchal culture in which we are immersed.

When young catalan authors such as Imma Monsó and Irish writers like Clare Boylan, Eilís Ní Dhuibhne and Katy Hayes comment critically on marriage, they often choose to do so in an ironic way. The style and the critique of marriage is something new to this generation. For example, in 'Getting Rid of Him', Katy Hayes uses numbers playfully to make her point:

> People rushing home to their husbands or wives or lovers. People behaving properly, normally. And I wondered why it is that we all want a mate. What is it about us that makes us want a mate? What was it about all these people rushing, many to unhappy homes, homes they were slaving to support, to relationships they were making work because, having invested so much, to acknowledge failure would be to die? . . . Why did people want to be in twos? What was wrong with threes, or fours? Or marauding gangs?[140]

The curious thing, she suggests, is that so many people arrange their lives in traditional relationships, despite the unfulfilling nature of the relationship which many marriages entail, and as a result they lose control of what they really want to do with their lives. In Carme Riera's 'Quasi a la manera de fulletons' (Almost Like in Melodramas), there is evidence of fundamental value shifts in relation to concepts associated with marriage:

> *Digue'm, que vol dir per a nosaltres adulteri? Per a ma mare té una accepció ben clara: pecat. Per a tu i per a mi que hem sobrepassat la moral a l'ús, no vol dir res; què és pecat? Adulteri, amant, infidelitat, engany, són paraules buides, el seu sentit pertany a una altra generació una mica vella ja per omplir-la del seu autèntic significat.*

> (Tell me, what does adultery mean to us? To my mother, it has a clear meaning: sin. To you and me who are beyond any morality, it means nothing; what is sin? Adultery, lover, unfaithfulness, fraud, they are empty words, their meaning belongs to a different generation, a generation that is too old to learn its real meaning.)[141]

These instances clearly reflect we are living a transitional period leading towards a more diverse and plural society. Heterodox attitudes to relationships and sex are expressed by the same author in the short story 'Marc-Miquel'.[142] The female protagonist loves both her husband Miquel and, in addition, her lover Marc, thereby breaking the taboo that women cannot love more than one person.

In 'That Bad Woman', Clare Boylan explores the humorous implications of female independence through reversing roles. If a married man tries to pick up somebody in a bar, it is not really funny but rather common. However, if a woman, in particular a middle aged woman, does so, it can be very funny indeed. Jude leaves her husband at home and goes to find an available man. She starts talking to one, Bernard, and when he learns she is married, he does not approve and reacts in a paternalistic way:

'Respectable married women don't pick up strange men in hotels. It isn't natural, you know.'[143] But Jude feels it is natural to her and certainly much better than sitting alone at home and 'worrying about whether I should make a sauce for the fish or grill it'. More seriously, she wants her body and her mind to keep pace because they have been apart for too long. But Bernard's response is disappointing: 'I'm not really sure I want to hear all this'.[144] The message seems to be that men are not open to listen to, never mind engage with, the complexities and forms of ambivalences of newer female subjectivity.

Most married women we have seen in stories written before the 1980s tend to describe sex as an unpleasant activity. Younger women writers seem to be much more comfortable sexually and describe sex as a pleasurable act. Katy Hayes, describing the work and fantasies of a petrol pump attendant in a magnificent story 'Forecourt', is more exuberant than most. When work gets a bit dull, the young woman simply masturbates:

> If I position the pump nozzle in such a way while I'm filling the petrol tank, and hold my crotch against the tubing, the vibrations caused by the petrol flowing through make me feel quite excited. It's a lovely tingly feeling. I could do it all day. Especially on a hot day.[145]

There are not many such explicitly written scenes in women's writing but even this is changing. In 'Something Formal' by the same author, the female protagonist says: 'When I was sixteen, at boarding school, we used to have competitions in the showers to see who could come first with the aid of the shower nozzles'.[146]

CONCLUSION

Marriage is widely recognised as the basic unit of Western societies. In glossy magazines and in films, marriage is often projected as an ideal situation. Far from the glamorous wedding ending as in a fairy tale, current feminist approaches are seriously challenging the assumptions which underpin the marriage institution. Contemporary women writers visit and revisit marriage perhaps more frequently than any other single theme. Female writers are concerned to deconstruct the concept of marriage and its associated meanings, showing how it has affected and circumscribed women's lives. In more recent times, they portray a world in a transitional period from a traditional family society to one constituted by different groups and individuals: heterosexual, homosexual, single parents, temporary relationships, married couples.

We may note an evolutionary pattern in Irish and Catalan female short-story writing. Before the 1980s, writers highlighted the more oppressive features of marriage, including extreme manifestations such as physical violence. Women are often portrayed as oppressed figures within the institution of marriage. Indeed, irrespective of whether they are in or out of marriage, female characters are seen as disadvantaged and dependent on men. Women seem to be defined in terms of being married or non-married. Since the 1980s, women writers continue to show an interest in deconstructing marriage but are also keen to create new spaces for women, new realities. They do so in a way comparable to postcolonial nations which try to redefine themselves after achieving independence. One manifestation of this is how young authors write openly about sexuality. Another is the fact that female characters are presented as more active beings. These authors challenge patriarchal reality. Young Irish women make particular use of irony in 'decolonising' themselves in their texts. This whole enterprise is much less common among Catalan authors, Imma Monsó being an important exception. Irony proves to be an effective technique whereby Irish women distance themselves from reality. In explaining differences between the two societies and the two literatures, it is important to remember that women's studies are much more developed in Ireland than in Catalonia, such studies having developed within the favourable context of the Anglo-American intellectual world.

It is noticeable that Catalan writers portray violence in more graphic and extreme forms. It is not easy to know why. In the specific case of Caterina Albert, representing an older generation of writers, this may have been related to the impossibility of expressing her probable homosexuality. She may also have contrived to make her text more 'masculine'. In the case of Mercè Rodoreda this might be related to her particular life experiences: the terrible problems of living in Barcelona during the civil war, followed by exile, poverty and further war in France later on. More generally, there is the comparatively more depressed status of women, particularly in terms of access to education, in Catalonia under the fascist dictatorship. Even if de Valera's Ireland was conservative, women still had more chances to achieve education and raise their expectations of life.

Among other characteristics of marriage, monogamy, which is a basic requirement of Western marriage, also finds itself threatened by a drift towards hidden relationships outside the marriage bond. One lover for life, it would seem, is not always enough for women or men, and feminist writings help us to understand why this might be so. In addition, such writings contest the traditional view which held women more responsible than men for sexual transgressions and hence deserving of more severe sanctions.

Using the colonial discourse to discuss marriage also sheds some light on the matter. This approach, which draws parallels between the wife and the postcolonial society, highlights the elements of conflict within marriage. But, it should be emphasised, both marriage and colonial societies have changed over time. Like former colonial societies, married women are now becoming more independent, not only economically, but also in terms of assertiveness. But both still inhabit an unequal world.

In this chapter we have seen how a society based on traditional families acts as a key colonising device in which women are losers because they become economically, emotionally and socially dependent on their husbands. All too frequently, after a brief honeymoon, there is a long period of non-communication, suffering and resentment, followed in some cases by violence because people feel trapped.

Running through many of the stories discussed here is a great longing for change. To varying degrees women characters are presented as suffering the restrictions of conventional marriage, as becoming increasingly self-conscious of various injustices, and as seeking to redress these.

Sketching alternatives to traditional marriage, be it in Catalan or Irish society, is more the domain of a newer generation of writers. Treating marriage and its discontents is a subversive enterprise, particularly in the context of societies where economic and family structures intersect and where prevailing ideologies of church and state endorse traditional family forms. Possibly the authors selected in this study found the genre of the short story a more discrete medium for the articulation of such critical ideas. Finally, as suggested in chapter one, there may be a connection between genre (short-story writing) and gender (women), though this has yet to be established. It may even be that Frank O'Connor's association of the genre of the short story with postcolonial countries could well be applied to the colonised gender.

CHAPTER THREE

Towards a feminisation of nationalism

Do you know Belfast has the most beautiful sunsets in the whole world?

Mary Beckett[1]

L'aire del matí, a Barcelona, és la cosa més bonica del món.
(The morning air, in Barcelona, is the most beautiful thing in the world.)

Isabel-Clara Simó[2]

INTRODUCTION

A CONCERN with national identity is a pervasive concern of writings in postcolonial societies. As Ashcroft puts it:

> A major feature of post-colonial literatures is the concern with place and displacement. It is here that the special postcolonial crisis of identity comes into being; the concern with the development or recovery of an effective identifying relationship between self and place.[3]

Most critics would agree that women and postcolonial countries share a condition of 'otherness'. In both cases identity is constructed in terms of difference rather than essence. Hélène Cixous, and before her Freud, refer to women as 'the black continent'.[4] Comparably, a recent historical account of the successful assimilation of Irish immigrants into nineteenth-century American society is entitled *How the Irish Became White.*[5] The success of the Irish in America was predicated on their differentiating themselves from African-Americans and gaining entry to the 'white race'. Back in Ireland, as Ailbhe Smyth puts it: 'Being Irish is about not being British'.[6] In Catalonia, a book called *No sóc espanyol*[7] (I am not Spanish), published in 2000, which includes interviews with a number of academics and writers arguing that their Catalan identity meant they were not Spanish, went through five printings in five months. Taking a longer historical view, Declan Kiberd explains the negative connotations associated with the idea of Ireland which stretch back to the times of the Anglo-Norman conquest:

Ireland was soon patented as not-England, a place whose peoples were, in many important ways, the very antithesis of their new rulers from overseas. These rulers began to control the developing debate; and it was to be their version of things which would enter universal history.[8]

History is always an issue in postcolonial countries. The colonial power wants to give an idea of history from the coloniser's viewpoint. At present, there is a huge debate in Catalonia regarding the kind of history children should learn at school after a Spanish institution issued a document saying that the history taught in Catalan and Basque schools is unduly nationalist. In Ireland, history also is a contested subject area, with compelling post-revisionist schools of thought.

In his book *Catalanofòbia*,[9] Francesc Ferrer i Gironès argues that Catalan nationalism exists because of the dislike Spanish people have always had of Catalonia. This phobia resulted because Catalonia was different from Spain and resistant to assimilation with it. In a similar way, English prejudice towards the Irish contributed to the development of Irish nationalism.

In the discourse of difference and identity, Edward Said's analysis of the two geographical entities, the Occident and the Orient, is very illuminating. Both terms, Occident and Orient, 'support and to an extent reflect each other', so 'all postcolonial societies realize their identity in difference rather in essence. They are constituted by their difference from the metropolitan and it is in this relationship that identity both as a distancing from the centre and as a means of self-assertion comes into being.'[10] Thus, as Ashcroft suggests, it could be argued that as long as those societies are created as a function of one another it is difficult to create a truly different reality: 'The struggle for power over truth in some senses "mimics" the metropolitan impulse of dominance'.[11] The danger is that postcolonial nations end up being imitations of the metropolis. However, the creativity which the writing brings about gives an opportunity to challenge that power and create new realities.

One might see certain parallels between the construction of women in dominant male discourses and representations of Ireland in the minds of the colonisers. In Ailbhe Smyth's words, both 'Irishness' and 'Womanness' are regarded as 'subordinating negative signs'.[12] In certain contexts, then, 'man' and 'coloniser' become interchangeable. It is interesting but disturbing to see to what extent difference features in the mind of the 'masculine coloniser'. Many texts at the end of the nineteenth and beginning of the twentieth centuries still talked about women's difference from men, and their consequent inferiority. The following is an example in a newspaper article published in Barcelona in 1889:

Desde su inteligencia a su estatura, todo en ella es inferior y contrario a los hombres. Todo en ella va de fuera a dentro. Todo es concentrado, receptivo y pasajero; en un hombre todo es activo y expansivo . . . En sí misma, la mujer no es como el hombre, un ser completo; es sólo el instrumento de la reproducción, la destinada a perpetuar la especie; mientras que el hombre es el encargado de hacerla progresar, el generador de inteligencia, a la vez creador y demiurgo del mundo social. Así es que todo tiende a la no igualdad entre los sexos y la no equivalencia; de modo que las mujeres, inferiores a los hombres, deben ser su complemento en las funciones sociales.

(From her intelligence to her length, all in her is inferior and opposite to men. All in her goes from outside to inside. All is concentrated, receptive and passive; in a man everything is active and expansive. In herself, the woman is not like a man, a complete being; she is only the instrument of reproduction, the one destined to perpetuate the species, whereas the man is the one in charge of making it progress, the generator of intelligence, at the same time as he is the creator of the social world. Thus, everything tends towards non-equality between the sexes and non-equivalence; thus women, inferior to men, must be men's complement in their social functions.)[13]

COLONIALISM, NATIONALISM AND WOMEN

Nationalism is a relatively recent creation, coming into being in most European countries during the course of the nineteenth century. But the relationships of subordination between England and Ireland, and Spain and Catalonia, reach deeper in time with nationalism in each case being a historically specific response to these evolving relationships. Hence it is necessary to begin with a more general discussion of colonialism, which may be illuminated by reference to postcolonial theory.

Are there parallels between processes of colonisation, in the conventional sense, and the subordination of women to men? Might the latter be viewed also as a form of 'colonisation', as some feminists would claim and as has been argued here (see Chapter Two) in the specific case of marriage? Edna O'Brien seems to think so. Take, for instance, her short story 'Honeymoon':

When they had driven for about three hours he decided that they should stop for tea. They stopped in a town where there had once been a dreadful battle and she told him what she remembered of it, from her schooldays. He was not a native and sometimes she got the feeling that he had no pity for those people, her people, who had for so long lived in subjugation and who like her were ashamed to confront themselves. He was twice her age, and she obeyed him in everything, even in the type of shoes she was to wear – completely flat shoes which as it happened gave her a pain in her instep.[14]

In fact, in Irish women's stories, we sometimes find couples in which the man is English and the woman is Irish, as if there was some suggestion of a colonial relationship binding the couple. In this case, Elizabeth's husband had decided to stop for tea because naturally he took such decisions for both himself and Elizabeth, even if the result was sometimes painful for her. Acting out the role of coloniser, he extended little pity towards subordinate beings: neither the Irish generally, women in particular, nor indeed his own wife (his possession). Here we are assuming that the nameless husband is English, like many male partners in Edna O'Brien's stories. Powerlessness is a feature of being colonised, as is a sense of shame, and Elizabeth, the protagonist in O'Brien's story, has experienced both these conditions. A long history of subjugation means that women find it hard to assert themselves, settling for a childish 'obedience' instead. Both postcolonial and feminist theories usefully alert us to the subtle forms oppression can take and, in particular, how it affects the confidence of the oppressed. Geraldine Moane has studied how the mechanisms of domination become institutionalised over time, to the extent that it becomes difficult for both the dominant persons and their subordinates to recognise them. She says: 'If these mechanisms are working well, they not only succeed in keeping the subordinates convinced that they deserve their position, or that, indeed, their subordination is natural and actually good for them'.[15]

A number of literary critics have linked colonialism with masculinity. They view the phenomenon of colonialism as a product of an unbalanced situation, wherein masculinity is associated with activity, strength and power. Femininity, on the contrary, has connotations of powerlessness. Ireland was seen as a woman whereas England, the metropolitan centre, was seen as masculine and the Act of Union (1800) was seen as a marriage. This marriage has been represented in various contemporary paintings and the bride looks sad. This kind of imagery is present also in Seamus Heaney's 'Act of Union' in which the Act is seen as a violation and described with arrogance by the coloniser. In this case, the speaker is male and the coloniser England: 'I am still imperially / Male'. Heaney goes on to present colonisation as a form of rape with long lasting consequences: 'No treaty / I foresee will salve completely your tracked / And stretchmarked body, the big pain / That leaves you raw, like opened ground, again'.[16]

The critic Ashis Nandy holds a similar opinion about gender imbalance and thinks that this is embedded in Western culture:

Colonialism, too, was congruent with the existing Western sexual stereotypes and the philosophy of life which they represented. It produced a
cultural consensus in which political and socio-economic dominance
symbolised the dominance of men and masculinity over women and
femininity.[17]

One would add that colonial structures are not a necessary condition for
male dominance, as this has a more universal character. The consequences
of colonisation can take a variety of forms. Considering that the real
motivation of colonisers is to enrich themselves at the expense of the
'object' communities, and not to facilitate development, colonisation has
had a distorting effect on the economies of these countries. But the
phenomenon goes far beyond economics: it is a 'state of mind'.[18] Long
centuries of colonisation create an inferiority complex among the
colonised. In the same way, being a woman in a patriarchal society is a
'state of mind'. Centuries of submission have resulted in women being
less confident than men in most aspects of life – socially, professionally and
also emotionally. Medbh McGuckian, among others, shows how this 'state
of mind' is reflected in postcolonial writing: 'The Irish poet will differ from
the English in his sense of security, though it depends whether the English
poet is a WASP, or a woman'.[19]

Albert Memmi explains how the colonised become objectified:

> What is left of the the colonized at the end of this stubborn effort to
> dehumanize him? He is surely no longer an alter ego of the colonizer. He
> is hardly a human being. He tends rapidly toward becoming an object. As
> an end, in the colonizer's supreme ambition, he should exist only as a
> function of the needs of the colonizer.[20]

A similar point has been made by feminist writers. Women are
subordinated to men, in a relationship of deference and dependence, in
which women's self-image is determined by male society. Women
'shadow' men. They are the object, not just of men's desires, but of their
will more generally. Memmi goes further. The colonised end up accepting
the vision the coloniser has of them – that is their own second-class
condition – and, rather than hating the coloniser, paradoxically, they feel
guilty about themselves and come to admire their oppressor:

> The accusation disturbs him and worries him even more because he
> admires and fears his powerful accuser. 'Is he not partially right?' he
> mutters. 'Are we not all a little guilty after all? Lazy, because we have so
> many idlers? timid, because we let ourselves be oppressed.' Wilfully created

and spread by the colonizer, this mythical and degrading portrait ends up by being accepted and lived with to a certain extent by the colonized.[21]

Once more, one might substitute women for the colonised. Traditionally, women have been considered and even labelled as 'the weaker sex' or 'the second sex'. How often have women worried about being too sensitive, too changeable, too contradictory – in short, different from men? Women, in real life as well as in fiction, have accepted their husband's violence towards them (as we have seen) and some have even felt they deserved it. In the extreme cases where women have been battered to death, it is significant that this has been preceded by long histories of beating and other forms of physical abuse. In one way or another, women have tolerated their degradation. Indeed, the abuse seems to have been accompanied, at least in some cases, by a sense of guilt about their 'failings'. Feelings of inferiority and insecurity feed into rationalisations of their plight.

There are other, more subtle ways in which women end up hating themselves rather than their aggressors. As a consequence of the male gaze, women have problems accepting their own bodies and, for instance, cannot face themselves in the mirror. In Maria Mercè Marçal's 'Joc de màscares' (Game of Masks), Laura has a strong dislike for mirrors. She keeps repeating that she does not like mirrors.[22] The mirror is also an important element in Mercè Rodoreda's writing. In 'Abans de morir' (Before Dying), when Marta is wearing her wedding dress, she looks at her reflection in the mirror and sees a ghost.[23] Her marriage eventually fails and she decides to commit suicide. Glancing in the mirror, she catches a glimpse of her own reflection and sees a ghost once more.[24] Feeling powerless, she says she feels sorry for the girl who is going to die. In another Catalan story, 'L'airet del matí, a Barcelona' (The Fresh Morning Air, in Barcelona), Teresa looks at her own naked body in the mirror. She cries because she feels old, fat and ugly. She says she feels defeated.[25] The mirror image appears in some Irish stories also. For example, Finnula, in 'Naming the Names', asks her partner to cover all the mirrors in the house.[26] She cannot face her own image.

In postcolonial discourse the word 'decolonisation' is often used to refer to the period between the achievement of independence and the present. Colonisation is an integral part of the history of many countries, a phase which in the end has to be transcended. Because colonies are created through violence, the eventual consequences are likely to be not only malign but also complex. During the early stirrings of the nationalist movements in Ireland and Catalonia in the middle of the nineteenth century, there was a strong admiration for, even idealisation of, the period before colonisation – early Christian Ireland in the case of Ireland, the Middle Ages in the case of Catalonia – when the language and the culture were strong and confident. The recovery of the language, for example, was considered essential. By contrast, women could never go to a 'before' period as a reference point because they have always been colonised and this is a fundamental difference from postcolonial countries. In the case of women, it is more difficult to find a model to follow. There is a clear identity problem. Just as people ask what it means to be Irish or Catalan, so women ask themselves what it means to be a woman. They know they have to be like men in order to compete with them but, at the same time, they want to be different and keep some of their distinctive selves. As for postcolonial people, the text is one of the 'fields of struggle' in which they can 'write back', subvert reality and be creative to find new realities. But the achievement of liberation for women is especially complex because of the absence of a historical reference point. However, through their writing they are trying to find new languages and new realities in which they feel more comfortable. For example, the exploration of female sexuality is also a desire to find essence, authenticity and comfort. About her poetry, Medbh McGuckian says: 'It's mostly moody and menstrual in a way a man's poetry never is'.[27]

Traditionally, men have greatly valued possession and, in particular, possession of territories. Hélène Cixous talks about the 'Realm of the Proper', through which masculinity is structured: 'Proper-property-appropriate: signalling an emphasis on self-identity, self-aggrandisement and arrogative dominance'. That leads to a masculine obsession with classification, systematisation and hierarchisation. Cixous links the 'Realm of the Proper' to a 'masculine libidinal economy', which is caused by a fear of loss and castration, whereas femininity would be associated with the 'Realm of the Gift', linked to generosity.[28]

History is full of examples of wars driven by the desire to annex territory, resources and people. In the typical case this involves murder, sexual abuse and the imposition of new ruling systems. Traditionally, women have been excluded from such acts of possession. Enclosed in their primary activity of caring and motherhood, they have developed an attitude of giving rather than taking. Incidentally, the word 'possession' is often used by men to describe sexual relationships, a usage rejected by women writers because of its connotations of conquest and even rape. In a related vein, some women writers have developed an interest in outcasts. Many Irish and Catalan short stories focus on marginalised beings, as the critic Anne Charlon has noticed.[29] For example, Caterina Albert's 'La vella' (The Old Woman) is about the marginalisation and neglect of an old woman by her relatives. The result is that she is later burned in a fire. Mercè Rodoreda's 'Ada Liz' is the story of the dilemmas and loneliness of being a prostitute. In several stories by Carme Riera and Isabel-Clara Simó, the handicapped, the defeated, prostitutes and children are the protagonists. Edna O'Brien's 'Dramas' is about the nightmare of a gay shop owner in an Irish community. Fiona Barr's 'Sun and Shadow' centres on the problems of a handicapped boy. By extension, these writers' interests in marginalised characters may also be seen to be interactively related to a concern with colonised countries and postcolonial nationalism.

It is hardly possible, at least in this century, to speak of colonialism without introducing nationalism. The two intersect, while feminist perspectives cross-cut each. Although important in their writing, it needs to be said immediately that nationalism is not the first priority of most Irish and Catalan women writers. More significant for many is the task of 'decolonising' themselves – that is, of constructing a new gender identity. Anne Charlon has noted:

> *De fet, tot i que la lluita catalanista serveix de base a tota l'obra de les novelistes, no en constitueix pas el tema essencial, ni el mes aparent. En canvi, la condició femenina, l'experiència femenina, els desigs de les dones i allò que elles refusen, són omnipresents en la literatura femenina catalana.*

> (Despite the fact that the Catalanist struggle serves as a basis in all the work of the female novelists, it is not the principal subject, nor the most apparent. However, the feminine condition, the feminine experience and women's wishes and also what they refuse are omnipresent in female Catalan literature.)[30]

By and large, women have not participated in the making of ideologies. This seems to be as true of ideas of nationality as of major belief systems, such as the various world religions. A qualification might be entered, though. Further research into the forging of modern nationalisms may uncover a more significant contribution by women than is usually allowed.[31] In any case, given the disproportionate role of men in authoring nationalism, it is less than surprising that most nationalisms should harbour powerful notions of patriarchy.

There is a case for saying that Catalan and Irish women are doubly colonised: both by reference to their status as women and by reference to their nationality. Women writers in Catalonia and Ireland have used literature to question both types of oppression. Sometimes they deliberately complain about it (as we have seen before with Edna O'Brien's 'Honeymoon' and we will see later in Eilís Ní Dhuibhne's 'Love, Hate and Friendship'.) The role of literature in the development of Irish and Catalan nationalisms has many similarities. For example, we can compare two representative poems: 'La Pàtria' (The Fatherland) by B.C. Aribau (1833) and 'A Nation Once Again' by Thomas Davis, published in the 'year of revolutions', 1848. Both poems harken back to an idealised past, as well as envisioning a future free from outside control. With their stirring rhetoric, they soon became anthems of nationalism, providing ideological resources for the nationalist struggle in their respective countries. But it does not happen only with those two poems – Irish and Catalan literature is full of national politics. Postcolonial writers, we may note, tend to evoke a precolonial version of their own nation, rejecting the modern and the contemporary, which is tainted with colonialism.

One of the dire consequences of colonialism is the loss of the indigenous language. Postcolonial theory makes plain what happens when a community loses this most important means of communication. The loss of the language gives rise to a lack of personal and communal confidence as it is such a vital arena where power can be subverted. The language question is a common feature among postcolonial peoples. Because of its importance, I will deal in detail with this particular aspect of colonisation in the next chapter, 'Decolonising language'. In the section which follows, I will attempt to focus more closely on the troubled relationship between women and nationalism as charted by different authors.

WOMEN AND NATIONALISM IN IRELAND

Before and during Independence a number of women were active in the Irish nationalist cause. Among these were Maud Gonne (better known in some circles as Yeats's friend than as a politician), the militant Constance Markiewicz, and the lesser known Helena Moloney, all of whom regarded violence as the only way to achieve independence. In 1913 Cumann na mBan, the female branch of the IRA, was founded. Carol Coulter claims that Irish women had a tradition of involvement in nationalist causes. In Ireland, as in other postcolonial countries, 'those politically active women of the early twentieth century came out of a pre-existing tradition of women's involvement in nationalist struggle'. She goes on to assert that nationalist agitation offered them an opportunity to become more involved in politics and public life. In her own words, they achieved:

scope for a wider range of activities in public life than that experienced by their sisters in imperialist countries, and that all this was then closed off to them by the newly-formed patriarchal state, modelled essentially on its colonial predecessor ... Not only in Ireland, but throughout the colonised world, women came onto the public stage in large numbers through the great movements of the beginning of this century.[32]

Whether these global generalisations would stand up to the scrutiny of historians is debatable, but in the case of Ireland it seems likely that the political participation of women has been inflated.[33] Margaret Ward seems a more reliable guide, emphasising the conditional nature of women's involvement. According to Ward:

> the high points of women's participation were also moments of exceptional political crisis, when women were either drawn into the movement because of the temporary (enforced) absence of men, or they were encouraged to participate because a strong, united front was desperately needed, and because women, when the military struggle began, were also needed for essential back-up services. At no stage were they accepted as equal members, as a closer examination of the role of those who seem to have transcended this limitation clearly demonstrates.[34]

Women were not accepted as equal. As a result, Inghinidhe na hÉireann was formed because of women's exclusion from other groups. Ward states:

> The only nationalist women's organisation which was completely independent – Inghinidhe na hÉireann – was formed because of women's exclusion from all other groups, and it existed during a period of general regroupment, when women's mobilisation was not even contemplated. The members of Inghinidhe had to fight for the right of women to participate alongside men; in effect, to alter the dominant consciousness concerning women's role within society.[35]

However, Ward and Coulter are in agreement that the achievement of political independence in 1921 marked a retreat from active engagement in politics. Women were no longer welcome: 'repeatedly in history (man) has tried to block women's presence in positions of power even to those women who risked their lives in their fight towards a free state'.[36] Coulter makes an explicit comparison between the disadvantaged position of the poor in Irish society, in terms of political participation, and women: 'Like the poorer sections of the society, they [women] found themselves excluded from political life in the new state'.[37] Also, the new state introduced a number of legislative measures which limited the rights of women and altered the statements of equality contained in the 1916 Proclamation and the 1922 Constitution. These included:

> discriminatory legislation relating to illegitimacy and divorce, the barring of women from jury service (a right they had under the previous British legislation), measures to restrict women's access to employment and equal treatment at work, both in the civil service and in industry, and laws relating to issues like contraception which bore especially heavily on women.[38]

Not only were women excluded, relatively speaking, from politics in the Free State but most Irish women writers and critics (Ailbhe Smyth, Rebecca Pelan, Eavan Boland, Angela Bourke, Gerardine Meaney, C.L. Innes, Carol Coulter and Edna Longley) agree that the construction of Ireland as a woman, with the qualities of passivity and silence as well as the unique function of maternity, was a misogynist construction. For young writers it is crucial to find new ideas of Irishness. Ailbhe Smyth elaborates the point:

> The idea of Ireland is especially complicated for women because colonised Ireland has conventionally been represented as a woman – a weak, vanquished victim . . . She symbolises 'Ireland' – and Ireland stands for 'Woman'. That is how 'men like to imagine her' and she has no space, no voice, no right to imagine herself differently – or even to imagine at all. As symbol, 'woman' is allowed no history, no story, no capacity for change – she is a given. Her particularity is overwhelmed by the primary demands of the nation. To be free, therefore, Irish women must find some way of extricating themselves from the double burden of patriarchy and colonization, whether consciously identified or not. But how can this be done? There is no one, easy answer. An important part of what Irish women writers are doing now is bound up with finding new ways of being a woman without denying 'Irishness', however they (variously) decide to define it.[39]

It is a difficult and challenging situation to create new identities as women and as Catalan and Irish. Smyth also rejects the usual associations conjured up in relation to women:

> to be 'outside history' or politics or citizenship . . . to be chaste, passive and invisible . . . to be Mother Ireland, the fertile source, the rich terrain, from which the 'nation', vampire-like, draws its sustenance, bleeding the blood of real women dry . . . to be idealised or romanticised . . . to be 'made immobile by oppression', choosing to be 'made active because of it . . . to be sacrificed in the name of the father or of anything else.[40]

Smyth thinks that in the 1990s there are new and different meanings of 'Irishness'. The new Irishness is plural, inclusive and eclectic. It is not owned by an elite ruling group. So Irish women are challenging traditional constructions of Irish identity.

On the same lines, Rebecca Pelan suggests that Irish women are domestically powerful but socially powerless. The image of the traditional mother conforms to the literary image of Ireland as woman – natural, passive and possessed: 'It is towards such images that contemporary Irish women writers have directed much of their attention in an effort to undermine and reject the model as having any value'.[41]

Eavan Boland sees nineteenth-century romantic nationalism as propagating the vision of women as both passive and mute and acting as a muse, an inspiration for men to go to war:

> Gradually, in inches, not yards, I began to realize that this idea of a nation, for all its lore and invention, had ugly limits . . . The heroine, as such, was utterly passive. She was Ireland or Hibernia. She was stamped, as a rubbed-away mark, on silver or gold; a compromised figure on a throne. Or she was a nineteenth-century image of girlhood, on a frontispiece or in a book of engravings. She was invoked, addressed, remembered, loved, regretted. And, most important, died for. She was a mother or a virgin. Her hair was swept or tied back, like the prow of a ship. Her flesh was wood or ink or marble. And she had no speaking part. If her harvests were spoiled, her mother tongue wiped out, her children killed, then it was for somebody else to mark the reality. Her identity was an image. Or was it a fiction?[42]

In 'Mayonnaise to the Hills', Angela Bourke is opposed to the vision of the land as a woman. On the contrary, the land as part of nature can stimulate fe / male sexuality:

> 'Hills are breasts, and the earth is a woman, and a woman is the earth and all that crap.'
> 'It's a bit pathetic though, isn't it?'
> 'Well, it is. But what I'm trying to say is I think landscape turns anyone on. Or it can – but men think sex belongs to them.' . . .
> 'But that's just what I'm saying! Plenty of women are thin – just look at you. And plenty of men are fat. It doesn't matter whether it's a man or a woman; the land can just do it to you. I once had an orgasm just sitting on a rock up here.'[43]

Bourke takes a more earthy and active line than conventional / nationalist notions of Mother Ireland would allow. She has little time for female passivity, including passivity in sex. Sexual behaviour is presented in terms of 'taking' the air and 'swallowing' the stars – that is, in an active rather than a merely 'receiving' mode.

Like other feminist critics we have seen, Gerardine Meaney argues that
the myth of Mother Ireland – the romantic vision of Ireland as a poor,
suffering mother – has paralysed or 'frozen' the country.[44] This motif of
paralysis is used by Edna O'Brien in 'Irish Revel' where the countryside is
literally frozen. Paraphrasing Joyce's 'The Dead': 'The poor birds could
get no food as the ground was frozen hard. Frost was general all over
Ireland; frost like a weird blossom on the branches, on the riverbank . . .
and on all the slime and ugliness of the world'.[45] If we compare the two
stories, in Joyce's 'The Dead', Gabriel is invited to a party and he is accused
of not being a good Irishman because he does not fully endorse Irish
nationalism. In 'Irish Revel', Mary is also invited to a party but she is
invited only to work as a servant. Mary's situation is worse than Gabriel's
because being a woman in Ireland is much more difficult that being a man.
Gabriel's arrival is greatly welcomed: '"O, Mr Conroy", said Lily to Gabriel
when she opened the door for him, "Miss Kate and Miss Julia thought you
were never coming"'.[46] By contrast, what Mary hears when she arrives, is:
'God, I thought it was someone important'.[47]

In the view of the critic Rebecca Pelan, Edna O'Brien engaged in
'writing back' to Joyce.[48] While O'Brien's version offers a less explicit
comment on the ugliness of Mary's world, frost is retained to represent
the brittle, cold reality of Mary's life as opposed to the soft, blankety snow
of Gabriel's – a distinction further reinforced by the fact that Gabriel's
contemplations and observations are made from within a comfortable
room, while Mary's take place outside as she cracks the frost with the heel
of her shoe. The implication seems to be that for women like Mary the
world of self-centred and self-indulgent contemplation is denied by the
cold, hard reality of their lives and in this world women are homeless and
dispossessed.[49]

C.L. Innes also reminds us that throughout the history of its colonisation,
Ireland has been represented by British imperialists, Irish nationalists and
artists as female; she is: 'Hibernia, Éire, Erin, Mother Ireland, the Poor Old
Woman, the Shan Van Vocht, Cathleen ní Houlihan, the Dark Rosaleen'.[50]
Trying to find an explanation, Innes quotes Richard Kearney, who
speculates that the change from fatherland to motherland has much to do
with dispossession: 'The more colonially oppressed the Irish became in
historical reality the more spiritualised became the mythic ideal of the
Motherland'.[51] In this male-centred ideology, being female has to do with
helplessness and material deprivation.

The dominant conservative ideology of the Republic of Ireland long
emphasised maternity as the primary female function, though this

consensus is clearly breaking up in recent times. Ailbhe Smyth has discussed how people in Ireland no longer accept the dictates of the Church and state without question, in particular since the early 1980s.[52] Still, the Republic remains one of the few countries of Europe where abortion is still officially banned and where divorce was not legalised until 1996. Even then, almost half of the voters were opposed to divorce. Abortion is still, of course, illegal in all but the most exceptional circumstances. The story 'Irish Revel' reeks of this atmosphere of social repression. In this story, Mary falls for an English artist because she really wants to escape from Ireland, anticipating in fiction the journeys Edna O'Brien, Julia O'Faolain and many other Irish women were to make in moving away to other more tolerant climes.

According to Meaney, the liberation of Ireland has not meant an end to the subordinate status of women within Irish society. The colonial consequences run deep in time, and a deterioration in the status of women may even have accompanied national independence because the ideology of the colonised has been taken from the metropolitan centre. Perhaps for revenge, the colonised men want to be the colonisers of women, in particular through controlling their bodies:

> Colonial powers identify their subject peoples as passive, in need of guidance, incapable of self-government, romantic, passionate, unruly, barbarous – all of those things for which the Irish and women have been traditionally praised and scorned . . . subject people, in rebelling and claiming independence and sovereignty, aspire to a traditionally masculine role of power. The result is that colonised peoples, often long after colonisation itself has ended, tend to observe or impose strictly differentiated gender roles in order to assert the masculinity and right to power of the (male) subjects . . . Anxiety about one's fitness for a (masculine) role of authority, deriving from a history of defeat or helplessness, is assuaged by the assumption of sexual dominance . . . Women in these conditions become guarantors of their men's status, bearers of national honour and the scapegoats of national identity. They are not merely transformed into symbols of the nation. They become the territory over which power is exercised. The Irish obsession with the control of women's bodies by church, state, boards of ethics and judicial enquiries, has its roots in such anxieties[53]

Irish women have found it more difficult to get involved in nationalism than their counterparts in Catalonia because Irish nationalism's main sign of identity was the Catholic Church, which was particularly repressive in relation to women. In Catalonia the Catholic Church was less deeply entrenched and was challenged by anarchist and socialist forces during the early decades of the twentieth century. During the dark night of Francoism, the Catholic Church was associated with the conservative and authoritarian power of the Spanish state, and hence its influence declined still further.

Ailbhe Smyth sees a clear tension between feminism and nationalism. She views them, in some respects, as antagonistic practices. Because of her Irish experience, she is acutely aware of the limitations of nationalism as far as women are concerned, but she is not prepared to throw overboard the nation state as a form of political organisation in favour of big superpowers. It may well be the only way to guarantee a basis for further advances:

> For all that, it does not automatically follow that we should abandon the possibility of a national consciousness and national structures which can ensure social, political, and economic rights for every member of the community. Living in an ex-colonial, peripheral, and economically under-developed state does not make you want to jump into the jaws of an all-enveloping 'open' multinational economy. I am acutely aware of the vulnerability of stateless communities in the contemporary geopolitical order, with its predatory superpowers, supranational cartels and corporations, and I do not for a moment underestimate the significance of national inde-pendence for those who have been deprived of it. It is a good deal easier to envisage renouncing what you have than giving it up before you've even had it. But nationness is not an absolute value nor a universal and fixed principle of social and political organisation. If, in some of its contemporary manifestations (as in Ireland), it is found to be wanting as a path to freedom for all, then it must either be abandoned or radically transformed.[54]

Writing from the North, in *From Cathleen to Anorexia: The Breakdown of Irelands*, Edna Longley disagrees with Smyth and offers a different perspective. She rejects nationalism, conceiving it as a 'prison more than a liberation'.[55] In her view, both nationalism and unionism in Ireland are simply dying ideologies. She says that the troubles in Ulster, with the hunger strike as the most extreme manifestation, have proven that the forms of ideology created both by the Republic and by Northern Ireland have failed. The Irish romantic ideal of Cathleen Ní Houlihan has become an anorexic figure which wishes its own death. It is what she calls the breakdown of nationalism. Mary Dorcey would agree with Longley in regarding both the south and north of Ireland as 'failed entities' under the patronage of external forces: the Catholic Church in the South and the British government in the North. Both these institutions are: 'prejudiced, fundamentally unjust, intolerant, undemocratic and financially impoverished to the point of bankruptcy'. Dorcey adds: 'To have grown up in either means to carry for life the scars of this, the burden of this ongoing bloody history'.[56]

Edna Longley goes on to criticise notions of being 'more' or 'less' Irish which crop up in Roy Foster's *Modern Ireland*, where Irishness is measured on a scale or spectrum: 'For some naïve readers some Irish writers and texts are still more Irish than others'.[57] Challenging conventional positions, Longley unleashes a strong attack on nationalism:

> So I think that 'Irishness' with its totalitarian tinge, ought to be abandoned rather than made more inclusive . . . Cultural change and changing aware-ness of culture, in the Republic and even in the North, have already exposed political Irishness (the 'ethos on which the independence movement was built').[58]

While not noted for her use of feminist approaches, Longley employs them here to challenge nationalism. For her, the traditional identification of Ireland and woman underlines the failure of nationalist ideology:

> Political images, like political language (from which they are never quite distinct), eventually exhaust themselves or prove incapable of renewal. I think this happens at the juncture where the image Women-Ireland-Muse meets contemporary Irish women. There, I believe, the breakdown of Nationalist ideology becomes particularly clear.[59]

The critique becomes clearer when she attacks the narrow, restraining nature of identities which offer only the duality of nationalist or unionist, each in opposition to the other. For Longley, female nature is more connected and avoids dualities in favour of plurality. In fact, she employs gender imagery to bring out the point:

> The image of the web is female, feminist, 'connective' – as contrasted with male polarisation. So is the ability to inhabit a range of relations rather than a single allegiance. The term 'identity' has been coarsened in Ulster politics to signify two ideological package deals immemorially on offer. To admit to more varied, mixed, fluid and relational kinds of identity would advance nobody's territorial claim. It would undermine cultural defences. It would subvert the male pride that keeps up the double frontier-siege. All this would be on the side of life – like noticing, redefining and again redefining, doing.[60]

The truth of the matter is that a concern with national identity is apparent among many Irish women writers. The meaning of Irishness arises again and again, while historic episodes, such as the Famine, the loss of the Irish language or emigration find their way into contemporary stories. The individual, as distinct from the society or the nation, is a particular concern. For example, Eilís Ní Dhuibhne shows her regret regarding the death of the Irish language. The disaster of the Great Famine is also mentioned: 'Other clues to her past are folk-museum stuff, school history stuff, too. The Famine. Seaweed and barnacles and herrings for dinner. A bowl of yellow meal given to a tinker caused her immediate death.'[61]

The more overtly political 'Love, Hate and Friendship', also by Eilís Ní Dhuibhne, is concerned with connections between the oppression of women and of the Irish. She uses postcolonial discourse to describe the Irish protagonist Fiona's infatuation with a man: 'Edward colonised her territory. Everywhere she looked in Ireland reminded her of him. He had taken over every place and every object in her life.'[62] In a patriarchal society, loving her means taking possession of her or, at least, this is how she feels. In exasperation, Fiona decries 'the way he claimed her world, the world that should have been her own'.[63] A parallel is being established here between traditional heterosexual love, which is not between equals, and colonisation. In the manner of many colonists, once he has exploited Fiona for his own selfish gain, he returns to the metropolitan London:

> a childish man, with a child's enthusiasm for new things and child's diffidence. And a child's dependence. He is the type of man who falls rapidly in love, pursues the beloved with utmost energy, almost with aggression, and then, just as quickly, falls out of love again.[64]

The man is the winner – what he wants he gets, preferably with no complications. He is allowed to be childish because he does not have to worry about the consequences of his 'conquest'; his power as a man makes him selfish and self-absorbed and makes him think only of his own gain. The colonial parallels become more obvious as we learn that he is English and she is Irish. Moreover, being a married man, with commitments elsewhere, he can only engage in a conditional and episodic relationship with her. He is using her in much the same way as Britain used Ireland over the centuries. He is a coloniser but often he is an absent presence. In language, which has resonances in terms of Irish history and postcolonial discourse, he is described as: 'An absentee landlord. Still, her imagination has surrendered her places to him, territory which he certainly doesn't want. Half the streets of Dublin are in his fiefdom.'[65]

There is, however, a clear difference between the portrayal of women in Edna O'Brien's 'Honeymoon', referred to earlier, and that found in the stories of Clare Boylan and Eilís Ní Dhuibhne. In O'Brien's story, the protagonist, Elizabeth, is a victim and maintains a passive attitude, despite the awfulness of her situation. It seems there is no way out for her. By contrast, in Ní Dhuibhne's story, Fiona is angry with her partner and considers that her predicament is his fault. Ní Dhuibhne belongs to that younger generation of Irish women writers who want to break with the past and construct more powerful and plural identities for women – identities based on essence rather than difference. Younger writers seek to fight patriarchy in the text at the same time as they want to resist colonialism.

One strategy for deconstructing reality is to turn a mocking face and show the 'contr/addictions' in the most 'serious' of ideologies. Using her unique sense of humour and mockery, this is what Julia O'Faolain achieves in one of her most compelling stories, 'It's a Long Way to Tipperary'. O'Faolain narrates the story of Captain Cuddahy, an Irishman who joins the British army in 1914. Having served for twenty years, he comes back to Ireland where he finds himself no longer welcome. The young narrator, Jenny, ironically explains that it was only a matter of a few years which separated the two friends, Captain Cuddahy and her father, but what happened in those particular years had been crucial. Captain Cuddahy had been 'guarding the Empire at a time when my father's generation of Irishmen was promoting a revolution against it'.[66] Some ideologies can change so quickly that, in a way, their 'seriousness' is subverted.

Cuddahy struggles to prove his Irishness by being a devoted Catholic. However, he secretly admires England and Englishness, perhaps under the influence of a postcolonial mind set. Not surprisingly, therefore, he marries an English woman: 'She was his idea of an English officer's lady and he was humble before her'.[67] Cuddahy, however, is restricted to being 'only an imitation English gentleman'.[68] A further complication is the fact that he cannot be a good Catholic either because she was a married woman, but he could not resist the 'temptation' and they were married outside the church: 'Cuddahy – good, plain, loyal and limited Cuddahy – was now a renegade Catholic as well as a renegade Irishman'.[69] At the end of the story, Captain Cuddahy's 'bisected patriotism' leads him to madness.[70] At that time, other ways of being Irish were simply not accepted.

Cuddahy, trapped between two cultures, has accepted the coloniser's assumed superiority. But his revenge is to 'colonise' his wife. He is quite explicit: 'I tried to ram Catholicism down her throat'.[71] At the beginning, his English wife, Emily, has an attitude of disdain towards the Irish and their religion. She has no Irish friends, not even Anglo-Irish ones.[72] Ironically, she believes Catholicism was a 'religion for servants'[73] because she has the coloniser's sense of superiority. But a radical change takes place. Instructed by a padre attached to her husband's regiment, Emily becomes a devoted Catholic, much to the delight of her husband. Reflecting his wider alienation from Irish society, Cuddahy had not been inclined to trust a local priest. '"I wouldn't let her consult one of those Tipperary bumpkins"'[74] is how he puts it. Inspired by Emily's conversion to his own faith, Cuddahy decides to leave the army in order to be with her. Cuddahy believes that with the new life 'she has found serenity and fulfilment in her religion . . . It has brought her peace of spirit.'[75] The perverse outcome, however, is that both go mad.

Thus Cuddahy, torn by conflicting ideological forces, becomes a victim of his circumstances. His fervent Catholicism takes on an exaggerated form when his Irishness becomes threatened. The latter is perhaps the more fragile or unstable of the two identities, given Cuddahy's earlier involvement with the apparatus of the colonial state and his difficulty in settling back into post-Independence Irish society. In the face of these dilemmas, a religious identity, as the main element of Irishness, is being substituted for a political identity. This obsession with religion may also be connected with colonialism in another way. Religious fundamentalism is common in postcolonial countries as a way of finding refuge and certitude, in the aftermath of great political and social turmoil. Emily's attitude towards Cuddahy moves to tenderness towards the end of the story. When asked in the asylum if he goes for walks in Tipperary, the only thing he can say is: '"Tipperary" . . . "it's a long way, sir, a long way to Tipperary" . . . "A long way to go"'.[76] Cuddahy could not make the journey in the new Ireland of the post-Independence period. O'Faolain might be suggesting that there is something absurd about grand narratives bearing on national identities. Cuddahy goes to war thinking that he is serving Ireland and when he comes back he is rejected and accused of being a bad Irishman. Though he attempts to find comfort in religion, the contradictions in his life prove overwhelming, culminating in madness.

Identities are perhaps not always clear-cut and there should be space for that too. In 'Epitaph', Edna O'Brien describes a similar situation of conflicting loyalties, with an even more tragic outcome:

> She was a widow at thirty, her husband having been shot by the Black and Tans. To make matters worse, her husband was partly on the side of the foe, since he worked for the constabulary and was something of a scab. Things get very twisted in this world, don't they; nothing is clear-cut. There he was blown to bits by the foe and yet not a hero, not a man for whom a ballad would be made up, or whose tragic fate would be an inspiration for other young men.[77]

There are obviously different ways of being nationalist. Maeve Kelly goes further than just questioning nationalism in 'The Sentimentalist'. She gives an anti-romantic vision of it. The speaker expresses herself rather coldly, accepting colonisation and the loss of the Irish language and the tradition with it. She is quite matter-of-fact about the historical past:

> I have no flair for languages. Since English has been imposed on us, for historical reasons, I accept it and consider it adequate for my needs, a vehicle for communicating thought. I concede that I may have lost something, subtleties of expression more in keeping with my cultural background, not to mention the heritage of tradition which is difficult to translate adequately. However, I have always been a pragmatist and I accept the reality of conquest. The new nationalist fervour associated with the revival of the language was boring to me. I despise passion, wasted emotions.[78]

On the contrary, her cousin Liza, who is English but goes to Ireland to live, 'threw herself totally into the Gaelic revival. She joined the Gaelic League, attended the Abbey plays and became a member of Cumann na mBan.' The speaker does not approve. She rejects 'big movements' and puts feminism before nationalism:

> It has always seemed to me that organized groups, military or civilian or religious, are death to the individual and therefore retard human development. It can be argued that for the apathetic mass such groups are necessary, but I believe that one strong-minded individual can achieve more on her own if she is prepared to sacrifice her life for her cause. I do not mean by that the futile sacrifice of death, which simply perpetuates myths and has no logical value. Martyrdom is the ultimate folly, the self-indulgence of the sentimental. I mean that one person, standing alone, against the convention of her times, must, if she applies herself, learn wisdom, fortitude and knowledge, and provide the vital link between the generations which must lead to the ennoblement of all womankind . . . I do not deny that the history of this country has been a tragic one, but the worst tragedy of all has been the number and variety of its saviours – most of them with foreign or English blood – which it has attracted. Liza saw herself as one of those saviours.[79]

Despite Liza's enthusiasm, the speaker is sceptical and says that, as a woman, there was no place for them in politics: 'she was not political, not ambitious, not scheming, and she was not a man. So there was no place for her among the new policy makers.'[80] Liza opens a Gaelic summer school and works there for fifty years. In her old age, she was little more than 'an embarrassing reminder to the few old nationalist members of the government'.[81] At the end of her life, Liza does not see the point in her cause and ends up feeling defeated and saying: 'Gaelic Ireland is dead'.[82]

As in O'Brien's example, nothing is black and white. Perhaps women's nationalism is more flexible and tends towards pluralism and diversity. The extreme of 'masculine nationalism' might be thought to be in Northern Ireland today, where violence still persists. In Northern Irish society, politics is very much the domain of men, whereas peace groups are seen as a more appropriate arena for women's activities. In this context it is worth mentioning that the creation of the Women's Coalition in 1996 was an important move. Its philosophy is one of inclusion, whereas its male counterparts still prefer to play the black and white card. Thus I would argue that women in Northern Ireland, generally speaking, have a tendency to be more accommodating and perhaps less violent than men, not least because there has not been a tradition of physical violence from women towards men. As portrayed in literature at any rate, women only resort to violence after having been abused for a long time and, even then, it is not that common.

'GET OUT OR WE'LL BURN YOU OUT': THE CASE OF
NORTHERN IRELAND

If for women in Catalonia and in the Republic of Ireland the main concern is to 'decolonise' themselves, for Northern Irish women writers violence itself has been a more immediate and pressing concern since the 1970s. The urgent cry is to stop violence, including domestic violence, and this has pushed other social and political concerns associated with women into second place. Women writers in Northern Ireland are mostly of a Catholic background (Mary Beckett, Anne Devlin, Maedh McGuckian and Fiona Barr). One of the most effective short stories by an Irish woman writer exploring violence linked to nationalism is 'A Belfast Woman' by Mary Beckett. For her, fanaticism, violence and death are the final consequences of a narrow and masculine idea of nationalism.

'Get out or we'll burn you out' is the opening line of the story.[83] It could hardly be more explicit or more uncompromising. This is nationalism and ethnic cleansing in its most extreme form. It is also the story of dispossession, which is a common theme in relation to postcolonial societies. Being expelled from one's own place has been and still is a common occurrence in Northern Ireland and, as a result, it is a frequent subject in women's writing from the North. Reaching back in time, Mary recalls: 'One of the first things I remember in my life was wakening up with my mother screaming downstairs when we were burnt out in 1921'.[84]

Mary is Catholic. In time she marries another Catholic but one whose father is Protestant. They move to a Protestant area. Mary quickly becomes aware of the small differences, describing her new neighbours as more independent and more distant, but realises that they are good people:

> They didn't come into the house for a chat or a loan of tea or milk or sugar like the neighbours in Glenard or North Queen Street but they were ready to help at any time. I didn't know the men much because they had work so they didn't stand around the corners the way I was used to. But when Liam was born they all helped and said what a fine baby he was.[85]

Fairly quickly, she notices that Protestants have jobs and also get better housing, while few Catholics have a job. But Protestants, as a social group, can change and stick together when problems arise. At the end of the story, when her house has been attacked, she says: 'Not one of the neighbours came out and all evening when I worked at tidying up and all night when I sat up to keep watch, not one of them knocked at my door'.[86]

In a graphic piece of imagery, violence is compared to weeds, as if it were a part of nature. Weeds and violence exist everywhere, in both Catholic and Protestant communities. Mary's father-in-law (a Protestant) comments on his garden: 'They're the plague of my life. No matter how much I weed there's more in the morning'.[87] Mary describes her grandfather's garden (he had also been burnt out):

> I told him about my grandfather and the big elderberry tree that grew behind the wee house he'd got in the country when he was burnt out in Lisburn. It wasn't there when he went into the house and when he noticed it first it was only a wee bit of a bush but it grew so quickly it blocked out all the light for his back window. Then one summer it was covered with black slimy kind of flies so he cut it down to the stump, but it started growing again straight away. One day when my father took Patsy and Joey and me down to visit him he had dug all around the stump and he was trying to pull it out with a rope. He told my father to pull with him. My father tried but then he leaned against the wall with his face pale and covered with sweat.[88]

The stump of communal hatred is deeply rooted in the two communities. Mary then thinks she has cancer. One might surmise that this is also a metaphor for violence and its endemic character within Northern Irish society. Out of fear and ignorance, Mary does not dare to go to the doctor. In the same way, out of ignorance, both communities fail to find peace.

Unexpectedly, at the end of the story, we discover Mary has no cancer. The nightmare of fear and paranoia gives way to a new consciousness. The story draws to a close with a call to Mary's house by a salesman:

> 'Do you know Belfast has the most beautiful sunsets in the whole world?' . . . do you know why? It's because of all the smoke and dirt and dust and pollution. And it seems to me,' he said, 'it seems to me that if the dirt and dust and smoke and pollution of Belfast just with the help of the sun can make a sky like that, then there's hope for all of us.' . . . And thinking of it I started to laugh, for it's true. There is hope for all of us. Well, anyway, if you don't die you live through it, day in, day out.[89]

This laughing end brings forward two issues: one is that love for your own country or city is the best homage you can pay it. Secondly, throughout the story there is a tone of stoicism which is present in many of Beckett's stories. Human nature can get used to almost anything, even to long-term violence. In my view, this story captures something very Irish: a stoicism laced with humour, sometimes black humour, which has its origins perhaps in shared experiences of poverty.

It is noteworthy that while Mary in the story is ashamed of the IRA, she does not blame her country. Violence is part of nature, like weeds or cancer. War is present everywhere, at some stage. Like death, it is part of humanity. It is not anybody's fault:

> I could swallow my own shame every time the IRA disgraced us. I lived with it the same as I lived with the memory of my own disgrace when I went for the teacher and ripped my arm. But William (her husband) had always been such a good upright man, he could never understand wickedness.[90]

Eileen, Mary's daughter, ends up leaving the country and tells her mother how ashamed she is of being Irish, whereas her son Liam stays. But Mary says:

> It's not right to put the blame on poor powerless people. The most of us never did anything but stay quiet and put up with things the way they were. And we never taught our children to hate the others nor filled their heads with their wrongs the way it's said we did. When all the young people thought they could fix everything with marches and meetings I said it wouldn't work and they laughed at me . . . It'll all lead to shooting and burning and murder.[91]

Beckett's point is to explain why violence exists. She seems to suggest here that Irish people are not violent because they are Irish, rather violence is a 'weed' or 'cancer' which is part of nature – of human nature, and in particular, of men's nature. There is not much that can be done and once it takes root it is almost impossible to eradicate. Like Maeve Kelly in 'The Sentimentalist', Mary Beckett is sceptical and does not endorse men's organisations, be they groups of demonstrators or paramilitary organisations. The end result is killing and destruction.

Fiona Barr's 'The Wall Reader' covers similar ground. Mary likes reading graffiti ('Shall only our rivers run free?', 'Peace in, Brits out')[92] as she pushes the pram in the streets of Belfast. At the end of the story, fearful of a message which has appeared on their wall, she and her husband are forced to leave the country just because of her friendship with an English soldier. Mary's new acquaintance with an English soldier causes her to be accused of being a 'tout'.[93] 'Touting is punishable by death: tradition has ordained it so'.[94] She cannot understand it: 'What have I done?' she keeps asking herself.[95]

As a woman, she is only a reader – a passive figure who observes what happens in the world and cannot do anything about it. However, nobody can stop her having an opinion, and she does not like what she sees. In this Northern story, issues of gender are to the forefront. At the end, when they have to leave Belfast, she describes the new family who buys the house as 'an ideal family': 'He too had an office job, but his wife was merely a housekeeper for him. She was sensible, down to earth, and not in the least inclined to wall-reading.'[96] In this society women are relegated to a second-class status with little power to change things. They also resent their isolation: 'If only someone noticed her from time to time'.[97] But Mary really wants to change the world, even if only in little ways. She rejects conformist notions and conventions, even in relation to her child. Not for her the dream that one day her daughter will marry a doctor and thereby better herself.

Mary has her own intimate needs. She is happy to have a friend; she feels valued. After all, friendship is what really counts: 'All her life she had longed to be remembered' but not through walls which are so destructive – rather through her new friend who would deliver her memory'.[98] Besides, her affection for the soldier suggests a lack of emotional communication with her husband.

Fiona Barr reacts to the bigotry produced in a deeply divided society. It is demonstrated by the absurdity of not being able to have a simple conversation with a person who happens to be a soldier and happens to be a man. (Her husband Sean is in fact jealous and resentful which is an interesting side view on masculine behaviour.) It makes no sense. On her way to Dublin, she remembers 'women who had been tarred and feathered, heard of people who had been shot in the head, boys who had been knee-capped, all for suspected fraternising with troops'.[99] Violence is disclosed as ineffective. Writing is held to be more effective. As Mary puts it: 'The brush is mightier than the bomb'.[100]

Violence is a masculine construction in which physical power is directly associated with sexual power: 'She thought of the thick-lipped youth who came to hijack the car, making his point by showing his revolver under his anorak, and of the others, jigging and taunting every July, almost sexual in their arrogance and hatred.'[101] As a woman, the generous action of being able to give life might help to explain her less violent disposition. Loving so much means she could not hate so much: 'She really did not care if they maimed her or even murdered her. She did care about her daughter. She was her touchstone, her anchor to virtue. Not for her child a legacy of fear, revulsion or hatred.'[102] Again this shows that after decades of violence, there is an awareness among northern writers of accepting death as part of life.

While women writers in Northern Ireland generally reject political violence in the literature they produce, there are exceptions, such as Brenda Murphy and Anne Devlin. Some of their characters sympathise with the republican armed struggle. (Brenda Murphy spent six years in jail on politically-related offences.)

'The Connor Girls' by Edna O'Brien deals with relationships between Catholics and Protestants in the southern context of de Valera's Ireland. Among the striking features of this story is the manner in which it combines issues of gender, admiration for the former colonial power and a sense of cultural inferiority. We see different games of power going on. These revolve around two axes: first, the Protestant family versus the Catholic village and, second, men versus women. In the two cases there is a mixture of antagonism and admiration from the colonised towards the coloniser, which is one of the expected consequences in terms of postcolonial discourse.

First, we see the secret admiration Catholics in the village have for the Protestant family. The Connors may be taken to represent the coloniser because not only were they Protestant and well-off but they celebrated things like the coronation and England's victory in the war.[103] Other hints of this colonial identification and local perceptions of their separateness abound. For example, the story opens: 'To know them would be to enter an exalted world'.[104] It continues: 'The Connor girls were not beauties but they were distinguished and they talked in an accent that made everyone else's seem flat and sprawling, like some familiar estuary or a puddle in a field'.[105] The awareness of the language is always an important element in colonisation. The Connor family, the girls and their father 'the Major', never mixed with the people in the village. Despite, or perhaps because, of this, the people in the village craved their attention: 'Those who had never had a salute felt such a pang of envy, felt left out'.[106] On sad occasions, 'local people who longed to be friends with them would rush out and offer their sympathy as if the Major was the only one to have suffered bereavement. But the more they sought attention, the stiffer became "the Major's" reaction. On meeting someone locally, he remained brusque and asked his daughters the name of the man or woman who happened to be talking to him.'[107] Even the Connors' dogs were 'thorough-breeds' and scared the other dogs.[108]

The speaker's family, whose surname we are never told, allows the girls to walk their dogs in their fields. The Connor girls talk to the father but 'ignored my mother who resented this'.[109] As colonisers, they talk to one of a parallel category, the 'coloniser man'. Moreover, just as the husband renames his wife on marriage, so the coloniser has the right to rename: the girls call someone Mick, even though his real name is Joseph. Despite being rejected, the mother still wants to invite them for tea and makes a big meal but they refuse and give a frivolous reason: 'they never eat between meals'.[110] Paradoxically, their offhand attitude inflamates her admiration still further.

One of the Connor girls starts a relationship with a new bank clerk in the parish. The people in the village change their attitude towards him immediately when they realise he is a Catholic who does not go to mass. He is sent a message: 'Go to mass or we'll kill you'.[111] The admiration towards Protestants also has some hidden hatred and, as a result, people do not accepted mixed marriages. The mother of the family who admires the girls so much says Catholic and Protestant should not intermarry. Still, they give Miss Connor a wedding present because, as colonial outsiders, the Connor girls can break with local conventions and set their own. Suddenly, the man leaves with no explanation. Later we learn that it was the Connor girls' father who had prevented the wedding. The would-be wife becomes depressed and ends up as an alcoholic. We could say, in gender terms, that the coloniser father figure has abused his power in relation to his daughter.

At the beginning of the story, we are made to believe that the roles are very clear and that the colonisers are the Protestant family and that the colonised are the Catholics in the village. But as the story unfolds we are exposed to other realities. The narrator is abused by her family who do not accept her and, ironically, her English husband ridicules the Protestant family. In an almost identical way, the members of the Catholic family abuse their power in relation to their daughter. The speaker leaves and marries a man 'who was not of our religion' and the family does not talk to her for years.[112] For them, being Protestant and not having a religion is the same. They invite the married couple back to the village only after she has a son. When she returns she is obviously worried as she steps out of 'her husband's car'.[113] Her husband's attitude is one of contempt towards her family, her village and even the Connor girls. The story ends by pointing out her loneliness. We could say she is colonised because she is an Irish Catholic and also because she is a woman. The combination leads to her deep loneliness and unhappiness.

It may also be noticed in O'Brien's story that there is complicity between these (fictional) representatives of the coloniser and the colonised. Village respect and deference in relation to the Connor family members serve to strengthen the position of the colonial outsider. A similar process may be at play where women marry men who exploit their power over them, and yet command respect and loyalty, as illustrated in the case of the two women (one Catholic, one Protestant) in this story.

Having developed some perspectives on Irish women's views of nationalism as reflected in the genre of the short story, including the complexities and contradictions these embody, I will now turn to Catalan writers. There may be similarities and parallels; equally there may be differences and incongruities. It is as well to indicate in advance that the literature on women and Catalan nationalism is in its infancy.

WOMEN AND NATIONALISM IN CATALONIA

Even though there are a number of similarities between Irish and Catalan nationalisms, there are two crucial differences. First, the Irish language was lost to most of the population during the eighteenth and nineteenth centuries. English was substituted in its place and adherence to the Catholic Church became the national badge of identity. By contrast, the Catalan language survived, protected by a strong middle class. It has become a vital shield for Catalan people in defending their identity and achieving self-confidence in the face of the centralist Spanish state and, later, fascist dictatorship whose aims were the destruction of cultural minorities like the Catalans, the Basques and the Galicians. Although some linguists say it is likely to disappear in the twenty-first century, Catalan nationalism has expressed itself more effectively through its language and

its culture than through politics. This is a crucial difference because overtly
nationalist concerns are much less apparent in comparison with Irish
literature. But the mere fact of choosing the officially-rejected Catalan
language in which to write, instead of the powerful and fashionable
Spanish, meant and still means strong commitment to a form of
nationalism. Still, like Irish nationalism, Catalan nationalism has turned
out to be a patriarchal discourse with a tendency to marginalise women.
The margin has produced other margins.

The second crucial difference between the two nations relates to
periodisation. Ireland has been politically independent for most of this
century. Despite the existence of a strong independence movement in
Catalonia, Primo de Rivera's dictatorship (1923–30) and the Francoist
rebellion from 1936 prevented its actualisation. The exception was a brief
period of autonomy in the 1930s. In post-Independence Ireland there was
a virtual unity of Church and State which had serious implications for Irish
women. As a result, many women writers reject or, at least, are critical of
the kind of nationalism which emerged. During most of the same period,
Catalan culture went through a difficult time, suffering persecution from
Madrid. That made it easier to be on the nationalist side which was also
against the authoritarian regime. To some extent women writers, and also
a number of men writers, felt protective of Catalan culture. The prevailing
patriarchal ideology was Francoist Spanish nationalism rather than Catalan
nationalism. Catalan nationalism had originated in the nineteenth century
and had been heavily influenced by Romanticism, with its designation of
women as passive figures. Also, as mentioned before, women have not
been the makers of ideologies and nationalism is no exception. Hence the
bias against women and women's interests, not only within Spanish
nationalism but also within Catalan nationalism.

During the Catalan revival period, women were used extensively as
objects in publicity materials. The revival period was largely the creation
of male writers.[114] In the nineteenth century, popular images of women
tended to be rural whereas in the 1920s the urban woman was deemed
more fashionable.[115] In literature we may note the character Teresa
(shades here of Cathleen Ní Houlihan), the protagonist in Eugeni d'Ors
popular novel *La ben plantada*. The title literally means 'the well-planted'.
It plays with meanings: a good-looking woman, the virgin Teresa and a
well-planted tree are all symbolic expressions of the Catalan nation and a
woman/mother at the same time. Teresa embodies the national qualities.
Eugeni d'Ors explains that the roots of this tree are very deep, just as his
speech comes from deep inside the land. The tree is oriented towards the

heavens, towards God. Thus, images of faith, motherland and the historic depth to the Catalan nation are fused together. Teresa is a model for Catalan women whose mission is motherhood and to transmit the values of the new century whilst remaining true to the traditions of the Catalan past.

There are some cases of bourgeois women active in '*catalanisme*' (Catalan nationalism), such as the women who published the magazines *Or i Grana* (1906) and *Feminal* (1907), but these publications were conservative, seeing women with a role solely within the confines of the home. For example, the first magazine's motto is quite explicit: '*El fonament de la Pàtria es la Família, el fonament de la Família es la Dona*' (The foundation of the Fatherland is the Family, the foundation of the Family is the Woman).[116] In Cristina Dupláa's words: '*ara . . . son elles les que accepten les regles del joc marcades, en molts casos, pels marits*' (now . . . they are the ones who accept the rules of the game, directed by their husbands in many cases).[117]

During the Francoist dictatorship (1939–75), Catalan women were among the most enthusiastic advocates of Catalan language and culture. Despite the prevailing climate, many women writers continued to write in Catalan, either from exile or at home. If we consider the difficulty of writing in Catalan during the dictatorship with hardly any possibility of getting published, then the use of an outcast language signifies a commitment to maintaining Catalan culture. Generally, women harboured the mother tongue, Catalan being the language of the home and the private sphere. This was also the sphere or space where women were most comfortable, most 'at home'. The political and cultural implications of this are spelled out by Kathleen McNerney:

> The private domestic space defines political community, in contrast to Castilian, the language of a superimposed public space. These differences do not necessarily imply hierarchical placement (i.e. Castilian would be the language for important matters, while Catalan, Galician, and Basque would be relegated to trivia); rather, they involve a politicisation of things feminine and domestic. For cultural and political minorities, domestic affairs, on impact with public affairs, acquire connotations they do not bear in the 'normal' order of things in modern societies. Domestic space becomes that of resistance.[118]

In Ireland, Carol Coulter also makes the point that in the Irish case the family was the 'locus of resistance'[119] to the colonial occupier because in that space one could speak one's own language, practise one's customs and express one's own opinions. The relevance of this to nineteenth, still less twentieth-century Ireland is muddied, however, by the knowledge that political freedom of speech was highly developed within the framework of the United Kingdom and that many Irish-speaking parents were noted for their concern to ensure their children became English speakers. The point seems more relevant to Catalonia. Cristina Dupláa says:

> *En els textos nacionalistes . . . la figura femenina simbolitza la pàtria i és la peça central de la família pel fet de ser transmissora de la història/tradició a les noves generacions*

> (In nationalist texts . . . the feminine figure symbolises the fatherland and is the centrepiece of the family by the mere fact of being the one who passes the tradition/history down to succeeding generations).[120]

Dupláa gives an explanation of the woman as symbol of the nation which is not unlike that of the Irish case. As the one who brings up the children, she is the carrier and transmitter of culture. The woman as the symbol of the nation is an idealisation derived from Romanticism, in much the same way as are sentimental images of the family. Dupláa writes: '*La dona/mare dins la casa acaba sent la dona/patria dins la nacio i, per tant el simbol de la continuitat i de la tradicio.* (the woman/mother within the house ends up being the woman/fatherland within the nation, thus the symbol of continuity and tradition).[121] However, the personification of the nation as a woman seems more pervasive in Irish writing. Why this might be so is not obvious, though it may be bound up with the greater resistance of Catalan language and culture and the dynamism of its economy, despite the colonial overlordship of Spain.

In Catalonia, women achieved the vote in 1931, a little more than a decade later than their Irish counterparts. However, traditional mentalities inhibited women from engaging actively in politics, and very few actually did.[122] Still, as Nash writes: '*El nacionalisme fou una de les vies mes importants de polititzacio de les dones catalanes.*' (Nationalism was one of the most important ways for women to enter politics).[123] Among the examples cited by Nash was the successful campaign by Catalan women for the release of political prisoners. This was in the late 1920s and the prisoners were released in 1930. Also, there were a number of women's associations which promoted the vote in favour of home rule in the referendum in 1931.

During the Spanish Civil War (1936–39) the situation changed dramatically. The war obliged a massive women's mobilisation in the anti-fascist struggle. New women's groups appeared, such as the *Grup de Dones contra el Feixisme i la Guerra* (Women's Group Against Fascism and War) in 1934, which was feminist and nationalist.[124] This movement helped to define women's identities. Whereas in Spain wives were subordinated to their husbands by law, under the short-lived autonomous government in

Catalonia wives enjoyed equal rights with their husbands. Women did not
need their husband's permission, for instance, to be able to work or occupy
active roles in society. Catalonia was also one of the first countries to legalise
divorce, in 1932, and abortion in 1936, so as to discourage backstreet
abortions and infanticide. The state also promoted contraception. That made
it easier for women to become involved with Catalan nationalism which was
more concerned about women's issues than the Irish one.

'*La gran derrotada de la guerra va ser la dona*' (Women were the real
defeated after the Spanish Civil War), as Montserrat Roig says.[125] All
women's rights and all legislation by the Catalan institutions were
invalidated. The married woman was reduced in law to the position of a
child, dependent on her husband in virtually all financial affairs for forty
years. Few women had jobs and/or education. Women's oppression under
the Francoist regime was welcomed by many Catalan men who were
happy to see women restricted. Many short stories of the period reflect
this grim reality. It is important to stress that, even those who were actively
resistant to Francoism, such as the Catalan left wing, accepted the circumscribed role of women.

During the Franco era most schools were Catholic, and in the literature
we have the same bitter reaction from women writers against the
misogyny of Catholicism as in Irish literature. The writer Montserrat Roig
tells of how some nuns hated girls for no reason other than their mere
existence.[126] In a similar way, Fiona Barr shows the hate a nun has for a
schoolgirl in her story *Sisters*.[127]

After the long era of Francoism, women had to begin afresh in the
1980s. It was not easy. For example, Montserrat Roig says women did not
voice opinions in university assemblies in either the 1970s or the beginning
of 1980, something that finds echoes in Ireland.[128] Nonetheless, women
went to demonstrations during the 1970s, were arrested and risked their
lives in the same way men did, yet were expected to serve coffees and to
type men's papers. What is worse, historians generally do not register
women's presence in public agitations. That was certainly Montserrat
Roig's experience. In one particular case, an important meeting which
took place in the early 1970s, 'la Caputxinada', the historian, justifies his
omission of women on the grounds that there were no women
mentioned in the police records.

Another writer, Isabel-Clara Simó, who is publicly committed to the
cause of Catalan independence, believes that the Catalan government does
not seek independence because memories of the Civil War are still fresh
and fears still persist.[129] Simó links the abnormality of both her gender and

her sense of national identity: '*M'agradaria poder deixar-me de plantejar la meva nació o el meu sexe com a problema* (I would like to be able to stop thinking of my nation or my sex as a problem).[130] She explicitly refers to the two colonised elements – the colonised nation and the colonised gender and establishes a link between the two. Of her country, she is critical rather than loving. The writer Montserrat Roig would also like to live in a normal society in which one loves one's country without mixed feelings of victimhood, pessimism and fear:

> *Vull forçar-me a viure com si em trobés en una societat sana i normalitzada. Voldria transmetre als qui venen al darrera aquesta sensació de societat sana i normalitzada. Estic cansada de transmetre la malaltia . . . Moltes vegades transmetem tot just l'agressivitat, la crispació i el sentit de víctimes. Vull que els meus fills estimin el seu país perque és el seu, perque a més és bonic.*

> (I want to force myself to live as if I was in a healthy and normalised society. I would like to transmit this sensation of a healthy and normalised society to the next generations. I am fed up transmitting the illness . . . Many times we transmit only the aggression, the nerves, and victimhood. I want my children to love their country because it is theirs and also because it is beautiful.)[131]

As with many other intellectuals in Catalonia, both women and men, Montserrat Roig says she could feel Spanish if Spain was a state made up of a collection of nations working towards a new society, in equal conditions.[132] As Ferrer i Gironès shows in *Catalanofòbia*, Roig thinks that Catalan nationalism is a result of not having been accepted by Spain.

Writing in Catalan alone was the best writers could do for the national cause considering that, due to the abnormality of the culture, there was a need to sustain Catalan and also because access to political life was difficult for women. As a consequence, feminist, linguistic and nationalist vindications have been deeply mixed. Oppression can provide an opportunity to deconstruct reality and to understand human groups who suffer. Maria Mercè Marçal takes such a tack by celebrating oppression in her short poem, 'Divisa' (Motto), which was very popular at the end of the 1970s and has become a national symbol.

There is also a willingness to find a common solution to the feminist and the Catalan struggles. According to Anne Charlon, this takes a variety of forms, based on female solidarity, and might include Catalan women writers 'winking at each other' through repeating the names of the main characters from other women's stories,[133] or writing new versions of the works of other Catalan women writers.[134]

Some writers of the beginning of the century, like Caterina Albert, were close to the national cause as her pen name, Víctor Català, indicates. However, Albert normally wrote about other themes in her short stories. She did not even want to publicise her opinions on literature. This was because at the beginning of her career she had been severely criticised for being a woman who used violence in her writing. As a consequence, in her introduction to one of her collections of short stories in 1907,[135] Albert strongly criticises the revival period. She sees it as provincial and narrow-minded because it did not accept her contribution as a woman writer, which was different and celebrated difference. For Albert it is crucial to leave the artist free to be able to create at ease. The fact that that was not the case in Catalonia was because Catalonia had not had a normal evolution: it was a postcolonial country. As early as the beginning of the century, Albert emphasised plurality in the construction of a Catalan culture and warned that if this was not going to be the case so the Catalan culture was not going to last.

During the period of the Civil War and after, most women's short stories were about the disgust they felt towards war. Women found it hard to understand the lack of dialogue and flexibility, the hate and ultimately the mass killings. Having lived through two wars, the Spanish and the Second World War in France where she was exiled, much of Mercè Rodoreda's fiction was about the effects of war: hunger, suffering and death. Rodoreda had been a nationalist activist, though more concerned with culture than politics, and this had led to her exile abroad.

In her last collection of short stories, *Viatges i flors* (Travels and Flowers), Rodoreda's purpose, she explains, is to deconstruct gender and the kind of bigoted nationalism that leads to war. The setting where the stories unfold reflects an allegorical world. The form is innovative, and the stories might be read as a type of magical realism. In the first part of the work there is a series of brief vignettes of the irrational and disruptive impact of war on men's but, in particular, on women's lives. There are fantastic images of doll-like lost girls suspended in time, old women whose sole function is knitting, rainbow-coloured new-borns whose spectrum fades to a single gender-identifying stripe, and men who hang themselves in a perverse ritual of family life. She imagines a series of nameless rural communities, steeped in traditional customs.

The first story sets the tone for the fantastic nature of the book. 'Viatge al poble dels guerrers' (Travel to the Warriors' Town) opens: '*Em vaig haver d'arraconar de pressa perque venien contra mi potser un miler de cavalls amb soldats al damunt armats amb llances*'[136] (I threw myself into a corner quickly because about a thousand horses with soldiers on them, armed with lances, were coming towards me). The world is against the individual. The irony, in this case, is that these soldiers do not hurt anybody; they do not inflict any injury. It is a farce in the same way as social reality, and gender reality, is a construction. The soldiers only want people to be afraid of them. They want their young wives to be waiting for them. The show is all about appearances, not reality. Another of the stories in this first part is 'Viatge al poble de les nenes perdudes' (Travel to the Lost Girls' Town). This story explains how entering the symbolic order for women means they cannot grow and are restricted to infancy all their lives.

In an exercise in deconstructing nationalism, Rodoreda's 'Viatge al poble dels guerrers' (Travel to the Warriors' Town), exposes the absurdities of patriotic symbols. The description of the flag of a departing army is repeated exactly upon their return in an identical cloud of dust: '*Vermella i blanca duia escrit amb lletres vermelles damunt del blanc i amb lletres blanques damunt del vermell, "Coratge", "Puresa"*' (Red and white, red print was written on white and white print on red: 'Courage', 'Purity').[137] Those kinds of words show masculine and inflexible values. Those are words which belong to the world of the masculine coloniser, whereas humility and hybridity fit more easily within a female vocabulary. Furthermore, the flags themselves seem to generate the passion with which the groups waving them march into battle. The narrator's monotonous and uncomprehending description tends to rob the whole enterprise of meaning or significance. The description of the army is theatrical: the constant drumming, the marching, the military uniforms. This is all a demonstration of masculine power, of preparing to make war and has little to do with the world of women.

There is a subversive incongruity between the male symbols of warfare and the imagery of women and marriage unfolded later in the story. The wives are waiting patiently and passively – the adverbs are rather stereotypical – although they are apprehensive for the fate of their menfolk. They are, of course, all young and pretty. How could they be otherwise inside the male imagination? Each wears a golden ring with a pearl on her toe. Slipping the ring from finger to toe is part of the ironic strategy deployed by the writer to illustrate the arbitrariness of social convention. Rodoreda described the title as a 'smile'[138] probably because of her playful demonstration that gender construction is totally irrational and theatrical. Nonetheless, she is also conscious that conventional constructions of masculinity are dangerous because they give rise to violence and war mongering.

At the end of 1970s, Isabel-Clara Simó published a collection of short stories, *És quan miro que hi veig clar* (It's When I Look That I Can See Clearly), paraphrasing a famous Catalan poem 'Es quan dormo qui hi veig clar' (It's when I sleep that I can see clearly). Being overtly nationalist, Simó is passionately concerned with the fate of the Catalan language. The stories are about the process of recovery of the Catalan language and culture which was actually taking place at that moment, after Franco's death in 1975. By then, many Spanish words had entered the Catalan language and Catalan linguists insisted on recovering the old Catalan words and making a collective effort to use them. This was difficult. People in Catalonia had been denied access to their native language in the schools and colleges, hence many had low standards of literacy. Through the medium of short stories, Simó demands flexibility for people to change the language. She brings to life the language enthusiasm of these transitional years, of people correcting each other in speech as part of the great collective effort to rehabilitate Catalan. Some of the stories illustrate the tensions which surrounded the struggle between Catalan and Spanish. These have social class as well as ethnic dimensions. Thus, in 'Em dic Jaumet' (My Name is Jaumet), Jaumet's mother, because she wishes to rise in the social scale, seeks to cast aside the cultural baggage of low-status Catalan. She begins to speak Spanish to her child, even renaming him Jaime (the Spanish version of his name). However, the child resists and does not want to use the Spanish language.

These various individual and collective acts are perceived by Simó as nationalistic, and the stories exude a sense of the necessity of remaking Catalan culture and politics in the aftermath of Francoism. There is also a palpable love of Barcelona. For Simó, Barcelona is simply the most beautiful city in the world:

> *L'aire del matí, a Barcelona, és la cosa més bonica del món. La gent va atrafegada, però d'una manera estimulant. El sol entra oblic per la mar I es veu que porta una càrrega d'oxigen que ho anima tot, i ens amara el cos de vitalitat I de ganes de fer coses . . . De vuit a nou del matí, Barcelona és la ciutat més bonica del món.*

> (The fresh air, in Barcelona, is the most beautiful thing in the world. People are busy but in a pleasant way. The sun gets into the sea obliquely and infuses a huge amount of oxygen which regenerates everything, and gives us vitality . . . From eight to nine in the morning, Barcelona is the most beautiful city in the world.)[139]

Moving forward in time to the 1990s, concerns about nationalism are less to the fore than in the period of euphoria surrounding the early days of democratisation. But in 'L'empelt' (The Graft), by Maria Àngels Anglada, the old theme of the fortunes and prospects of the Catalan language springs afresh and shows the collective fear with the possible death of the Catalan language. The story is initially framed against the background of the death of another Latin language – Dalmatian – which became extinct towards the end of the nineteenth century. In 'L'empelt' only one woman on the island home of the language is still able to speak Dalmatian. She is old. She is going to die soon. With her passing, the language will also die. The death of the language will change the world, its landscape and nature:

> *Els penya-segats ja no seran els mateixos, sense ella, ni ho serà la plata de les oliveres, ni els peixos diferents que bullen a les xarxes en la derrera agonia, ni serà igual l'escassa pluja ni el cop d'ala de cada vent, de cada ocell.*

> (The cliffs won't be the same, without it, nor the silver of olive trees, nor different fishes which twist in the nets in their last agony, nor the light rain, nor the movement of the wings of every bird.)[140]

The story then takes a futuristic turn, and we find ourselves in the twenty-first century. Many minority languages are disappearing worldwide, threatened by the dominance of English and Anglo-American culture. Latin languages find themselves under particular threat. A Dutch linguist, Ernst Heyltjes, whose favourite language is Catalan, travels to Catalonia to help save the language. There has been a *coup d'etat* whose main aim is to extinguish the Catalan language. (The echoes here of the Francoist era are deliberate.) Elsewhere in Europe there have been strong cultural revivals; in the case of Wales, this long-submerged nation has even achieved political independence. But in Catalonia the native language is facing extinction. The Dutch linguist finds a shepherd, Jordi, who happens to be the last native speaker of Catalan. Finding Jordi had not been easy. The visit has to be in secret as the Central government no longer allows the study of Catalan. Listening, enraptured by the speech he is recording, the Dutchman feels there is no music as beautiful as the sound of those romantic words. But the political reality is harsh in the extreme:

> *durant anys i panys s'havien persegit, empresonat, mort, els parlants obstinats. En altres casos, tècniques de rentat de cervell, individuals i collectives, esporàdiques i continuades, havien estat emprades amb eficàcia.*

> (For many years, Catalans who had obstinately clung to the language had been persecuted, imprisoned, killed. In other cases, at the level of individuals and groups, sporadic and continuous techniques of brainwashing had been used effectively.)[141]

Driving along Catalan roads, the Dutch linguist finds police checkpoints all over the place. Suddenly he is kidnapped by a group of Catalans. He discovers that they are part of a resistance movement against the new regime and are trying to maintain the Catalan language underground. The eventual outcome is not important to the point being developed here. What matters is that the author, Maria Àngels Anglada, is touching on deep anxieties in Catalan society regarding the survival of the language, even in post-Francoist times. Is the living language of Catalonia facing death in the future? If, so what of the riches of Catalan literature and culture, which may also disappear with the spoken tongue? Unlike the Irish case, the centrality of the native language to a sense of cultural and national identity is underlined.

The relationship between women and politics, and male chauvinist reaction to such involvement, is conveyed in a number of stories. A good example is Merry Torres' 'Dones soles' (Lonely Women), which focuses on women's resistance to oppression. Written in 1995, it is the story of a women's rebellion. The action takes place during the International Exhibition which was staged in Barcelona in 1929. On the last night of the event, there is a spectacular music and light show at the Montjuich Fountains. Special guests on the occasion. This spectacle, in fact, still exists. Special guests on the occasion include the King and the General Primo de Rivera, the Spanish dictator who ruled between 1923 and 1930, all male authorities. (Like Franco some years later, Primo de Rivera banned public manifestations of Catalan culture, including the use of the Catalan language, Catalan institutions such as the government and Parliament, the Catalan flag and even Catalan folklore.) On the night in question, three women disrupt the great spectacle, by actually getting into the fountains. They are immediately arrested and taken away by the police. A journalist in the pay of the regime, reporting on the scene, describes the women who were disrupting the event as lunatics who should be looking after the house, like good wives and mothers. He describes women as weak, little equipped for abstract thought, whose subjugation is due to their fickle-mindedness as evidenced by their flirtation with women's emancipation. In the journalist's opinion, these protests are due to bad external influences, such as the fashion for women to wear trousers which is creeping in. He compares the event at the Fountains to another which took place some years before, a Catalan uprising, which, in fact, happened in 1926. It seems that Torres is seeking to relate the two: Catalan nationalism and female protest. Both male and Madrid authority are being questioned. However, it is only fair to add that women writers in recent years have been less interested in developing a female perspective on Catalan nationalism than in exploring other themes. In this there are similarities with contemporary Irish women writers who are also ranging across more extensive thematic landscapes.

CONCLUSION

Being doubly colonised, the main concern of Irish and Catalan women writers has been to decolonise themselves. Nationalism figures importantly in this writing agenda. In these respects, there are similarities between Catalan and Irish writing. But there are also significant differences. The degree of concern with these issues is more pronounced in the Irish case. However, the shift away from overtly nationalist concerns among the newest generation of Irish and Catalan women writers reduces the contrast. In Catalonia national identity has been expressed mainly through the use of the Catalan language, whereas in Ireland national identity has been expressed in more explicitly political terms.

Like most ideologies, nationalism is patriarchal. Its romantic inspiration created the vision of Ireland/Catalonia as a weak and passive woman in need of help and salvation. Once the new Irish Free State was created, women were shut out of an active role in politics. De Valera's Ireland, with its emphasis on Catholicism, was very much male-centred, although in truth this represented continuity rather than change in Irish society. While women writers show themselves to be critical of a heritage of colonial domination in both societies, they are less than sentimental about purely nationalist concerns. Still, there is a sympathy with the nationalist cause, in its political or cultural manifestation, or both, due in part perhaps to a parallel sense of also being 'colonised'. In the Catalan case, the very fact of writing in Catalan, which most Catalan women writers did, was in itself a nationalist act, expressing commitment to preserving Catalan culture through the use of the Catalan language.

One of the consequences of colonisation is a problem with borders. We see this in the case of Northern Ireland and the Irish Republic, with a large minority of Irish nationalists living in the North and hence within the United Kindgom. In terms of ethnicity and language, Catalonia spills across the Catalan and Spanish border into France, a territory known as North Catalonia. In a similar way, women are also unhappy about their 'borders', as regards the activities to which they have traditionally been restricted – those of motherhood and caring.

I would argue that the situation of Catalan writers was worse than the Irish one during the twentieth century because of war and poverty and the yoke of various dictatorships. The latter account for almost half of the century, (1923–1930 and 1939–1975). Moreover, the limited educational opportunities available to women were available only in Spanish, so that they became or remained illiterate in their own language. Hence the prominence of language issues in Catalan nationalism, and the links forged between women's concerns, national autonomy and language change.

Most of the women writers selected in this study see little glory in violence. They are strongly critical of violence in Northern Ireland, the violence of the Spanish Civil War and the Second World War. They reject the intolerance born of masculinist ideologies, including nationalism. Rodoreda clearly associates war with masculinity. A woman in one of her stories says: '*Tot el mon . . . es ple de guerres i els homes embogeixen per anar a la guerra*' (All the world is full of wars and men are crazy to go to war).[142] Women reject the symbols of bigoted nationalism and war – flags, military music, party emblems – just as some reject the symbols of traditional marriage (as we have seen in Chapter Two). They prefer a much more open idea of nationalism, just as they like to think of gender roles in a much more open way.

The subject-matter of this book is contemporary women's short stories in Catalonia and Ireland, the aim being to draw out and explore common-alties of female experience in the two societies. One important aspect of this experience, both historically and in contemporary times, is the relationship of women to nationalism. This is not a static relationship, as we have seen in this chapter. There is evidence, particularly in the 1980s and 1990s, that women have a desire to move on, leaving behind tradi-tional views of nationalism. They seem keen to create new ideas of Irishness or of being Catalan: identities in which plurality, openness and inclusion are the basis and where women feel free to have relationships, to have abortions, to pursue careers – in short, to live life with intensity.

CHAPTER FOUR

Decolonising language

No sabia si encara era persona o si només era una bestiola.
(I didn't know if I was still a person or just a little animal.)
Mercè Rodoreda[1]

Cathy was often wrong, she found it more interesting.
Anne Enright[2]

INTRODUCTION

IMPOSING a new language on a society is one of the most effective ways of gaining power over it. It colonises the heart of that society. Acquiring the new language means absorbing the new culture and the values which go with it.[3] The new language comes to be considered as more prestigious than the original one, which becomes secondary, marginalised. As the authors of *The Empire Writes Back* argue:

> One of the main features of imperial oppression is control over language. The imperial education system installs a 'standard' version of the metropolitan language as the norm, and marginalises all 'variants' as impurities . . . Language becomes the medium through which a hierarchical structure of power is perpetuated, and the medium through which conceptions of 'truth', 'order', and 'reality' become established. Such power is rejected in the emergence of an effective post-colonial voice.[4]

In the past, it was thought that language was only a way to express thoughts. Structuralism has shown that language is the means by which reality is constructed and where power remains hidden. It is the most intimate sign of the identity of a community. In most cases colonisation has involved control over language because this ensures control over the colonised peoples' construction of reality. A number of authors seem to agree on that:

> Colonialism imposed its control of the social production of wealth through military conquest and subsequent political dictatorship. But its most important area of domination was the mental universe of the colonised,

the control, through culture, of how people perceived themselves and their relationship to the world. Economic and political control can never be complete or effective without mental control. To control a people's culture is to control their tools of self-definition in relationship to others . . . The domination of a people's language by the languages of the colonising nations was crucial to the domination of the mental universe of the colonised.[5]

Moreover, the postcolonial discourse is centred on a struggle for power, namely 'that power focused in the control of the metropolitan language. Power is invested in the language because it provides the terms in which truth itself is constituted.'[6]

For the colonised, renouncing the native language and adopting a new one has serious and longlasting implications. Using the romantic language of his time, Thomas Davis said: 'To lose your native tongue, and learn that of an alien, is the worst badge of conquest, it is the chain on the soul'.[7] Albert Memmi writes: 'The first ambition of the colonised is to become equal to that splendid model and to resemble him to the point of disappearing in him',[8] and that, obviously, includes language. It presupposes admiration for the coloniser; at the same time 'rejection of self and love of another are common to all candidates for assimilation . . . Love of the colonizer is subtended by a complex of feelings ranging from shame to self-hate.'[9] This self-hate is mentioned with concern by some Catalan critics such as Ferrer i Gironès[10] and Víctor Alexandre.[11]

The Irish historian, Gearoid O Tuathaigh, argues along the same lines that the loss of the native language induces a trauma among the colonised because it represents a loss of the native culture, together with the shame of being conquered. The acquisition of the colonial language and new names for geographical places involves a crucial acquiescence in the colonial structures:

> The abandonment of a language . . . involved a disorientating rupture in cultural continuity at several levels: not only an alienation from landscape (place names) and inherited historical narratives and communal myths, but also a deep psychological trauma (at an individual and collective level) caused by the loss of a rich inherited matrix of wisdom and knowledge (knowledge of self and of the world.) This elemental trauma had been exacerbated by a number of features particular to the language change in Ireland: that it was the outcome of conquest (military and political), so that the abandonment of the native communal language in the face of the dominant new language of the conqueror (in law, commerce, politics, administration etc.) became internalised as part of the shame of being conquered, of defeat, dispossession, humiliation and general impoverishment. (The general syndrome among a conquered people – the self-disparagement and shame, the contempt for the

native culture felt by many of its carriers in the face of their need to come to terms with a seemingly invincible new culture sustained by a new ruling group – is now well-documented in the literature on colonialism, from Memmi and Fanon to Said.)[12]

My objective in this chapter is to show how women have been disempowered by a phallogocentric language, in a similar manner as the postcolonial language, and thus find themselves in a situation which has some parallels with language questions in postcolonial countries. Women, and women writers in particular, like colonised countries, have been penetrated by and subordinated to a new linguistic order. A growing consciousness of the significance of language in the construction of social reality has led some women writers to employ new linguistic devices in redressing the bias in language use.

As the authors of *The Empire Writes Back* point out: 'Women, like postcolonial peoples, have had to construct a language of their own when their only available "tools" are those of the "coloniser"'.[13] In fact, some feminists would argue that language is a masculine construction, as the linguist Dale Spender has suggested in *Man Made Language*. Women writers have therefore challenged masculine forms and uses of language and have tried to create different forms of writing to make new spaces in which to develop their own voices. Women writers try to create a new voice in their 'adventure' of writing back. As Hélène Cixous says: 'a language of 1,000 tongues which knows either enclosure nor death'.[14] In a similar way, postcolonial writers also have an uneasy attitude towards the colonial language. We may recall Joyce's much-quoted statement on this subject. While in the presence of the English dean of studies, Stephen Dedalus wonders about the English language:

> the language in which we are speaking is his before it is mine . . . I cannot speak or write these words without unrest of spirit. His language, so familiar and so foreign, will always be for me an acquired speech. I have not made or accepted its words. My voice holds them at bay. My soul frets in the shadow of his language.[15]

By implication, there is a sense of loss of another tongue – the Irish language. This loss is a wound for Joyce, even though his family was English-speaking. Like Joyce, the issue of language is vital for the Catalan writer Montserrat Roig. She gives an example in relation to her beloved grandmother: '*No la vaig perdre del tot quan es va morir, me'n quedava la llengua*' (I did not lose her completely when she died, her/our language remained).[16] The language is compared with a member of the family. That shows how powerful the Catalan language is for many Catalan writers. It gives a meaning to life which we could almost qualify as religious. Roig adds: '*tot escriptor que ha de canviar la llengua és un escriptor . . . ofès, un escriptor que no acaba mai de sentir-se a gust, intranquil.*' (Every writer who has to change her/his language is offended, never completely at ease, restless).[17] For some this meant a need to re-engage with Catalan literature, to update its vocabulary and forms of expression, to free it from archaic formalism. Let us listen for a moment to the male poet Narcís Comadira:

> *El fet d'haver-me trobat de jove que la meva llengua estava prohibida i contaminada, que els seus autors, aquells que havien de configurar el meu imaginari, eren clandestins i que sobretot, molta de la literatura que havia d'anar descobrint era tronada i amb una llengua anacrònica i allunyada de la meva llengua real, em va encaminar a remenar llengua, . . . Moltes vegades penso que si jo hagués estat anglès, posem per cas, potser no hauria escrit.*

> (The fact of having found out when I was young that my language was banned and contaminated, that its authors, those that were supposed to shape my imagination, were suppressed and that, much of the literature that I was going to discover was weak and burdened with an anachronistic language that was far from my every-day speech – this spurred me to work on the language. Often I think that, had I been born English, for example, maybe I would not have written.)[18]

Little by little, the Irish have been making English their own language, beside, or in place of, the Irish language. Some women, however, have been trying to 'demasculinise' the symbolic order. Both situations are uncomfortable and both processes seem to be long and difficult. Literature is certainly a viable terrain for that experimentation. In the case of women, Julia Kristeva refers to those attempts as efforts to 'break the code, to shatter language, to find a specific discourse closer to the body and emotions, to the unnameable repressed by the social contract'.[19]

L'ÉCRITURE FÉMININE OR FEMALE WRITING

According to French feminists (Hélène Cixous, Luce Irigaray and Julia Kristeva), language is oppressive to women because it is phallogocentric: the 'law of the father' is embedded in its deepest structure. The symbolic order has been based on a systematic repression of women's experience, which has been inscribed in the language. In this phallogocentric culture, man is a unified, self-controlled centre of the universe and a coloniser (white, European and ruling class):

The rest of the world, which I define as the Other, has meaning only in relation to me, as man/father, possessor of the phallus . . . To speak and especially to write from such a position is to appropriate the world, to dominate it through verbal mastery. Symbolic discourse (language, in various contexts) is another means through which man objectifies the world, reduces it to his terms, speaks in place of everything and everyone else – including women.'[20]

Thus the text gives women and postcolonial peoples an opportunity to create and explore new realities and construct new languages, but these are not the monopoly of women. Male writers can also contribute to the process. A consequence of this phallogocentrism is that for the woman writer, words sometimes are not available to define women's experiences. Toril Moi explains this phenomenon:

One specific argument within the study of sexism in language is the question of naming. Feminists have consistently argued that those who have the power to name the world are in a position to influence reality . . . It is argued that women lack this power and that, as a consequence, many female experiences lack a name.[21]

To be able to express themselves, women often have to use surreal and alternative types of language. For example, in Eilís Ní Dhuibhne's 'The Inland Ice', Polly, an unhappy wife, feels confused. She knows that there is beauty inside her but she cannot enjoy it. She describes the inner part of an icecap in Greenland as if she were describing the inner part of herself. This frozen atmosphere which Ní Dhuibhne is using to describe the feminine world is close to the one Edna O'Brien had used in 'Irish Revel': 'Underneath, however, the ice has formed shapes like stalagmites, and when you peer under you see that they are blue and turquoise, silver, jade and other subtle, shining, winking colours for which you have no name'.[22] They have beautiful colours but they are known only by analogy – they have no name like the many parts of her being which have no name. There is no language to describe the hidden/beautiful/female parts of herself. Significantly, the frozen environment, similar to the one Edna O'Brien described in 'Irish Revel', symbolises the unfavourable world women have to live in. In Ní Dhuibhne's 'The Shapeshifters', Angela's mother does not know the names of her own body, 'for the intimate parts of the body, the intimate details of sexuality' because they are 'dirty and taboo'.[23] We have a similar example in Montserrat Roig's 'Mar'.[24] The nameless protagonist cannot find a word to describe a lesbian love relationship she had with a woman called Mar:

No ha estat escrita la paraula que defineixi el que va neixer el dia en que la vaig veure per primera vegada . . . i tampoc jo sóc capac d'inventar-ne una.

(The word which defines what was born the day I saw her for the first time has not yet been written . . . and neither am I able to make one up.)[25]

By contrast, men are quick to name things and are particularly adept at making up crude words and phrases to stigmatise relationships between women.

Later the protagonist says: '*No m'adonava, aleshores, que hi ha una barrera, més enllà dels diners, més enllà de les idees, i que aquesta barrera es la del llenguatge.*' (I didn't realise, then, that there is a barrier, beyond money, beyond ideas, and that this barrier is the one of language).[26] Any currently existing language, in the view of some feminists, is foreign to women. It belongs to the coloniser – that is men. Lacking a 'native tongue' and in search of it, French feminists seek women's essence in the most intimate part of themselves, their sexuality, which they call the 'jouissance', the re-experience of the physical pleasures of infancy which have been systematically repressed. This can be compared with the exploration of the Early or Middle Ages by Catalan and Irish revivalists to find the roots of the culture before colonisation. Seeking to explore their infancy can be seen as a utopia more than a reality but the radical school of French feminists sees it as the only way to find the 'authentic' self. Women have not been able to express their own sexuality fully because they have been mere objects of male desire (virgins or prostitutes, wives or mothers.) Hence, women need new and non-phallogocentric languages to be able to express themselves. Women's uneasy position in relation to language leads to frustration. Yet it might be helpful to them to play around with language. Richard Kearney has suggested that James Joyce's uneasiness with the English language may account for his exceptional capacity to deconstruct and reconstruct it.[27] Women, who are somewhat similarly situated, may be in a position to turn these tensions to creative advantage. So the problem is not so much with the language *per se*, as with how language is used. Indeed, Toni Morrison has suggested that a marginal position allows deeper insight: 'I think the range of emotions and perceptions I have had access to as a black person and a female person are greater than to those who are neither'.[28]

However, the Irish writer Mary Dorcey does not accept the idea that language was originally a masculine construction. On the contrary, Dorcey says that women were the ones who created language: 'women invented and developed language and . . . men adapted it to their uses to make it seem as if they do'.[29] She argues that girls talk, read and write at an earlier age than boys and that women are the ones who teach and transmit the language between generations. However, Dorcey adds that when language came to be written, men had differential access to it and altered the structure of grammar in their favour so that it become an instrument of domination.[30]

In my view Dorcey's last point is crucial and leads us back to French feminism. The symbolic order has been created by men because they have been the main constructors of reality. It is the case that languages, in particular Latin languages, reflect a masculine view of the world, according to the Catalan story writer Carme Riera.[31] This is now changing but the process of women becoming the makers of reality must necessarily be a long one. Still, today's women who are creating art and literature are offering fundamental challenges to a narrow and single-sex perspective on social reality.

The language, form and content of many women's short stories have one thing in common: a subversive tendency. Many women writers want to challenge the phallogocentric nature of the culture which has silenced their voices. They subject it to criticism; they sometimes offer alternatives for change. Some common characteristics are to be found in their writing. A realist style is frequent and it responds to an urgent need. As Ailbhe Smyth puts it, it offers women writers 'freedom to give a name and substance to the long unspoken, always unwritten, realities of their lives'.[32] Towards the last phase of her career, Mercè Rodoreda was greatly attracted to the use of fantasy writing. Young Catalan and Irish writers, such as Imma Monsó, Anne Enright and Katy Hayes are also now using more experimental forms. They employ a multiplicity of voices and frequently evoke images of sensuality, invoking smells, taste and touch. An ironic tone is also common, in particular among the younger writers. I will explore these features further, before expanding on the Catalan case.

As colonised subjects, women have to deny, sometimes 'destroy', themselves in order to secure their acceptance by men. As we have seen, the consequences of this are lack of confidence, self-hate, rivalry between women and, in particular, confusion. The linguistic consequence is that women frequently speak in a multiplicity of voices and they struggle to achieve a sense of balance and to know what they really want. They are not afraid to show their weaknesses. We may recall Luce Irigaray's famous idea that women have sex organs everywhere has some relevance here. She transforms the suppressed weakness into strength. About women's language, Irigaray writes:

'she' sets off in all directions leaving 'him' unable to discern the coherence of any meaning. Hers are contradictory words, somewhat mad from the standpoint of reason, inaudible for whoever listens to them with readymade grids, with a fully elaborated code in hand.[33]

It is important to also remember the sentiments of Simone de Beauvoir who stated that women are not born but made. As fellow human beings, men also have multiple voices but, as victors, they develop a complex of superiority which gives them a sense of clairvoyance. However, as women writers show, that is only an illusion. They are simply afraid of showing weakness.

The desire to invite the reader closer and to feel included is common to many women's short-story writing. This reduces the distance between the writer as the authoritarian voice, and the reader as the passive being. The preference for first-person narration, frequent in women's writing, encourages the reader's identification with and closeness to the protagonists and their emotions, and it works well within the privacy that the genre of the story provides. Mary Dorcey offers something a bit more experimental which is the use of the second person. This also helps draw the reader closer. In her collection of short stories, *A Noise from the Woodshed*, she uses this technique in five out of the nine stories. Even though the intention is a positive one, some readers may find the technique a little disconcerting.

The second characteristic of women's language is the speaking voice. Most precolonial cultures had an oral tradition, so their postcolonial literatures have a strong oral influence – that is to say, they use the speaking voice. Historically speaking, women have been slower to develop their writing skills because they have had more limited access to education.[34] Possibly this is one reason why women seem to be more at ease using the speaking voice as a writing device. More importantly, the speaking voice offers spontaneity, which is much valued by women writers as a means of achieving directness. Indeed, Mary Dorcey refers to the speaking voice of 'ordinary women' and, as a contrast, Dorcey defines men's writing as a 'thinking' voice. She cites Joyce's 'stream of consciousness' as a thinking voice. Dorcey explains the speaking voice in her own writing:

> There is no thinking voice. The voice is always a person talking, addressing itself aloud to a listener. And it is this assumption of a listener that is all-important. I think that women probably have fewer inner monologues than men because we talk to each other so much more. We share our thoughts and feelings to such an extent that the characteristic voice for a woman is the speaking voice. I think this is one of the many aspects I have always

found false in the Molly Bloom soliloquy (which isn't one, women don't think like that.) Molly would be saying all this, not thinking it, which in effect we know she did, she talked it all out to Joyce, which is why he got to write it down. If she had been happy to think it the world would never have heard of it.[35]

That 'speaking voice' is certainly the one Dorcey uses in her collection of short stories, *A Noise from the Woodshed*. This is her experience with women in her life:

> It is the very root of my desire to write this talking of women that I heard all about me from my earliest years – the voice of my mother, my grandmother, my aunts and their friends – this great sharing that women do across the generations – not locking themselves up in studies to write and think, but working and sitting in the kitchen talking. I write in a speaking voice which presupposes a listener and invites the reader into a dialogue. It makes the reader an active force in the telling of the tale or poem in the way that women's conversation does, whereas men 'think aloud' at others.[36]

For Dorcey, the primary reason for playing with words, breaking them down, making new forms, patterns and associations, is to allow the reader to hear better, to be close to the writer and, in so doing, to become more active:

> It is an effort to get behind the given or assumed daily meaning of words to the real or more vivid or essential or forgotten meaning. Any technique that helps people to hear better is valid . . . Another manner is to write such plain, unadorned, bare language, with so much space between each word, that the reader or 'listener' hears the words quite differently from usual.[37]

I have drawn attention earlier to the sensuousness of women's texts, in particular the importance of smell and touch. This is a characteristic of the new writing, though it is striking that the use of another sense, that of sight, is less evident. This may not be coincidental. It is quite possible that women are responding to the use and abuse of the male gaze in the phallogocentric order in which women are reduced to being mere objects of male desire. While it is not my intention to compare female and male texts, there does seem to be a difference in terms of these qualities of writing. It is as if women were seeking to find forms of language that allow them to express themselves more freely and also to challenge assumptions implicit in the phallogocentric symbolic order. These strivings might also be seen as manifestations of what some French feminists call 'a return to the female body'.

Young Irish writers seem to be particularly attracted to the use of irony, and one wonders why. It could be that young women have distanced themselves sufficiently from an oppressive reality to be able to mock it. For example, when women do things which are traditionally done by men, the result is funny. This is the case of sexually liberated women in the stories of Eilís Ní Dhuibhne, Clare Boylan, Anne Enright and Katy Hayes. Even the titles of some collections of short stories are indicative: *Eating Women Is Not Recommended* by Ní Dhuibhne and *That Bad Woman* by Boylan.

In the following section I will discuss women's writing in Catalonia, but this is preceded by a brief historical sketch of the position of the Catalan language. Because language connects with so many other areas of life, the fortunes of the Catalan language have been touched on before. But it may be helpful to provide a more integrated discussion at this point.

CATALONIA AND THE LANGUAGE QUESTION

Despite the systematic banning of the Catalan language for centuries, it has managed to survive and is still the language used by most people and by most women writers in Catalonia.[38] Even in a democratic system, it can be argued, there is still resistance from the Spanish central government to the promotion of the three minority languages in Spain (Catalan, Galician and Basque). The Spanish constitution proclaims, in its third article, that Castilian is the official language of the state and it then mentions the 'other' ones: 'The other Spanish languages will also be official in the respective autonomous communities'.[39] It is significant that they are not named. The year in which the Constitution was written (1978) followed one of the blackest periods in Catalonia. Forty years of dictatorship meant:

> the practical disappearance of the cultural infrastructure that had been created over a century. As part of the victor's attempt to return Catalonia to the fold of the 'true Spanish soul' (*reespanolizacion*), the Catalan language was banned from public use and from education, and practically all signs of Catalan identity were outlawed. Most of the intellectual elite was forced into exile or was repressed and silenced, and all Catalan-identified cultural activity had to go underground.[40]

Catalan was largely maintained in private spaces but people had to use Spanish in all areas of public life. A number of women writers who stayed behind in Catalonia after the Civil War gave up writing altogether, as in the case of Maria Teresa Vernet and Carme Montoriol. Most of those who went into exile wrote little, partly because of the problems of making a living in a foreign setting. Mercè Rodoreda, in exile during much of her productive life as a writer, described the impact of her linguistic isolation in an interview: *'escriure en catala a fora es com voler que floreixin flors al pol nord.'* (writing in Catalan abroad is like wanting flowers to grow at the North pole).[41] Moreover, the Catalan language lost prestige by comparison with Spanish, and some upper-class Catalans began to change the language of the home in favour of Spanish. Nonetheless, some sectors of the bourgeoisie sponsored or financed publishing in Catalan and some books managed to get published. For example, in 1976 the number of books published in Catalan regained the level reached in 1936 (just before the war), that is, around 800 titles, and the first newspaper in Catalan since the end of the war, *Avui*, appeared. It is also important to remember that between one and two million people from the south of Spain moved into Catalonia after the 1950s. These migrants were sometimes prejudiced against the Catalan language, not least because many of them did not even know about its existence before coming to Catalonia. Some felt no need to learn Catalan. In a sense, this is the kind of problem which faces stateless nations.

With the advent of democracy and the Catalan Parliament, a Department of Culture was set up. This was a major step in the process of cultural and linguistic normalisation:

> 'Cultural normalization', the cultural policy of contemporary Catalan nationalism, aims at constituting Catalonia as a 'normal' society: that is, a society in which Catalonia's own language would be hegemonic, in which citizens would share a common sense of (Catalan) national identity based on their cultural traditions, and which would be comparable to any other modern European society in terms of cultural infrastructures, habits of cultural consumption, and the balance between high and mass culture.[42]

Under the new dispensation the rise in the number of Catalan publications was phenomenal. Some 800 titles were published in 1976 and 4,500 published in 1990. However, it is important to add that this process of 'normalisation' is still continuing. Set against an international context of economic and cultural globalisation which is neither sensitive to nor favours minority languages and cultures, the process is not easy. Moreover, being in the shadow of the powerful Spanish language does not help:

> Other problems derive from the collision of two cultural markets (Spanish versus Catalan) in the same territory, which places Catalan products in a position of inferiority; this has been aggravated by the introduction in 1989 of the three private television channels, which broadcast exclusively in

Spanish. Finally, the conflict between Spanish and Catalan nationalisms remains, leading to hostility on the part of the Spanish state towards the development of an audio-visual space common to the Catalan-speaking territories in their entirety.[43]

Perhaps a history of marginalisation of their own language is one of the reasons Catalan people have displayed a special interest in minority languages.[44] Montserrat Roig explains the difficulties she had as a child in finding that her own language was invisible at school. Like the other children of her generation, she learned to read in Spanish even though her language at home was Catalan:

> *La revelació que existia una llengua 'real' em va venir als quatre anys, quan les monges m'obligaven a llegir unes paraules que no entenia . . . Creia que les monges inventaven una llengua per a dominar el territori del meu jo i les meves paraules. Eren el poder. I el que elles havien inventat ja no tenia res a veure amb la meva magia. Mai 'una mesa' podia ser una 'Taula'. Era una altra cosa que no significava res perque jo havia perdut la forca del conjur. M'havia convertit, en certa manera, en una autista. Així neix la diglossia que encara estem patint els que no vam ser educats en català; la llengua parlada i la llengua escrita entren en fricció i fan perdre, als parlants, capacitat d'expressió.*

> (The revelation that there was a 'real' language came to me when I was four, when the nuns obliged me to read words which I did not understand . . . I thought that the nuns were making up a language to dominate my territory and my words. They had the power. And what they had already created did not have anything to do with my magic. Never a *'mesa'* (table in Spanish) could be a *'taula'* (table in Catalan.) It was something different which did not mean anything because I had lost the strength of the spell. Somehow I had become an autistic child. This is how diglossia was born which the ones who were not educated in Catalan are still suffering. There was friction between the speaking language and the written one and this caused a loss of ability of expression to the speakers.)[45]

As a language under colonial pressure, the Catalan language did not develop a regular grammar until 1913. Indeed, that is common among colonised languages; some of them still do not have standard grammars, for example the Sard language, and Breton. The Basque language created its own as late as the 1970s. Other grammar regulations were written much earlier; Spanish and French grammars were published as far back as the sixteenth century.

It is striking, therefore, that one of the most accomplished writers at the beginning of the century, Caterina Albert, did not accept the new grammar and continued writing as before. Her argument was that the new rules limited the expressive powers of the language and could impoverish it. She used a vast vocabulary that she had collected from country people. Some of the more archaic words used by her were in fact contained in the *Diccionari General de la Llengua Catalana*,[46] though they were *only* used by her. Possibly the fact that the rules were written by men made her distrustful and was part of the reason why she did not accept them. Rejection of standardisation may have been a form of resistance. Incidentally Caterina Albert used a male pseudonym, Víctor Català,[47] throughout her long literary life so as to feel freer from conventional prejudices regarding women and women writers. This may have been particularly important in her case, given her fascination with violence (which would have been regarded as peculiar in the case of a female author.)

Despite the fact that Catalan had been banned in education and that it was very difficult to publish during the long era of Francoism, most Catalan women writers decided that Catalan would be their only literary language. There was a strong commitment by women writers to cooperate in restoring and improving Catalan as a literary language. Anne Charlon makes this point, but adds that this might have occurred at the expense of creating a women's language:

> *Les novelistes catalanes no han volgut . . . crear una llengua 'femenina' tal com ha fet Julia Kristeva per exemple . . . Això s'explica pel fet que la recuperació del català enfront de la repressió representava una tasca prioritària*

> (Catalan novelists have not created a feminine language like Julia Kristeva has done . . . The explanation for this is that the recovery of the Catalan language was a priority task)[48]

Earlier I suggested that, as a colonised group, women were keen to use Catalan as a means of resistance to colonisation, thereby making the text a 'field of struggle'. Montserrat Roig has said: '*Una manera de transgredir les normes és escrivint*' (One way of transgressing the rules is writing.)[49] The Catalan writer and politician Maria Aurèlia Capmany gives another reason to explain why Catalan women were drawn to use their language: '*Pel fet de ser una llengua oprimida, no era un gran negoci escriure en català, era, doncs, una activitat de dones*' (Being an oppressed language, it was not good business to write in Catalan; that made it a woman's activity).[50] It was certainly not possible for a writer in Catalan to become a professional writer. During the first years of the dictatorship, these Catalan writers risked their lives.

Even today in Madrid, there is ignorance of and resistance to accepting the Catalan language as a language of culture. The young Catalan writer

Imma Monsó describes her experience in Madrid and makes an interesting link between this resistance and a reluctance to accept women. The occasion was when she was presenting the translation into Spanish of one of her novels:

> *A Madrid no feien altra cosa que preguntar-me com era que escrivia en català, si m'expressava tan be en castellà. No ho feien amb mala intenció es que realment no ho entenien. I tornem al mateix: la llengua, com el fet de ser dona, també forma part de la meva condició.*

> (In Madrid they were asking me nothing else but why I wrote in Catalan, and also if I was able to express myself in Castilian. They did not have a bad intention but, really, they could not understand it. We go back to the old story: the language, like the fact of being a woman, is also part of my condition.)[51]

The use of the mother tongue can be an effective means of resisting the coloniser's language, as Kathleen McNerney explains:

> If masculinity and femininity occupy opposing spaces in Western thought, the public and the private respectively, in the specific case of minority languages the private feminine space has defined the survival of these vernaculars. For the nationalist Catalan, Galician or Basque speaker, it is, or has been, the mother tongue. The private domestic space defines political community, in contrast to Castilian, the language of a superimposed public space . . . Domestic space becomes that of resistance.[52]

BETWEEN TWO ELEMENTS

An extreme example of the way in which language may be subverted is to be found in some of Mercè Rodoreda's fantasy stories. As mentioned before, a realist language is common in women's stories, although there is the exception of Mercè Rodoreda who, during the second part of her literary career, used a surreal style of writing, describing a world of dreams which then changes into nightmares. For example, 'La salamandra' (The Salamander) is a good example. This is the tale of a girl who is seduced by a married man. However, she is the one who pays the price of this illicit liaison, becoming emotionally dependent on him. He takes advantage of the situation and she finds it hard to resist. Overcome by his advances and her own confusion, she submits:

> *Ell s'havia aturat una mica lluny i jo no sabia que fer, però tot d'una em va venir por i vaig arrencar a correr . . . ell es va plantar al meu davant amb els braços*

estesos a banda i banda perquè no pogués fugir . . . vaig mossegar-me els llavis per no cridar pel mal que tenia en el pit amb tots els ossos com si estiguessin a punt de trencar-se. Em va posar la boca al coll i allà on va posar-la vaig sentir una cremada . . . les fulles em deien coses que tenien sentit però que jo no comprenia.

(He'd halted a little way off and I didn't know what to do, but suddenly I got scared and started to run . . . He planted himself in front of me, with his arms stretched out on both sides so I couldn't escape . . . I bit my lip so I wouldn't cry out from the pain in my chest and all my bones were feeling like they were about to break. He put his mouth on my neck, and it burned where he put it . . . the leaves were telling me things which made sense but which I didn't understand.)[53]

Nature, emblematised by the leaves, is telling her to stop but she cannot make sense of its cautions. The tragedy quickly unfolds, as the burn on her neck predicts. When his wife discovers them together she accuses the girl of being a witch. The other villagers follow her lead. At first they are content with persecuting her with threats and cruel suggestions; dead animals are nailed to the door of her house. Finally they burn her at the stake. In this way, Rodoreda describes a misogynistic society in which the people in the community show deep cruelty towards women. (One can find comparable examples in Irish stories such as those of Edna O'Brien in particular.) Symbolically, salamanders are associated with fire. In Classical antiquity, this amphibian was believed to be able to live in fire without being burned and to be able to put out fire through its extraordinary coldness.[54] It was also said that the salamander was born in fire.[55] In fact, in the story, as the flames touch the girl's body, she turns into a salamander. But the vital point is that the change in form does not change her lot. She still thinks and feels like a human being. The pain burns incessantly.

As we have seen in other stories, the young or inexperienced female protagonist is used by a male coloniser who later abandons her. In fact, he only wants to prove his power by 'possessing' her and that is why he uses her. Love is always destructive for women in Rodoreda's stories. Love of the man becomes a point of vulnerability. The man implants himself in her very being and she loses her strength; it is like physical colonisation. It also has sexual connotations of penetration: '*Em vaig adonar tot d'una que ja no esperava res; vivia tota girada enrera amb ell dintre meu com una arrel dins la terra*' (I suddenly realised I had no hope left. I lived facing backwards, with him inside me like a root in the earth.)[56] Moreover, although he is the active one in pursuing her, she is the one who reaps the consequences. Thus, while the male is the instigator of the drama, society takes its revenge on the woman.

Following the ordeal at the stake and now metamorphosed into a salamander, the girl is drawn to her lover's house. Even if transformed into a salamander, the amphibious woman still looks for her lover, despite the difficulty and the danger of such a visit. Compounding her problems, it is physically difficult for her to move in her new shape. Once in his house, she hides beneath the bed where her beloved sleeps with his wife, happily and peacefully. She endures hearing him telling his wife that she is the *only* one, just as he used to tell her. As in other women's stories, for such men, lying is part of the repertoire for exercising control over women. Flattery and deceit, when deemed appropriate, are also part of the resources of colonial powers.

The unrelieved gloom of the narrative intensifies. On discovering the salamander under the bed, the wife of her former lover puts a burning torch into her face and hacks at her with a broom. Children come and throw stones at her, almost severing one of her claws. The claw is later torn off by an eel. At the tale's end her desolation is complete. Lying in the mud at the bottom of a pond, she wonders whether she is still a person or only a little animal. Does she belong in water or on earth? Does she belong anywhere? There is a deep feeling of solitude, definitely one of the major themes in women's writing, and a deep feeling of confusion. She lacks reference points, does not know what she is, where she is or what she should do. She finds herself in a foreign world. In fact, the writer herself, Mercè Rodoreda, said that the only thing she had in common with one of her major characters was the fact of feeling lost in the middle of the world.[57] That is the way the poor little animal, the salamander, feels:

> Tot i que no era morta, no hi havia res que fos viu del tot, i resava fort, perque no sabia si encara era persona o si només era una bestiola, o si era mig persona i mig bestiola, i també resava per saber on era, perque hi havia estones que em semblava que era a sota de l'aigua, i quan era a sota de l'aigua em semblava que era damunt la terra i no podia saber mai on era de debó.

> (Even though I wasn't dead, there was nothing inside me that was totally alive, and I prayed hard because I didn't know if I was still a person or only a little animal, or if I was half person and half animal. And also I prayed to know where I was, because at times I felt like I was underwater and when I was underwater, I felt like I was on the ground, and never knew where I really was.)[58]

This sense of confusion, of a diminished and uncertain sense of identity, is common in women's writing. Their otherness and second-class citizenship create prejudices against them and makes them foreign and misunderstood, even to themselves. The narrator in 'La salamandra' is not even sure about basic things. She does not know if she is still as completely human as her consciousness indicates, since she knows how to behave as an amphibian. In this story Rodoreda dramatises both the feeling of being an outcast in an alien, hostile world and the double standard that prevails in that world. Indeed, she describes the world of the outcast, of the defeated, of the colonised – the world of women. Going back to the story, the girl's sexuality is sinful, 'unnatural', and she is considered responsible for her lover's fall. She has 'bewitched' him, even though he is the one who actually pursued her. The unemotional, matter-of-fact tone Rodoreda employs heightens the impact of the story. The few occasions when she mentions her fright and anguish are, consequently, all the more striking.

As an animal which crosses habitat boundaries, the salamander is an apt figure for the writer herself. Rodoreda was exiled during most of her life, living between two cultures and two languages, in a sense inhabiting two 'elements'. The use of the metamorphosis responds to the wish to escape and liberation for her characters and for herself. According to her, metamorphosis is something natural and people's souls experience it.[59]

Like many other Catalan female writers, Mercè Rodoreda uses the speaking voice in most of her short stories. As Emilie Bergmann observes: 'Almost all of Rodoreda's fiction is narrated in the first person in a colloquial style imitative of spoken Catalan'.[60] Extensive use of dialogue, which is common in women's stories, is also present in Rodoreda's writing. For example, 'En el tren' (On the Train) starts in the middle of a conversation: ' . . . no, no, tal com li ho dic, mai no he pogut dormir en el tren, m'ensopeixo una mica pero . . . ' (no, no, as I told you, I have never been able to sleep on the train, I rest a bit but . . .).[61] In this particular story, we may also note her use of the device of one-way dialogue in which we hear just one side of the conversation, the person being addressed remaining silent. The presence of an addressee is acknowledged in the speaker's direct interpolations to a second person. Rodoreda's 'L'elefant' (The Elephant) has a similar beginning:

> Per què no s'acosta una mica més? Posi's sota el meu paraigua . . . A vostè l'he vist altres vegades, tot passant, davant la gàbia dels serpentaris.
>
> (Why don't you come a little closer. Get under my umbrella . . . I've seen you before, walking up and down in front of the serpent-eater's cage.)[62]

'Zefarina' a story about a poor and exploited maid, is a monologue and 'El Parc de les Magnòlies' (Magnolia Park) takes the form of dramatic dialogue. In these stories, the impression of speech is successfully created through the limited range of vocabulary, the frequent use of popular words and sayings and the intentional repetition. Syntactically, the stories show a clear preference for simple sentences, usually joined by the conjunction 'and'. The abundance of punctuation marks emphasises intonation as a vehicle of oral expression. The apparent linguistic simplicity of these stories is a trademark of the fiction of Rodoreda, which mimics the oral speech of ordinary people, a common feature in women's literature. Moreover, the preference for first-person narration encourages the reader's identification with and closeness to the protagonists and their emotions, and it works well within the privacy that the genre of the short story provides.

A young writer who uses dialogue extensively is Imma Monsó, the author of a short story called 'Neu al cervell' (Snow in the Brain). Her style is experimental. Through an apparently simple dialogue between two youngsters, Claudia and Bart, Monsó achieves a deep analysis of the differences between women's and men's subjectivities. There is an enormous difference between Claudia and Bart. Claudia is mentally very active, she has a variety of sujectivities and loves talking about them and their apparent contradictions, whereas Bart is simple, a 'unified' being, and loves silence and 'listening to how it snows in his brain'. Her energetic mind is complex and full of curiosity whereas nothing much seems to be happening in his.

Claudia is the main speaker in the story, challenging patriarchal assumptions that women are passive. With a touch of humour, she tells Bart of the variety of voices she has inside:

> *hi ha coses que m'agraden i m'agrada que m'agradin, les que no m'agrada que m'agradin, i les que m'agradaria que m'agradessin però no m'agraden . . . Per acabar hi ha les que no m'agraden i ja m'esta bé que no m'agradin. M'entens?*

> (there are things which I like and I like liking them, the ones I like but I don't like I like them, and the ones I'd like to like but I don't like . . . Finally there are some which I don't like and I am happy about not liking them. Do you understand?)[63]

The language, though colloquial, has an abstract meaning and it is not always easy to follow. But it does make sense. Claudia is giving an account of the complexity and plurality of her different voices, which are sometimes in tension with her surroundings. By contrast, Bart sees himself in more straightforward terms and is perhaps lacking in depth:

> *jo sóc més conformista, segurament. Vull dir que si una cosa no m'agrada, com ara per exemple una pel.lícula o un llibre o una persona, doncs senzillament ho accepto.*

(I am more conformist, probably. I mean that if I don't like something, such as a film or a book or a person, then I simply accept that fact.)[64]

Women's situation is much more difficult because they feel obliged to make changes. That is why Claudia has to create a public persona. At one point she explains that there are two Claudias inside her: Claudia, and what she ironically calls Claudiocopy. The latter is a copy of herself made by significant others in her life. Both are within her but she prefers Claudiocopy as the public persona for Claudia. Claudia recognises that this copy is important for Claudia's identity and to know that she herself really exists. Her two 'I's are quite separate and have opposite interests. For example, Claudiocopy hates writing whereas Claudia loves it. In this example Monsó is alluding to the experience of women being silenced in terms of cultural production and writing in particular.

Claudia endeavours to find her true identity. She is aware she cannot rely simply on her own perception: '*Sóc incapaç d'experimentar la meva propia identitat. No em trobo, no em localitzo, no em delimito*' (I am incapable of experimenting with my own identity. I cannot find myself, I cannot locate myself, I cannot delimit myself.)[65] As I have mentioned before, her position as 'other' helps her to deconstruct a humanist and masculine construction of subjectivity, as we have seen before with Rodoreda.

Claudia wishes she could discover a stable nucleus within. She wishes she could say 'this is me' even if this core was something tiny: '*Som tan fràgils! Tan inestables, confusos, dividits, fets a trossos, dispersos.* (We are so fragile! So unstable, confused, divided, made by pieces, dispersed.)[66] This reads like lines from a deconstructionist manifesto.

Bart does not have these fragmented forms of consciousness. He reckons himself to have been born bounded and unified: 'un home d'una sola peça' (a man made of one piece).[67] Claudia is not sure this is good, and indeed is a shade suspicious. She rejoices in the advantages of her position: she can feel more, she experiences fluidity, even if at times it is a bit scary or tiring, but this is better than being a 'marmolet' (a little piece of marble). Men should be the ones who change to be more like women, she suggests. They should also help to change the symbolic order. In fact, Claudia shows that Bart is not as well integrated as he claims he is. Because of his dominant position, by virtue of his male status, he is simply not aware of what he truly is.

Women have more self-knowledge and find it easier to admit their weakness. This is the advantage of being in a situation which is marginal. A woman does not feel obliged to prove herself constantly. Claudia is demonstrating that positions of dominance are not necessarily advantageous, and may even be limiting. She shows that the complexities of being a woman are challenging and creative. For this young writer being a woman is good, whereas for the generation before, that of Rodoreda, it was much more destructive and painful.

At the end of the story, this portrayal of the male gender is echoed in a newspaper report on the death of the president, which could well be an image of the end of the dictator Franco himself: '*L'expresident mantenia el seu posat de sempre: hieràtic, d'esfinx, perfectament autoritari fins després de mort.*' (The ex-president maintained his usual expression: hieratic, sphinx-like, perfectly authoritarian even in death).[68] Man, the coloniser of women, is powerful even after death, not least because he betrays no sense of doubt or uncertainty, but it is fake, it is only a mask. Women subjects have faith in him, or at least that used to be the case. The subversive suggestion seems to be that the power they thought men had, and which makes men attractive to women, is based on illusion.

Other authors portray other aspects of women's confusion. In 'Joc de màscares' (Game of Masks), again we are dealing with disguises, Laura is not sure even if she likes making love to men. It is hard to separate out real feelings from what women have been conditioned to feel:

> No sé ben bé ni si m'agrada a mi. En el fons és massa difícil saber que és el què t'agrada de debó i què t'agrada perque als altres els agrada que t'agradi.
>
> (I don't even know whether I like it. Deep down it is too difficult to know what you like truly and what you like because the others like you to like it.)[69]

A similar theme surfaces in Rodoreda's 'Pluja' (Rain). Marta is at home waiting for her lover but she keeps wondering if she loves him and if she really wants to see him, even as she prepares to receive him. Impulsively, she leaves the house with a note excusing herself. A similar situation faces Miss Hawkins in Edna O'Brien's 'Christmas Roses'. Both women retreat from men, finding solace in their own company.

The patriarchal culture does not tolerate lesbian love but we have several representations of this 'sexual transgression' in both Irish and Catalan short-story writers. In fact, in virtually all female writers, both heterosexual and homosexual, there is some reference to lesbian love which may suggest a current of bisexualism in women's writing. Take Carme Riera's 'Te deix amor la mar com a penyora' (I Give You, my Love, the Sea as a Token). This was written before Franco's death, which marks it out as especially deviant. The nameless protagonist of this story remembers a love relationship she had in the past with her teacher, but it is not until the last lines of the story, when she pronounces the name of her ex-lover, that we realise that her lover was a woman. Another example is Isabel-Clara Simó's 'La taula set' (Table Seven). In this story, Lluïsa, a waitress, cries because one of her customers is 'touching her up' while she is serving her meals. Again, it is not until the very end of the story that another waitress tells Lluïsa the same has happened to her, the difference being that she actually liked it. Sometimes settings for lesbian love are disguised in carnival times. As early as 1907, Caterina Albert described lesbian love in her story 'Carnestoltes' (Carnival). Almost a century later, Maria Mercè Marçal wrote 'Joc de màscares' (Game of Masks). This story, which is dedicated to Carme Riera because of the similarities to 'Te deix amor la mar com a penyora', describes the love between a student, Laura, and her teacher, Júlia. If in men's literature the gaze dominates the description of the loved one, in this case, Júlia keeps remembering Laura's words. At the end, Júlia muses: '*Servo poca memòria del seu cos. Pero em resten els mots, incorruptes com cossos enterrats en la neu*' (I keep little memory of her body. But her words remain, uncorrupted like bodies buried in the snow).[70] The emphasis is on words and feelings rather than physical beauty and sex.

I have referred to the abundance of descriptions of smell and touch in Irish and Catalan women's texts. According to Anne Charlon, smells are crucial in Catalan women's writing. She divides them into two groups: smells of nature, generally associated with physical happiness and contentment, and smells from the marketplace and kitchen.[71] Whereas smell and touch are common, sight is less important and it can even work against women. The point is strongly suggested in M. Aurelia Capmany's 'El temps passa sobre un mirall' (Time Goes By in a Mirror).[72] In this story, a nameless young woman feels very uncomfortable when men stare at her. She misses the freedom she had as a child when nobody looked at her in an overtly sexual way.

An older writer, Caterina Albert, recalls touch in the first lines of 'La Jove' (The Daughter-in-Law).[73] The protagonist in this story, Beleta, is a baker and the story starts by describing what she feels when she is kneading the dough to make bread. She compares it to the act of fondling a woman's breast:

> El panet de llevat, estufat i dur, d'una duresa flonja, tenia forma i turgències de pit de dona, i la Beleta sentia una sensació agradosa moixant-lo i fent-lo saltar entre les seves mans.

(The leaven roll, quilted and hard, with spongy hardness, had the shape and turgidity of a woman's breast and Beleta felt a pleasant sensation making it jump in her hands).[74]

Isabel-Clara Simó fuses an appreciation of aromas and flower imagery in her text. In the title of one story she enquires: 'Saps que Barcelona fa una olor meravellosa de bon matí?' (Do you Know that Barcelona has a Wonderful Fragrance Early in the Morning?).[75] The second part of Mercè Rodoreda's *Viatges i Flors* is made up of little stories about magical flowers such as 'Flor ballarina' (Dancing Flower) and 'Flor desesperada' (Desperate Flower). Each type of flower expresses different kinds of human experience. For example, 'Flor blava' (Blue Flower) is about a white flower which is dyed by an insect and instantly becomes blue. It has connotations of sexual relationships between women and men. Rodoreda's description of flowers often recalls the female sexual organ and female sexuality in general. However, more often than not, it is a depressed, unfulfilled sexuality. For example, in 'Flor fossil' (Fossil Flower), Rodoreda says: '*Xopa de por, una flor de maduixa anava perduda i no sabia que fer.*' (Full of fear, a strawberry flower was lost and did not know what to do.)[76] It may not be too fanciful to suggest this refers to the colonised female subjectivity. 'Flor d'aigua' (Water Flower) is the description of a flower which has petals with a spoon shape. These collect water for the plant. When the plant has enough water, it sheds the flowers, which then die. The petals may be seen as the feminine element, whereas the selfish plant is the masculine element, using the flower solely for its own benefit. 'Flor sense nom' (Nameless Flower) loved everything since birth, even the most unpleasant beings such as worms in wet ground, the lizard's tail and ants. One day the strong wind rushed against the flower which kept repeating 'they are taking me away', but the wind (the masculine element) kept pressing and took some letters of its alphabet away and altered their order so that what she said made no sense anymore. She was condemned to a state of being incomprehensible to others. Symbolically, this seems to recall issues of gender oppression and the problems of women being able to articulate their condition.

It is not only the fragrance of flowers which is to be found in modern short-story writers in Catalan. In the collection by Isabel Olesti *Dibuix de dona amb ocells blancs,*[77] almost all the stories start with smells of some kind, from those of body sweat, to coffee, perfume and food. Preoccupation with smell is reflected even more prominently in the collection of short stories by Núria Serrahima, where the title of the volume itself is *L'olor dels nostres cossos* (Our Bodies Smell).

Earlier I discussed the position of the Catalan language, and then proceeded to explore some characteristics of women's writing, in particular the use of language and literary devices in Catalan literature. A similar approach is applied to the Irish case in the section that follows.

IRELAND AND THE LANGUAGE QUESTION

Once the Irish Free State was constituted in 1922, decolonisation was a priority for the new government, although the process had been initiated earlier. This took a variety of forms. A principal aim was to recover the Irish language in a project which has been called variously 'the formation of an Irish mind' or 'the de-anglicisation of Ireland'.[78] This process gathered momentum in the early 1930s with the election of Fianna Fáil under the leadership of Eamon de Valera. In his speeches, de Valera articulated Thomas Davis's idea that the recovery of the Irish language was the surest defence against the nation's absorption into an English world. The language was a badge of national identity and also a bridge to past generations of Irish people. Moreover, 'the more we preserve and develop our individuality and our characteristics as a distinct nation, the more secure will our freedom be and the more valuable our contribution to humanity'.[79] The independence of Ireland had to be more than political; it had to be cultural. However, the dream was bordering on the utopian as, by the 1920s, only a small minority of the Irish people were Irish speakers. In practice, religion had taken over long before as the real symbol of Irishness.

It is interesting to note that the decline of the Irish language was not caused by laws prohibiting Irish, as in the Catalan case, but rather it was due to a more indirect process. In 1800 half of the population of Ireland spoke Irish but the dramatic decline of the language took place during the nineteenth century. By the time of the creation of an independent Irish state hardly anyone was a monoglot Gaelic speaker outside a few remote and impoverished areas in the west of Ireland. The processes which undermined Irish were several: immigration during the seventeenth century with a quarter of the population of Ireland in 1700 being of recent Scottish or English colonial origin; the process of commercialisation which favoured English; the dominance of English in the legal, religious and political spheres; widespread migration, and the Great Famine which selected the poor, who were disproportionately Irish speakers. We could say that the Irish language disappeared more as a consequence of neglect than direct persecution.[80]

Despite the best efforts of the new Irish state, English remained the language of the overwhelming majority of Irish people. Irish intellectuals have conflicting opinions about the question of the language. Gearoid O Tuathaigh says that, during the nineteenth century, trying to eliminate the English language was out of the question and could actually have been prejudicial: 'English had already become so embedded in the social and cultural fabric of the majority of the people that any sustained attempt at replacement would itself have involved rupture and a new form of cultural coercion'.[81] For Seamus Heaney, being Irish and writing in English is not worrying: 'I am convinced that one can be faithful to the nature of the English language and at the same time to one's own non-English origins'.[82]

Maeve Kelly takes a caustic view of the Irish language in her short story 'The Sentimentalist', at least through the principal character Jo, who mocks the language's enthusiasts. Jo's English cousin, Liza, comes to Ireland: 'Typical of the convert, she threw herself totally into the Gaelic revival. She joined the Gaelic League, attended the Abbey plays and became a member of Cumann na mBan.'[83] Liza spent her life teaching Irish until she was about to die, whereupon she confesses to Jo that she had been right all along: 'Gaelic Ireland is dead'.[84]

Jo had often disagreed with her cousin and had justified her position thus:

> Since English has been imposed on us, for historical reasons, I accept it and consider it adequate for my needs, a vehicle for communicating thought. I concede that I may have lost something, subtleties of expression more in keeping with my cultural background, not to mention the heritage of tradition which is difficult to translate adequately. However, I have always been a pragmatist and I accept the reality of conquest. The new nationalist fervour associated with the revival of the language was boring to me. I despise passion, wasted emotions.[85]

Jo accepts the English language but her distance and coolness suggest some sense of loss. However, to Jo and probably to Maeve Kelly too, being sentimental has its dangers. Sentimentality might develop into political violence, which she abhors. Death simply perpetuates myths and has no rational value: 'Martyrdom is the ultimate folly, the self-indulgence of the sentimental'. In Kelly's mind, the individual, perhaps through writing, can better help 'womankind' (she indicates that the term includes men.)[86] Worse than the difficulties of the Irish past are the 'saviours' it has attracted, 'most of them with foreign or English blood'.[87] She concludes that the ones who have caused most violence in Ireland have actually been outsiders.

Even if the Irish language is almost gone, some Irish women writers, like Catalan writers, prefer Irish as a vehicle for their writing. That is the case of the poet Nuala Ní Dhómhnaill, who celebrates writing in her native Irish and finds that Irish has the advantage of being less phallogocentric than English. She makes the point that the Irish language and women have been oppressed in a similar way. She says:

> I think I'm very lucky in being Irish because the Irish language wasn't industrialised or patriarchalised. And many things, including this idea of a deeper quality, this negative femininity, this Hag Energy, which is so painful to mankind, hasn't been wiped from our consciousness, as it has in most cultures. Irish in the Irish context is the language of the Mothers, because everything that has been done to women has been done to Irish.[88]

Even if they use English, some Irish women writers regret the loss of the Irish language. In 'The Flowering', the character Lennie says:

> The oral tradition. What oral tradition? It went away, with their language, when the schools started. Slowly they are becoming articulate in the new language. Slowly they are finding a new tradition. If there is such a thing as a new language and a new tradition. Do you have to invent them? Like you have to invent history? Invent, discover, revive? You too can transform yourself. Utterly.[89]

Spoken language comes with an accent. Edna O'Brien notices that the accent of Protestants in Ireland, the descendants of the colonists, was considered to be 'posh'. About 'The Connor Girls', she writes: 'The Connor Girls were not beauties but they were distinguished and they talked in an accent that made everyone else's seem flat and sprawling, like some familiar estuary or a puddle in a field'.[90] As noted earlier, there is present here an admiration for both the tones and the language of the coloniser.

Anne Enright is the author of '(She Owns) Everything', a story which is a good example of the use of experimental language which is characteristic of her writing. The title in brackets suggests the author is familiar with new theories of language. The brackets isolate the subject and the verb, making the object of the sentence the most valued element, whereas traditionally in the hierarchy of syntax the verb and the subject dominate. In effect, the title indicates that the story is challenging the conventional hierarchy of language. So does the first line: 'Cathy was often wrong, she found it more interesting'. Cathy explicitly locates herself as a woman on the 'wrong' side, adding that she actually prefers this position. In effect, she mocks the traditional priorities of syntax and language use.

This is another author, a member of a younger generation of writers, who celebrates marginality.

Like other young writers, Enright has frequent recourse to humour, much more so than is the case in Catalan literature. For example, in the story Cathy was wrong about the taste of bananas, and about where her life ended up. By including 'important' and 'non-important' things side by side, Enright questions the criteria used to categorise reality. As language is itself a construction, it can be challenged and changed. But the important thing is that she loves changes: 'corners, surprises, changes of light'.[91] What Cathy and indeed Enright want are deep changes.

In '(She owns) Everything', Cathy works in a universe of handbags, gloves and umbrellas. She loves it. She even uses that mundane vocabulary to describe something as sublime as falling in and out of love. While engaged in selling, she likes thinking of the relation between women and their tastes. One day, she realises that she has fallen in love with one of her customers who 'seemed to pick her up with the same ease as she did an Argentinian calf-skin shoulder bag in tobacco brown . . . '.[92] But the customer does not buy the bag after all which, in this particular language, means that Cathy is unrequited. It is probably the first time Cathy has fallen in love with a woman. Subsequently, she feels confused and makes mistakes, selling the wrong bags to different women customers. She comes to realise 'she just didn't know anymore'.[93] It's time for change again. She gives up her job. Changing is good but is also difficult and painful.

In other stories Enright describes women who lack confidence and cannot take decisions (echoes of the Catalan Imma Monsó here): those who end up buying royal jelly when they try to buy a blouse, who cannot buy a perfume unless it is for somebody else, or who buy two identical coats but of a different colour. More dramatically, some cry in the lingerie department, or laugh while trying on hats. Enright dwells on these female characteristics, making them loveable.

Many of Enright's stories are humorous, often touching on sex as a taboo subject. In 'Revenge', the protagonist says: 'My husband and I are the kind of people who put small ads in the personal columns looking for other couples who may be interested in some discreet fun'.[94] In 'The House of the Architect's Love Story', a frustrated wife says: 'I am unfaithful with my husband's money . . . My husband earns forty thousand pounds a year and has a company car. This is one of the first things he ever told me. But I fell in love with him anyway'.[95]

Gender presumptions and prejudices are also challenged in comic ways by Katy Hayes, but the humour tends to be softer than in Enright's work.

Thus her girls might break conventions and wrestle instead of playing with dolls. A child cries out: 'I don't understand why my mammy makes me go to ballet lessons. I hate ballet lessons. I much prefer wrestling.'[96] In 'Something Formal', Claudia and her boyfriend John are invited to a dinner party. Claudia feels uncomfortable talking to a conservative woman, Mrs Collins. Then Claudia starts talking about the abortions she has had, her female lovers, and even masturbation:

> I did seriously consider having a baby last year, because I was pregnant. Nothing makes you consider having a baby like being pregnant. But I didn't feel it was right for me at the time so I had an abortion . . . I was with a female lover at the time, but the pregnancy was the result of a one night stand with another old flame of mine.[97]

Mrs Collins does not know what to say and she burbles: 'So, are you a l-l-lesbian?'. Claudia's boyfriend finds the scene amusing. That means that he accepts her and her wiliness to change. This is a totally different kind of male character. As in many of her stories, Hayes uses humour to expose the contradictions of unbalanced gendered relations. The struggle is not so often against her male partners as against older generations who put pressure on young women to fall in with traditional patterns.

As in Catalan women's literature, modern Irish women's writing employs a sensual language of smells. A good example is Angela Bourke's *By Salt Water*. These stories have salt water in common which takes different forms: the sea, tears, sweat, the amniotic fluid where we first swim. In 'Ohio by the Ocean', Eithne misses the smell of salt when she is beside a lake, even if it is as big as the ocean. She thinks:

> The air was limp and lifeless without salt; even the setting sun looked dull . . . A sudden smell distracted her from what he'd said. She couldn't breath deeply enough, trying to catch the vivid pungency that drifted through the car and out again . . . Eithne tried to recall the exhilaration of that smell. It was in her memory tonight as they made love: wild and warm, far from fruit salad with marshmallows, and napkins embroidered with shamrocks.[98]

That smell also brings back to Eithne memories of her mother. In the same author's 'Mayonnaise to the Hills', there are more references to smells. Lucy says: 'I walk along the road and smell the turf smoke and the salty air and I want to open my mouth and my nose wider and wider to take it in'.[99]

Bourke's *By Salt Water* has its counterpart, in terms of salt and sea imagery, in Montserrat Roig's story 'Mar' (which stands for sea as well as being the name of a woman). And the only Catalan publishing company specialising in women's writing was called 'La sal' (Salt.) It is noticeable how often images of salt water and salt air crop up in women's writing. The tanginess of ocean breezes and the sea itself have a direct sensual feel, as well as a deeper symbolic significance forming part of 'the return to the body'. The Irish poet Medbh McGuckian lets us into the secret when she reveals that the subject matter of her poetry is 'the sea and its flux, the world of water and matters that females dominate, or that dominate them'.[100] In fact, for Hélène Cixous water is the feminine element *par excellence* because it reflects the comforting security of the mother's womb. It is also important in her writing which, like fluid, is constantly changing.[101]

Hardly surprising in view of the title, Edna O'Brien's 'Paradise' is something of an aromatheraphist's dream: 'There were flowers in the room. They smelt of confectionery. In the bathroom a great glass urn filled with talcum powder. She leaned over the rim and inhaled.'[102] In Mary Dorcey's 'Flower for Easter', the speaker says: 'The smell closed in on you as you walked up the staircase; the thin blue odour, as it seemed to you, that rose from everything you touched . . . Why do hospitals smell like this?'[103] In the same story there are several descriptions of flowers:

> The pollen covered your fingers with its golden dust and the smell of them rose in waves that made you giddy. And then you had come to the final one. It was red. You touched the tip of the black tongue, it quivered at your touch, you smoothed the stiff curve of its petals. It was yours. You plucked it.[104]

Perhaps the marginal position of women in society, including women's relationship to language, gives women writers a vantage point from which to observe the power of language and its role in constructing reality. In this context, representations of Northern Ireland and its terrible realities demand close scrutiny. The power of language flows like a stream through Anne Devlin's disturbing short story 'Naming the Names'. The story starts with a list of place names: 'Abyssinia, Alma, Bosnia, Balaclava, Belgrade, Bombay'. Lists of names are repeated on several occasions throughout the story. These are names of streets in West Belfast where the action takes place in the late 1960s. Finnula says that she used to name them in a skipping song.[105] Names are very important, and according to Hélène Cixous, those who have the power to name the world are in a position to influence reality.[106] Reality for people born and brought up in West Belfast is intimately connected to these names and to everything these connote, including sectarianism and violence.

Finnula has an Irish name, although Jack, her boyfriend, renames her Finn, which is a male form. She is a young woman who works in a second-hand book shop on the Falls Road. The beginning of the story announces what is important for Finnula: her national identity and the man she loves. She says: 'It was late summer – August, like the summer of the fire'.[107] Everything is connected with being republican, that is, with having a past of oppression. For example, the month of the year, August, makes her think of the summer of the fire. She also says: 'He hadn't rung for three weeks'.[108] As in many other stories by Irish women writers, the loved one is an Englishman who displays the insensitivity of the coloniser. Once Finnula tells Jack she is in love with him, she is in his power. He, however, has no problem in telling her he has to marry somebody else but wants to go on seeing her. The coloniser has no problem in colonising several territories. He is selfish, does not worry about the others, feels no guilt, no suffering.

Finnula wants to leave the claustrophobic world of Belfast's violence but her past does not allow her to. She tells Jack that she likes spiders because her granny used to say that a spider's web was a good omen: 'It means we're safe from the soldiers!'[109] In fact, like a spider's web, that old saying of her grandmother's, or that skipping song she used to sing about the names of streets of West Belfast, trap one in a universe of prejudices which cannot be escaped. Those values, however wrong some of them might be, haunt the mind because they have been embedded in childhood. This early socialisation is what directs Finnula down a sectarian pathway. Being an outsider, Jack cannot understand and he says to her: 'Sometimes I think . . . you live in a dream, Finn'.[110]

The story does not follow a chronological order; rather it tracks Finnula's memories, which do not fall into any obvious order. Salman Rushdie talks of the technique of 'circling back' – he says that the traditional orality is not linear: 'An oral narrative does not go from the beginning to the middle to the end of the story. It goes in great swoops, it goes in spirals or in loops, it every so often reiterates something that happened earlier to remind you, and then takes you off again, sometimes summarises itself.'[111]

In Devlin's story, there is a deliberate atmosphere of ambiguity. Finnula seems to be involved with the IRA, but we cannot be sure. At the end, it is suggested that she may have been responsible for Jack's death. In the police station she is questioned over and over again about the names of other people involved in his killing: '"And the names? The names of the people involved?" There are no names. Only places. "Perhaps you'll tell us the names later."'[112]

When she is interrogated further about members of the organisation, she keeps repeating the names of streets. She explains: 'Naming the names: empty and broken and beaten places. I know no others.'[113] Because she knows no others she has no choices. Language and names determine the bleak outcomes. Beyond the terrorists, perhaps it is the culture of the streets which is the real killer.

CONCLUSION

In Catalonia and Ireland women writers reveal some affinity with their native languages, although in other respects the two cases are quite different. In the Catalan case, it has been difficult to write in Catalan because the language has been banned and excluded from the educational system during most of last century. Furthermore, it has been difficult to publish in Catalan. Nonetheless, women writers have used that language almost exclusively.

Few Irish writers write in Irish because most of them have been brought up as English speakers. However, most show some concern over the loss of the language, albeit sometimes in a backhanded way, as with Maeve Kelly.

From a feminist point of view, language is a masculine construction which leaves a constricted space for women to express themselves. Language belongs to the male coloniser. But, as in postcolonial countries, women are 'writing back' in an attempt to decolonise language. In this 'writing back' there are some common aspects which respond to a common effort to challenge the 'foreign' language. For example, a 'speaking voice' is frequent in these texts, perhaps because it is a terrain in which women feel comfortable. Traditionally, women have not had equal access to education so they developed oral skills more fully than written ones. There is sometimes a sense of the writer inviting the reader to enter into the dialogue, thereby avoiding the hierarchy in which the writer is the active creator while the reader is only a passive figure who contemplates what the powerful writer has to say. Moreover, oral language, being less rationally constructed, allows the semiotic to flow freely and this is a vital achievement for women's writing.

There is an important difference between the cohorts of writers born in the 1930s and 1940s and those born in the late 1950s and 1960s. Those in the first group tend to portray female characters who, as colonised beings, cannot be much more than passive victims. Their suffering makes them paralysed and frozen, like the ice described in Edna O'Brien's 'Irish Revel'. They are used and abused, to the extent that there is more than a hint of masochism on the part of those who have undergone a long period of oppression. In most of these cases the style is one of realism because the motive is to highlight injustice of the 'colonial' situation. Exceptionally, the language is surreal, as in Mercè Rodoreda's *Viatges i Flors* (Travels and flowers). Both Catalan and Irish writers use a sensual language in an effort to express women's sexuality. Irish writers, it may be suggested, show a greatert facility with the use of irony and humour in deconstructing patriarchy.

Younger writers such as Imma Monsó, Anne Enright and Katy Hayes are drawn towards experimental modes of writing. Literary theory, particularly in the form of deconstruction, seems to inform some of the writing. For example, it is common to hear a variety of voices in their female characters. Their marginal position, it may be suggested, helps them to explore language, sometimes in a playful way. Female characters tend to be more complex or multi-layered in terms of consciousness. Male characters, by contrast, are presented as being simpler, more direct in their motives and responses. In some cases, their behaviour is exploitative and possibly violent.

Both postcolonial Catalonia and postcolonial Ireland have a native language to use as a frame of reference, even if the fortunes of Irish and Catalan have been different. Women, so far as we know, have never had a language of their own. This may not even be desirable, in that few advocate gender apartheid. But it does mean that women writers do not have an alternative medium, as they struggle to decolonise languages impregnated with masculine concepts. Thus the two kinds of 'decolonisation' – in the gender and socio-political spheres – are different, with the likelihood of different outcomes. What those outcomes may be is a matter for conjecture.

CHAPTER FIVE

Conclusions: 'Inventing women'

Because fundamentally I believe it to be right. We should have the freedom to do what we want, not what everybody else wants. It's not easy, but it's right.

Katy Hayes[1]

ONE of the central objectives of this book has been to create an awareness of inherited structures of power and authority which impinge painfully on women in Catalonia and Ireland. It has also aimed to delineate the restricting processes involved in some key areas of women's private and social lives and, by laying bare these structures and processes, to call them into question. The reflecting mirror is short-story writing by women in the two societies, supplemented on occasion and as seems appropriate by reference to other societies and other literary genres, including history. A central contention of the work is that women are 'doubly colonised' in their status as women and as postcolonial subjects.

In *Inventing Ireland* Declan Kiberd observed that Irish people have used and should be using still their imagination to 'invent Ireland' in an effort to overcome its history of colonisation. In this task, the postcolonial writer has a crucial role of 'writing back', producing texts committed to cultural resistance,[2] presenting counter discourses against traditional, imperial and dominant assumptions. The same could be applied to the Catalan writer or to the woman writer. Contemporary Irish and Catalan women short-story writers are certainly part of this process of 'writing back' and of 'inventing women'.

Before elaborating on the conclusions, it may be helpful to recall some of the main themes from the four central parts of the book. The first chapter, 'The Short Story in Ireland and Catalonia', discusses the prominence of the genre of the short story in the two countries. As postcolonial societies, each has had to struggle to maintain its cultural, economic and political identity. Lacking in resources, the short story was often easier and cheaper to publish. In both cultures it was difficult for authors to become full-time professional writers. The short story has the great advantage that it does not require a large and sustained commitment of time. It can be squeezed into crevices of time stolen from other routines of work. There are all sorts of explanations. Raymond Carver said he wrote short stories because he was drunk a lot of the time and his kids were driving him crazy, and a short story was all he had concentration for.[3]

In Ireland, oral culture, ranging from traditional tales to ordinary conversations, has left a deep imprint on the writing of the modern short story. Though less pronounced in the Catalan case, possibly because of the more urban, industrialised nature of Catalonia, folklore and fables have been an imaginative resource for creative writers. The speaking voice, which is another reflection of oral culture, is an important device in the construction of such stories in both literatures.

There seems to be a link between orality, short-story writing and women's writing. Women's culture has been closer to orality because historically women have had more limited access to education. As Mary Dorcey says, girls start talking earlier and women are the ones who transmit the language between generations. The culture of women, and the dominant means of communicating between women, depend more on conversation than writing.

But the really key points are the marginality of the genre of short-story writing and women's relationship to that genre. Perhaps there is a connection between the two, drawing women to this literary medium? To an extent, women writers, as colonised subjects, have a tendency to lack confidence. In the public arena, including literary production, some women begin their literary careers by writing short stories; sometimes, at the end, they go back to them. This is the case for Mercè Rodoreda and Monserrat Roig. Many combine the use of the short story and the novel such as Edna O'Brien and Julia O'Faolain. A major Catalan short-story writer, Pere Calders, observes that the short story offers a huge sense of freedom.[4] Freedom is very much welcomed by postcolonial subjects who are learning to push back the conventional barriers that have previously hemmed them in and are searching for new terrains. Perhaps they also welcome a form of writing which facilitates subversion. Certainly Frank O'Connor felt that the genre could attract marginalised population groups – in our terms postcolonial subjects, be they women or the inhabitants of formerly colonised territories.

Marriage is one of the fundamental social institutions in most societies, historically and in contemporary times, and it is the subject of Chapter Two. Not surprisingly, many Irish and Catalan writers have treated the subject in the course of their work. What is more unexpected is the extensive critique of marriage which is embodied in many of the short stories examined here. Marriage is the personal destiny of most women (and men), hence the notion of 'compulsory marriage'. Even if society is changing, and nowadays there are new options for women, the implications for them can be malign. However, that is not to say the alternatives, until recently at any rate, were any better. Economic and social dependency marked the position of women within marriage, while their position in the labour market was a disadvantaged one, even as compared to single women. Economic and social dependence opened the way to abuse, something which is highlighted in a number of the stories featured here. The parallels with colonised countries, in terms of the abuse of power by the strong over the weak, are plain to be seen.

On the whole, women are portrayed as sexually powerless within marriage. Among older writers, this is often implicit rather than explicit, sex being a taboo subject. The younger writers show few such inhibitions, plunging into the difficulties of women's sexuality within the context of a patriarchal order. The stance is sometimes ironic, occasionally brightly humorous. An analogue to the loss of female sexual power may be the loss of a native power to speak, as in the loss of the language in postcolonial countries (the question of language is discussed more fully in Chapter Four). Marriage, as conventionally structured, is experienced as being designed to empower and satisfy men. New currents of social change, reflected especially in women's writings since the 1980s, seek to modify traditional relationship structures, including marriage. There is a striving for new ways in which women may relate emotionally to men: to break free from patterns of behaviour which suggest roles more akin to those of the coloniser and the colonised. Where growth and change are not possible, women are prepared to walk away from men. 'Goodbye to you now'[5] says the girl in Eilís Ní Dhuibhne's 'The Search for the Lost Husband', just as Marta writes a farewell letter to her husband before leaving in Nuria Pompeia's 'L'ordre i el matrimoni' (The Order and Marriage.) Women are starting to explore alternatives: they enjoy friendship, work, art, and in some cases they embrace or take refuge in lesbian relationships.

The tendency of older women writers to show women as passively experiencing and enduring, the objects rather than the authors of their personal histories, is firmly rejected by a newer generation of voices, sometimes with playful irony. The fatalism of feeling, the bitter-sweetness, the woman enthralled to the whims of husband or lover: these qualities are much less evident in the stories of Imma Monsó, Anne Enright and Katy Hayes. A further shift of style and sensibility is apparent in the successful use of irony and humour, which is more common in the Irish stories. The use of such devices signifies the taking back of power, directly on the part of the woman author and indirectly in relation to her female characters.

The third chapter, 'Towards a Feminisation of Nationalism', shows how Catalan and Irish women writers engage with nationalism while at the same time rejecting masculine constructions of nationalism, such as the image of the nation as a passive woman who has to be saved or died for. It is instructive to be reminded that even when independence or autonomy is achieved, postcolonial countries continue to marginalise groups such as women. Eamon de Valera, the father figure of the modern Irish state, famously remarked on the eve of political emancipation: 'Labour must wait'. Significantly, it wasn't even necessary to add: 'Women must wait'.

The relationship between women writers and nationalism is a complicated one, and one must be cautious about generalising, not just between two societies but even within the two societies. Edna O'Brien, for instance, who is overtly nationalistic in her public statements as is Isabel-Clara Simó in Catalonia, represents the concerns of nationalism and nationality (as well as women) in a very different way from that of a younger writer like Maeve Kelly. Still, there are commonalties. On the basis of the stories examined here, one may conclude that the authors are drawn to a liberal nationalism: one which is open, inclusive and recoils from violence. To use a contemporary political reference point, this could be the core statement of the Northern Ireland Women's Coalition, formed in 1996 to promote new values and new approaches within the male bear pit of Northern politics.

It is difficult to dissent from Thomas Davis's view that losing the most precious sign of cultural identity for a community, that is, its language, means losing an important part of its roots. The theme of language, in relation to former colonial societies and in relation to women, forms the subject matter of Chapter Four. The imposition of the coloniser's language guarantees long-term colonisation and makes decolonisation more difficult. That has been one of the greatest cultural difficulties Ireland has had to go through. The ambivalence of various Irish women writers in relation to the Irish language suggests the complexity of the question. The situation in Catalonia, at least on the surface, is more clear-cut. Despite the historic banning of the Catalan language, Catalonia has managed to maintain its language, at least until now. However, in recent decades being placed formally in the same position as the powerful Spanish language means, in effect, 'competing' with it. As a result, some linguists have grave forebodings regarding the future viability of Catalan, despite a partly favourable state framework for its development in recent times.

Like Irish nationalists (obviously Ulster unionists would see the world differently), women find themselves using a 'foreign' tongue.[6] In the light of feminist critical theory, one might suggest that women writers experience frictions or difficulties in being obliged to work within this phallogocentric language. To achieve greater authenticity, it seems necessary to 'decolonise' it first. That is one of the most difficult challenges women writers have to face, not just in Ireland or Catalonia, but wherever women put pen to paper. So, in these short stories we find women, especially younger writers, trying to use language in ways that allow them to subvert a phallogocentric system. Paradoxically, the less centred position of women seems to facilitate artifice and wit. Indeed, there may be some similarities between the way Irish writers in English have successfully adapted and domesticated the language of the former colonial power for their own needs and the way women writers are revising and re-visioning the English language. In this respect, Catalan women writers, who are deprived of the huge dynamic of the Anglo-American literary industry and its associated literary studies, are lagging behind.

Among a number of the women writers we have encountered here, there is a deliberate resort to a multiplicity of voices. The omniscient voice, the patriarchal author speaking, is noticeably absent. These multiple voices may well contradict each other, in an attempt to portray the complexity of women's inner world. Who fears to speak of contradiction! The use of a fantastic language may also be used to deal with a world of uncertainty and confusion, as in Merce Rodoreda's perplexing *Viatges i Flors* (Travels and Flowers).

Let us turn now to issues of critical theory. Peter Barry sees the connection between postcolonialism and French feminism in particular as being only natural.[7] The evidence of this study is that the two perspectives, far from being antagonistic, are mutually reinforcing. It is worth setting out the characteristics the two approaches have in common. For example, each seeks to give voice to social groups or categories which had little or limited opportunity to write before. Each gives confidence to those on the margins because each accords due respect to the artistic endeavours of such individuals and groups, rather than acquiescing in the cultural imperialism which views the European or Anglo-American world as the storehouse of all that is best in human creativity. Feminism challenges the patriarchal judgement that the literary canon should be composed mainly of male Western writers. Thus, feminism and postcolonialism are allies in the challenge to the way in which traditional canons have been constituted.

Peter Barry establishes three historic phases in postcolonialism. The first is the 'adopt' phase, in which postcolonial writers begin to accept the authority of the coloniser's models (especially in the novel.) The second is the 'adapt' phase, in which the aim is to adapt the coloniser's form. In the final phase, postcolonial writers are independent 'adepts' in the form. Barry adds that a stress on 'cross-cultural' interactions is a further characteristic of postcolonialist criticism. As a matter of fact, the three phases closely parallel the development stages of feminist criticism defined by Elaine Showalter: a feminine phase (1840–80), in which women writers imitated dominant male artistic norms and aesthetic standards; then a feminist phase (1880–1920), in which radical and often separatist positions were developed, and finally a female phase (1920 onwards) which focused specifically on female writing and female experience.[8]

Geraldine Moane explains the historical processes involved whereby the colonised (woman) comes to accept the ideology of the coloniser (man). The ideology of domination becomes hidden and normal:

> Systems of domination, or hierarchical systems which are not consensual, rely in part on mechanisms of control for their maintenance. Initially, use of violence is a fairly brutal and obvious mechanism. However, over generations of domination mechanisms of control become more pervasive and more subtle, focusing on control of economic, political, and symbolic systems. Over time, the mechanisms become institutionalised and shrouded by ideology such that it becomes difficult for both the dominants and the subordinates to recognize them. If these mechanisms are working well, they not only succeed in keeping the subordinates in their place, they convince the subordinates that they deserve their position, or that, indeed, their subordination is natural and actually good for them.[9]

In terms of hierarchical systems as they affect women, it may be noted that (at least until recently) patriarchy was more invisible than most other forms of domination. Moane identifies various mechanisms of control within colonialism which are worth spelling out: 'violence, economic exploitation, sexual exploitation, exclusion from power, control of ideology and representation, and fragmentation or "divide and conquer"'.[10] The parallels in the case of the treatment of women, and also as reflected in a number of the short stories discussed in the course of this book, are evident enough.

One of the worst manifestations of colonialism, in the literal sense as applied to former colonial societies or in the metaphorical sense as used to dramatise the oppression of women, is when the oppressed internalise the ideology of their oppressors – the oppression becomes hidden. The result is guilt, admiration for the domineering other and self-abnegation. This outcome is portrayed dramatically in the case of the woman in Mary Dorcey's 'A Sense of Humour' who believes she is worthless in every respect. She claims no rights, not even the negative right not to be beaten or insulted. She comes to believe that she deserves to be beaten; that only he, priest-like, can absolve her. Again the word 'whore' appears, almost naturally. The ideology of male dominance has penetrated her psyche to the extent that she cares for and admires men much more than she loves her own womanhood. As Montserrat Roig has said, women's challenge is to learn to love their own sex, women's sex.[11] This is something which seems to come easily to men, presumably because of a different socialisation, but which takes time and courage for women.

The ideology of domination is closely tied up with violence which is a feeling of inferiority in relation to the coloniser. Violence is a consequence of oppression. Colonisation involves violence. Male domination also involves violence. According to Mercè Rodoreda, war is a product of gender imbalance. Acts of violence swim to the surface of many of the short stories explored here. As Monica McWilliams says, it is easier for women writers to denounce war than domestic violence because the latter is hidden in the 'marriage ideology' in which the wife is the possession of the husband. Thus, this kind of violence is seen as normal.

Some of these stories illustrate an important psychological consequence of domination – what we could sum up as an 'inferiority complex', reflected, for example, in the language of the colonised. Take, for example, O'Brien's 'The Connor Girls'. The people in the village admired the accent of the Protestant girls: 'they talked in an accent that made everyone seem flat and sprawling, like some familiar estuary or a puddle in a field'.[12] We also find examples of an 'inferiority complex' in relation to the Catalan language. A Catalan author who writes in Spanish, Ana Maria Moix, claims that Catalan is not an intellectual language and therefore not comparable to Spanish. As evidence for this, she complains that Catalan is written in the same way as it is spoken.[13] In my view, this sense of inferiority is a hangover from the era of colonial domination, not just in the political but in the cultural sphere as well.

Both feminism and postcolonialism detect an unequal power structure, coloniser-man / colonised-woman, and, in this recognition, they provide the first step towards escape. The colonised has to acknowledge the injustice first so as to be able to change the situation. The process of

decolonisation is not easy because one of the consequences of colonisation is a sense of confusion and uncertainty about one's identity: 'What
am I?', 'Where should I go to?'. A young woman might realise that she
should prepare herself not just for marriage but might have trouble
knowing what to do instead. Should she imitate men and their approach
to making their way in the world? Or should she evolve some new
strategy? In one of Eilís Ní Dhuibhne stories, we find that the dream of
the wedding still remains:

> Many girls she knew then worked in department stores, in restaurants.
> They became secretaries . . . convinced that their destiny was to be taken
> care of by a husband. This was in the 1970s, a time when you might have
> expected more ambition in young women . . . She felt if she were married,
> all the other problems of her life would fade into insignificance.[14]

But change comes slowly and is inevitably difficult and painful. Even
the pathway to equal opportunity in the workplace has been strewn with
difficulty. Entry into, or continuing participation in, the labour force has
posed problems for married women, even in the climate of reform since
the 1970s. In the same story, the female protagonist, Emily, ironically
notes: 'Once married women began to stay on at work, all promotions
stopped. It has nothing to do with discrimination against women, it's just
a coincidence. If anyone suggests otherwise, the management laughs and
says they are prejudiced and hysterical.'[15]

Change for women has been particularly stressful because it has extended
beyond the workplace to the most intimate areas of life – those of feelings,
emotions and sexuality. In the stories studied here, we are reminded again
and again of women reflecting on their position in life, having doubts and
questioning many fundamental tenets: 'Sometimes I don't believe that
sexuality is as easily boxed as society likes to think';[16] 'And I wondered why it
is that we all want a mate';[17] 'Do you ever wonder who you are?';[18] '*És massa
difícil saber que és el que t'agrada de debó i què t'agrada perque als altres els agrada
que t'agradi*' (It's too difficult to know what you like really and what you like
because the others like you to like it).[19] We could situate these processes
within a transitional phase of society in which women are located at the
forefront of change.[20] In these stories we have seen cases of women looking
at themselves in the mirror and experiencing unhappiness. What is reflected
back to them is a sense of incompleteness which can hardly be divorced from
the phallogocentric order to which they belong.

Both feminism and postcolonialism, it has been suggested here, have
the power to illuminate. But it is important to acknowledge that each, and

in particular notions of postcolonialism, have attracted their share of criticism. Some regard the dichotomy between the coloniser and the colonised as too simple, and in certain historical circumstances it would be hard to dismiss this view. Some of the later, more sophisticated formulations of postcolonial theory take on board the idea of a greater range of experiences which are not easily summed up in terms of a dichotomy. Catalonia and Ireland each possess their own distinctive, though hardly unique, experiences and characteristics, which is why a fair amount of space has been given to a discussion of the specific historical circumstances of the two societies.

A further objection is that postcolonialism leads into an uncritical acceptance of nationalism, whatever its manifestation or orientation. Some of these can lead to violence, as we have seen. Some critics would see nationalism itself as simply a reflex, if oppositional, response to colonialism. Thus, rather than being liberating, postcolonial practices may well mimic the politics of the colonial power. A creative debate between discourses on nationalism and postcolonialism is now developing and may lead to more fruitful reformulations in the future. It should be remembered, though, that the postcolonial paradigm has generally celebrated hybridity, which saves it from being simply a disguised form of nationalism. Just as postcolonialism and feminism have radically changed our view of societal structures and relationships, so they have also revolutionised our reading of texts, in the process uncovering and promoting new meanings and practices.

In the 1960s Frantz Fanon saw the independent nation as the eventual and desired outcome of anti-colonial struggle. But the story does not end there. We notice in relation to Ireland and Catalonia that once they had achieved a substantial degree of autonomy, they did not stop being 'colonisers' themselves. They both reproduced the politics of centralisation and exclusion. Postcolonial criticism has increasingly turned its attention to the 'margins of the margins'. As Colin Graham points out, postcolonialism is switching its focus to gender, class, ethnicity and localised history, all of which it can employ to fracture the homogeneity of the nationalist discourse.[21] We have seen that a number of the short stories studied here chose outcasts as their protagonists.

Postcolonialism has also been criticised for creating a sense of victimhood. This, it is claimed, can be disabling. But surely it is necessary to acknowledge situations of discrimination, disadvantage and subordination as a first step towards some kind of emancipation. Alcoholics cannot get rid of their illness unless they recognise they have an illness. In a similar way, women cannot change their lot, either individually or collectively, unless they recognise how they have been locked into structures of domination, both in the household and the wider society. Obviously their condition and status have varied over time and between societies, but there is a remarkable thread of continuity which cannot be ignored.

The relevance of postcolonial theory to the Irish case has been attacked by the revisionist historian Líam Kennedy. As this theoretical approach has hardly begun to be applied to Catalonia or Catalan Studies, there is no comparable critique on the Catalan side. In 'Modern Ireland: Post-colonial Society or Post-Colonial Pretensions?',[22] Kennedy argues that Ireland cannot be compared to Third World countries which are the usual focus of such theorising. Ireland, in his view, is located solidly within the First World. The recent phenomenon of the Celtic Tiger economy serves to consolidate this position of relative affluence. Viewed historically, he sees little difference between, on the one hand, the position of Ireland in relation to England (later the United Kingdom) and, on the other hand, the experiences of other regions of Europe and their incorporation into larger, centralised states. Catalonia, Schleswig-Holstein, Brittany, Alsace and Lorraine are cited as cases in point. In terms of this perspective, most regions of Europe have experienced forms of colonialism at some point in time, distant or otherwise.

Kennedy's arguments are based primarily on an appeal to economic considerations and are perhaps at their strongest in ridiculing the idea that Ireland and contemporary Third World countries have much in common economically or socially. But postcolonialism is not confined to the economist's agenda, and one might note in the case of Catalonia that despite being the most industrialised and economically advanced region of the Iberian peninsula in the nineteenth century, it was still subjected to domination from Madrid. The issue is really about power relationships and not only about economics. Perhaps it is important to remember at this point that postcolonial theory was first formulated to describe the reality of Third World countries rather than European countries. However, in time it has come to be used to describe other forms of colonisation and abuse.

Though there may be some dispute about the content of the term, there is no doubt that Catalonia and Ireland experienced colonisation. In both cases the colonial power sought to produce a society which bore a strong resemblance to the metropolitan country. In the case of Ireland this was accompanied by the loss of the native language. In Catalonia, paradoxically, the systematic persecution of Catalan failed to dislodge it from the private sphere, from whence it re-emerged. In each, though, there is cultural self-questioning and problems of identity, as is richly reflected in the creative literature of the two societies. Political subordination did not result in the suppression of the Catalan enterprise, but some would see the economic underdevelopment and depopulation of Ireland in the nineteenth century as a product, in part, of its imperial link with Britain.[23]

The scepticism of historians, however, is not shared by literary critics. One of the seminal thinkers in terms of postcolonial ideas, Edward Said, discusses Yeats against a backdrop of colonialism in 'Yeats and Decolonisation'.[24] Fredric Jameson has found such a perspective helpful in exploring Joyce and Dublin.[25] Other notable exponents include Declan Kiberd, Seamus Deane and the Field Day group. In Peter Barry's general introduction to cultural theory, it is noteworthy that Ireland is his first example in the postcolonial section.[26]

There is ample evidence that the paradigm has fruitful potential, as suggested by these various applications in relation to Irish literature and culture. Such potential has yet to be unlocked in Catalonia. Still, it may be that the Irish and the Catalan cases, because of their historical specificity and their distance from Third World postcolonial societies, are best approached through atypical rather than 'straight' readings of postcolonial theory, as has been suggested by Colin Graham.[27]

As mentioned in the introduction, postcolonial theory offers a new way of reading texts. It may be said that postcolonialism and feminism have delivered a double shock to existing ideas about what constitutes literature and how the canon has been constructed. In addition, they have helped open up the riches of non-Western literatures and women's writings, which have been undervalued, sometimes actively, in the past. Not only are the texts changing but the ways of reading them have also been changing under the impact of postcolonial and feminist ideas. The two perspectives prove complementary, as suggested earlier.

Throughout this work, it has been shown that both women and colonised peoples are made out of 'otherness' rather than 'essence', and that this gives rise to crises of identity and fulfilment. In the case of Catalan and Irish women, they are doubly colonised because they have experienced both conditions simultaneously. Their work to reconstruct themselves is bound to be especially difficult. Clearly there is a major challenge in constructing new identities in a world which is changing rapidly. There is, inevitably, a price to pay. Solitude and confusion make frequent appearances in women's writing, the outcome of poor communications with male partners and an unequal status in society. Traditional codes of behaviour limiting females and males, including the institution of traditional marriage, seem increasingly under strain and ill-adapted to the ways of a changing world. In some of the stories studied here, women are consciously seeking new ways of finding emancipation, even if the personal price to be paid for abandoning conventional patterns of behaviour is high. This quest is more true of the younger authors who have come to the fore in the 1980s and the 1990s. Better educated, and with brighter prospects, they are much better placed than earlier cohorts of women writers to challenge the various power structures which limit them, be they the after-effects of colonialism or the distorting implications of patriarchy. However, the resistance they encounter should not be minimised.

Thus short-story writing, particularly by younger women authors, might be viewed as part of their 'writing back'. It constitutes an enterprise which serves to subvert the established masculine order, not least through acts of imagining. Imagined realities, by creating alternative possibilities of the mind, are a step in the direction of empowering women. These may relate to the public or private spheres: relationships, marriage and the family, gender identity, work, national identity and national language. Significantly, many of the women writers who have emerged during the 1980s and the 1990s portray women in the active rather than the passive voice. The stories in Katy Hayes's *Forecourt* sometimes create the impression that we live in a postfeminist world, because women are so empowered that there is less need to be feminist and women can take for granted the gains secured by earlier women's struggles. The same might be said of her Catalan counterpart, Imma Monsó. However, there may be a danger of complacency in taking such ideas too literally.

Is it fair to present women and postcolonial subjects in much the same breath? Some would argue that analogical reasoning of the kind employed here is inherently wrong. Stephen Howe, for example, argues that it is ironic that in an age when empires, including the Soviet empire, have collapsed, the concept of colonialism 'as universal image of all forms of oppression seems to be spreading. It has been inflated to include women, social classes, ethnic minorities, and almost any other imaginable group.'[28] Howe sees this as little more than a claim to property rights in victimhood and presumably would be disappointed by the increasing use of postcolonial thought since he wrote in 1992. It must be conceded that the colonial concept, and its application to particular groups and time periods, is open to abuse. The concept has its limitations when applied to relatively affluent societies such as Catalonia or Ireland, though it is worth emphasising that to point to a colonial past is not the same thing as claiming that Ireland or Catalonia were akin to Third World countries as was suggested in some of the earlier and cruder formulations of postcolonial theory. The latter position is untenable, particularly in relation to material conditions, but the political and cultural subordination of the two countries to metropolitan powers can hardly be wished away. The task for postcolonial writers is to explore the legacy of a type of colonialism that belongs to the First World that is distinctive in the sense of taking place *within* Europe rather than beyond its perimiters.

The more relevant point is the usefulness of colonial images and metaphors to the position of women within Western societies. Like all forms of comparison, the parallels can be pushed too far. However, I believe it is a useful tool both to uncover and fight oppression. Clearly there is a *quantitative* difference between the material conditions of women in Catalonia and Ireland and men or women in the postcolonial societies of Africa or Asia. No one would deny this. Equally, one would recognise that the position of women has changed over time. It is now considerably better than it was in the age of Franco or de Valera. But we must avoid present-mindedness, especially in relation to social and cultural matters. It is important to bear in mind that some of the more substantial gains have been made relatively recently. Moreover, many forms of oppression remain, ranging from cultural expectations which limit the role of women in society to physical assault and rape. If a sense of perspective is maintained, a comparison of the processes which emanate from colonial domination and those which emanate from patriarchal power structures can prove mutually illuminating.

This leads into a final, and perhaps unexpected outcome. On the basis of the experience of this work – exploring the genre of the short story as practised by women writers in Ireland and Catalonia – maybe there is a case for bringing the two bodies of theory deployed here into a closer, more formal relationship. One might coin the term postcolonial feminism to suggest close and fruitful connections between the two sets of perspectives and to emphasise the role of women in the intellectual enterprise. Currently postcolonial theorising is the product mainly of men (Albert Memmi, Frantz Fanon, Edward Said, Bill Ashcroft, Gareth Griffiths) and a few women (Gayatri Spivak, Helen Tiffin). A reformulation of the two bodies of theory with close reference to each other, or the development of some major kind of synthesis, would be a mammoth task and, thankfully, does not fall within the remit of this work. But it may be worth considering.

Perhaps it is appropriate, as we enter a new millennium after the most violent century the world has known, to finish on a future-oriented note. Writing back, decolonising, inventing women, inventing men, reinventing Irish and Catalan cultures all these are challenging projects which involve struggles that extend forward in time. They are struggles which could be mutually reinforcing and ultimately emancipatory for both women and men in colonial and postcolonial countries. As Julia Kristeva says: 'Call it "woman" or "oppressed classes of society", it is the same struggle, and there cannot be the one without the other'.[29] If pursued, this suggests a more colourful, varied and optimistic basis for human relations in the years to come.

Appendix

Caterina Albert 'Víctor Català' (L'Escala, 1869–1966). Daughter of a lawyer from a rural, land-owning family, she never married, managing her family property after her father's death. She always used a male pseudonym, 'Víctor' for masculine strength and 'Català' for nationalism. The label 'naturalism' has been attached to her fiction, and her unmarried state led to the frequent characterisation of Albert as a 'masculine' writer.[1] Here I study mainly her last two collections of short stories, published after the Spanish Civil War: *Vida Mòlta* (Battered Life) (1950) and *Jubileu* (Jubilee) (1951). In this way I am trying to be consistent in time with the other writers. These late productions have been little studied.

Maria Àngels Anglada (Vic, 1930–99) studied Greek literature in the University of Barcelona. She published novels: *No em dic Laura* (My Name is Not Laura) (1981), *Sandàlies d'escuma* (Foam Sandals) (1985); poetry: *Columnes d'hores* (Hours Columns), and short stories: *La daurada parmelia i altres contes.*

Imma Monsó (Lleida, 1959–) studied French literature at the University of Barcelona and linguistics at the French universities of Caen and Estrasburg. Her first novel, *No se sap mai* (You Never Know) (1996), has been translated into Spanish. She has published a collection of short stories, *Si es no es* (Almost) (1997).

Núria Pompeia (Barcelona, 1942–) is a cartoonist as well as a writer. She has published in Catalan and Spanish: *Pels segles dels segles* (For Centuries and Centuries) (1975), *La educacion de Palmira* (Palmira's Education) (1972), *Mujercitas* (Little Women) (1975), *Cinc Cèntims* (Five Cents) (1982) and *Mals endreços* (Untidy) (1997).

Carme Riera (Palma de Majorca, 1948–) moved to Barcelona to study at the University of Barcelona where she lectures in Spanish literature. Riera is currently one of Catalonia's leading writers. She has published three collections of short stories, *Te deix, amor, la mar com a penyora* (I Leave You, My Love, the Sea as a Token) (1975) and *Jo pos per testimno les gavines* (I Offer the Seagulls as Witnesses) (1977), *Epitelis tendríssims* (Tender Epitheliums) (1981) and the novel *Una primavera per a Domenico Guarini* (A springtime for Domenico Guarini) (1981), which won the Prudenci Bertrana prize.

Mercè Rodoreda (Barcelona, 1908–83) Recognised in her lifetime as one of the greatest short-story writers and novelists in Catalan, Mercè Rodoreda received important awards early in her career and in 1980 was awarded the highest distinction for a Catalan writer, the Premi d'Honor de les Lletres Catalanes, for her entire work. She is an acknowledged model for many Catalan women writers, for her creation of an authentic narrative voice to express women's inner struggles and for the connections she makes between exile and women's lives. Her works have reached an international audience. In 1939 she went into exile in France. From an arranged marriage in 1928 with one of her uncles, Rodoreda had a son, whom she left in the care of her mother when she fled Spain. She had already separated from her husband. During the Second World War Rodoreda worked as a seamstress in Limoges and Bordeaux. After the war she moved to Paris and then to Geneva. Rodoreda shared her life in exile with the Catalan writer Armand Obiols until his death in 1971. She re-established residence in Barcelona in 1979. Her novels and collections of short stories include: *Vint-i-dos contes* (Twenty-two Short Stories) (1958), *La Placa del diamant* (The Time of the Doves) (1962), *La meva Cristina i altres contes* (My Christina and Other Stories) (1967), and *Viatges i flors* (Travels and Flowers) (1980).

Montserrat Roig (Barcelona, 1946–91) had a varied life as a journalist for newspapers and television. She is the author of collections of short stories: *Molta roba i poc sabó* (Many Clothes and Little Soap) (1970), *El cant de la joventud* (The Youth Chant) (1989) and novels, *L'hora violeta*, (The Violet Hour) (1980), *L'òpera quotidiana* (The Daily Opera) (1985). As a journalist she published a volume on the Catalan people in Nazi camps, *Els catalanas als camps nazis*. (Catalans in Nazi Camps) (1977).

Isabel-Clara Simó (Alcoi, 1943–). From 1972 to 1983 Simo edited the Catalan magazine *Canigó*. She won the Victor Català award for her collection of stories *És quan miro que hi veig clar* (It's When I Look that I Can See Clearly) (1978) and was a finalist for the Ramon Llull award in 1982 for her novel *Julia* (1986). Her collections of short stories include: *Bresca* (Honeycomb) (1985), *Alcoi-Nova York* and (1987) *Dones* (Women) (1997); the novel *T'estimo Marta* (I Love You, Marta) (1989) and two detective novels: *La veina* (The Neighbour) (1991) and *Una ombra fosca com un núvol de tempesta* (A Shadow Dark as a Storm Cloud) (1994).

IRISH WRITERS

Mary Beckett (Belfast, 1926–) was a teacher in Ardoyne, Belfast, until her marriage in 1956 when she moved to Dublin. She began writing short stories when she was twenty-three, but stopped writing for twenty years whilst rearing her five children. In 1980, her collection of stories, *A Belfast Woman*, was published, to be followed by her novel, *Give Them Stones*, in 1987. In 1990 *A Literary Woman* was shortlisted for the Hughes Irish Fiction Award.

Angela Bourke (1962–) A lecturer in modern Irish at University College Dublin, she has published stories in Ireland and America. She was the 1992 winner of the Frank O'Connor Award for Short Fiction. She is the author of *By Salt Water* (1995).

Clare Boylan (Dublin, 1948–) is the author of four novels and two other volumes of short stories. Her novels include *Home Rule* (1992) and its acclaimed sequel *Holy Pictures* (1983), as well as *Black Baby* (1988), which is due to be filmed.

Non-fiction works include *The Agony and the Ego*, essays on the art and strategy of fiction writing, and *The Literary Companion to Casts*.

Anne Devlin (Belfast, 1951–) has won considerable acclaim for her television plays: *The Long March*, *A Woman Calling* (winner of the Samuel Beckett Award), *Naming the Names*, and for her stage play, *Ourselves Alone* (1986). She is the author of *The Way Paver and Other Stories* (1986).

Mary Dorcey (Co. Dublin, 1950–) has lived in England, France, the USA and Japan. Her first collection of poetry, *Kindling*, was published in 1982. Since then her stories and poems have appeared in numerous journals and anthologies in Britain, the USA and Ireland. She is the author of *A Noise from the Woodshed* (1989) and *Moving into the Spaces Cleared by our Mothers* (1991).

Katy Hayes (1965–). *Forecourt* is Hayes's first collection of short stories; the title story, 'Forecourt' won the Golden Jubilee Award in the Francis MacManus Short Stories Competition on RTÉ in 1993. Her first novel is *Curtains* (1997). She is a theatre director, whose work has been commissioned by the Abbey Theatre.

Eilís Ní Dhuihne (Dublin, 1954–) works as an assistant keeper in the National Library and she also lectures in Irish folklore. Her publications include a novel, *The Bray House* (1990), which was short-listed for the Irish Book Awards. Ní Dhuihne has published a book for children, *The Uncommon Cormorant* (1990), which was nominated for the Bisto Children's Book awards. Other books are *Eating Women Is Not Recommended* (1991), *Hugo and the Sunshine Girl* (1991) and *Viking Ale* (1991).

Edna O'Brien (Tuamgraney, Co. Clare, 1932–) was educated in Galway and Dublin. In 1951 she married, settled in London in 1959 and was divorced in 1967. She achieved a literary sensation with her first three books, *The Country Girls* (1960), *The Lonely Girl* (1964), *Girls in Their Married Bliss* (1968), a socially and psychologically realistic trilogy dealing with young women coming to maturity in a puritanical and hypocritical Ireland. All three were banned under the Censorship Act. O'Brien's subsequent work is typically concerned with relationships. Her short-story collections include *The Love Object* (1968), *A Scandalous Woman* (1974), *Returning* (1982) and *Lantern Slides* (1988). Her novels include *August Is a Wicked Month* (1964), *A Pagan Place* (1971), *Night* (1972), *The High Road* (1988), *Time and Tide* (1992) and *House of Splendid Isolation* (1994). She has adapted a number of her stories for the stage and screen.

Julia O'Faolain (England, 1932–). Daughter of the writers Seán and Eileen O'Faolain, Julia O'Faolain studied at University College Dublin, the University of Rome and the Sorbonne. She has translated Italian works and has published a volume on history, *Not in God's Image: Women in History from the Greeks to the Victorians* (1973). She has published several novels and volumes of short stories including *We Might See Sights* (1968), *Godded and Codded* (1970), *Man in the Cellar* (1974), *Women in the Wall* (1975), *No Country for Young Men* (1980), *The Irish Signorina* (1984) and *The Judas Cloth* (1992).

Notes

INTRODUCTION

1 Colm Tóibín, 'Playboys of the GPO', *London Review of Books*, 18 April 1996, 14.

2 In Northern Ireland the aim of almost every political party has been either promoting the union with Britain (British nationalism) or breaking the union with Britain (Irish nationalism). The three significant exceptions have been the Northern Ireland Labour Party, the Alliance Party, and, in more recent times, the Northern Ireland's Women's Coalition. In the Irish Republic all political parties, to varying degrees, subscribe to Irish nationalist ideals. In pre-independence Ireland, however, there was also a unionist party with minority support in regions of southern Ireland. In Catalonia, the main two parties represent either Catalan nationalism (*Convergència*) or integration with Spain (*Partit Socialista de Catalunya*). There are also more radical, and milder, versions of them.

3 Tóibín, 'Playboys', 14.

4 The Catalan government was imprisoned after proclaiming its sovereignty within a Spanish Federal Republic in October 1934.

5 Catalonia has also experienced partition, but a long time ago. The northern region of Catalonia was incorporated into France under the Treaty of the Pyrenees in 1659.

6 Around 400,000 were exiled in 1939 yet around 300,000 went back to Catalonia later that year.

7 Ania Loomba, *Colonialism/Postcolonialism* (London: Routledge, 1998), 2.

8 Ibid., 2, 3.

9 Irish literature, history and culture have been studied under the postcolonial banner by a number of authors (Declan Kiberd, Seaumus Deane, Terry Eagleton, Colin Graham, Gerry Smyth). Postcolonial theory is something newer in Catalonia but the word 'colonisation' has been used lately to describe the Catalan experience (Ferrer i Gironès, Víctor Alexandre, Salvador Cardús, Joan Brossa). Indeed, the poet Joan Brossa says: 'Catalonia is the last Spanish colony, that is why they will not let it go'. Víctor Alexandre *Jo no sóc espanyol* (Barcelona: Proa, 2000), 346.

10 Even if the Irish language was not officially banned, it is possible to argue that it was lost as part of the wider consequences of colonisation.

11 Ferrer i Gironès, Francesc, *Catalanofòbia. El pensament anticatalà a través de la història* (Barcelona: Edicions 62, 2000), 370.

12 Ibid., 382.

13 In relation to Ireland, as I mention in the main text, I have concentrated on Irish nationalism rather than on Irish or Ulster unionism or Protestantism.

14 Bill Ashcroft, Gareth Griffiths and Helen Tiffin, *The Empire Writes Back: Theory and Practice in Post-colonial Literatures* (London: Routledge, 1989), 172.

15 Ibid., 2.

16 Maria Aurèlia Capmany, *Ara* (Barcelona: Plaza y Janés, 1988), 92–3.

17 Ashcroft, *The Empire Writes Back*, 164.

18 Maria-Josep Ragué-Àrias, 'La sang del castell', *I tornarà a florir la mimosa* (Barcelona: Edicions 62, 1984), 20.

19 Ashcroft, *The Empire Writes Back*, 193.

20 Ann Owens Weekes, *Irish Women Writers: An Uncharted Tradition* (Kentucky: The University Press of Kentucky, 1990), 9.

21 Kathleen McNerney, ed., *On Our Own Behalf: Women's Tales from Catalonia* (Lincoln: University of Nebraska, 1988), 4–5.

22 Ashcroft, *The Empire Writes Back*, 33.

23 Ibid.

24 Ibid.

25 Toril Moi, 'Introduction', *Sexual/Textual Politics: Feminist Literary Theory* (London: Routledge, 1994), 13.

26 Ashcroft, *The Empire Writes Back*, 174–5.

27 Maria Mercè Marçal, *'Divisa'*, *Cau de llunes* (Barcelona: Selecta, 1976). Translated by Sam Abrams, *Survivors* (Barcelona: Institute of North American Studies, 1990), 103.

28 Colin Graham, '"Liminal Spaces": Post-Colonial Theories and Irish Culture', *Irish Review* 16 (1994): 29–43.

29 Ashcroft, *The Empire Strikes Back*, 168.

30 Ibid.

31 Ibid.

32 Víctor Alexandre, *Jo no sóc espanyol* (Barcelona: Proa, 2000) 172.

33 McNerney, *On Our Own Behalf,* 18.

34 Líam Kennedy, *Colonialism, Religion and Nationalism in Ireland* (Belfast: Institute of Irish Studies, Queen's University, 1996).

35 Marta Pessarrodona, 'Una manera de ser', *Avui*, 16 August 2000, p. 14.

36 Alexandre, *Jo no sóc espanyol*, 179–80.

37 Ernest Lluch, 'Esfuerzos inútiles i melancolía', *La Vanguardia*, 31 December 1998.

38 Anne Charlon, 'Dona catalana, i a més novel.lista' *Catalan Review* 7, 2, 1993, p. 46.

39 However, as Irigaray notes in the case of women, 'their dispersion among several classes makes their political struggle complex, their demands sometimes contradictory'. Luce Irigaray, *The Sex Which is Not One* (Ithaca, NY: Cornell University Press, 1985), 73.

40 Weekes, *Irish Women Writers*, 218.

41 Ibid., 16.

42 Ibid.

43 Patricia Boyle Haberstroh, 'Literary Politics: Mainstream and Margin', *The Canadian Journal of Irish Studies* 18, 1, July 1992, 189.

44 Ashcroft, *The Empire Writes Back*, 174–5.

45 Ibid.

46   Ailbhe Smyth, 'Ireland', *Bloomsbury Guide to Women's Literature*, Claire Buck, ed. (London: Bloomsbury, 1992), 40.

47   Weekes, *Irish Women Writers*, 212–13.

48   Literary theory in Catalonia is in its infancy: Jordi Llovet, ed. *Teoria de la Literatura* (Barcelona: Columna, 1996), 9.

49   Kathleen McNerney and Cristina Enriquez de Salamanca, eds., *Double Minorities of Spain: A Bio–Bibliographic Guide to Women Writers of the Catalan, Galician, and Basque Countries* (New York: Modern Language Association of America, 1994).

50   Marta Cièrcoles, 'Drets d'autora', *Avui*, 23 April 1998, 18.

51   McNerney, *Double Minorities*, 8.

52   In order to give an example of this, I should mention a recent study on literature in Spain which includes 83 novelists and all of them write in Spanish (Fernando Valls, *La narrativa española, de ayer a hoy* (Madrid: Ministerio de Cultura, 2000). There is not even one single author who uses the Galician, Basque or Catalan language. What makes matters worse, the study has been funded by the Spanish Ministry of Culture.

53   McNerney, *Double Minorities*, 9.

54   Quim Aranda, Interview with Mary Nash: 'A la dona encara no se l'escolta', *Avui*, 23 January 2000.

55   One of the few studies on Catalonia as a postcolonial nation is by the Australian Stewart King, 'Orquestando la identidad: estrategias postcoloniales en l'Opera Quotidiana de Montserrat Roig', *Proceedings of the First Symposium on Catalonia in Australia,* Robert Archer and Emma Martinell eds., (Barcelona: PPU, 1998), 59–76.

56   Marta Nadal, *Vint Escriptors Catalans* (Barcelona: Publicacions de l'Abadia de Montserrat, 1997), 91.

57   Raymonde Popot, 'Edna O'Brien's Paradise Lost', *The Irish Novel in Our Time*, Patrick Rafroide and Maurice Harmon, eds, (Villeneuve d'Ascq: Publications de l'Universite de Lille, 1975–76), 260.

58   Nuala O'Faolain, 'Irish Women and Writing in Modern Ireland', *Irish Women: Image and Achievement. Women in Irish Culture from Earliest Times*, Eiléan Ní Chuilleanáin, ed. (Dublin: Arlen Press, 1985), 131.

59   Edna O'Brien, *Lantern Slides* (London: Penguin, 1990). This is the most recent collection of short stories by Edna O'Brien.

60   Luce Irigaray, *The Sex Which is Not One*, 90.

61   Edna O'Brien, 'Honeymoon', *'A Scandalous Woman' and Other Stories* (London: Penguin, 1976), 95–6.

62   Moi, *Sexual/Textual Politics*, 156.

CHAPTER ONE

1   Mercè Rodoreda, *Cartes a l'Anna Murià 1939–1956* (Barcelona: Edicions l'Eixample, 1991), 90.

2   Vicent Alonso, *Entre la poesia en prosa i el conte literari* (València: Universitat de València, publications de l'Abadia de Montserrat, 1992), 141.

3 Ibid., 142.

4 Ibid., 6.

5 Jaume Aulet, 'Mercè Rodoreda i els seus vint-i-dos contes' *Actes del I Símposi Internacional de Narrativa Breu*, Vincent Alonso et al., eds. (València: Universitat de València, Publicacions de l'Abadia de Montserrat, 1998), 459.

6 Walter J. Ong, *orality and Literacy: The Technologizing of the Word* (London: Methuen, 1982) 10, 49.

7 Ian Reid, *The Short Story* (London: Methuen, 1977), 1.

8 William Trevor, ed. *The Oxford Book of Irish Short Stories* (Oxford: Oxford University Press, 1989), xiv.

9 Valentin Iremonger, ed. *Irish Short Stories* (London: Faber and Faber, 1960), 9.

10 Joan Triadú, 'El conte el gran desheretat de l'edició catalana', *Serra d'Or* (Barcelona: Octubre, 1972), 693.

11 Frank O'Connor, *The Lonely Voice: A Study of the Short Story* (London: Macmillan, 1962), 18.

12 Ibid., 17.

13 O'Connor was writing in 1962. This view would require heavy qualification from at least the early 1960s onwards and seems out of date in the Ireland of the Celtic Tiger.

14 Ashcroft, B., Griffiths, G. and Tiffin, H. *The Empire writes back: Theory and Practice in Post-colonial Literatures* (London: Routledge, 1989), 115.

15 Albert Balcells, *Catalan Nationalism: Past and Present* (Cambridge: Macmillan, 1996), 15–16.

16 Eliseu Trenc Ballester and Alan Yates, *Alexandre de Riquer: The British Connection in Catalan Modernisme* (Sheffield: The Anglo-Catalan Society, 1988), 11.

17 Ballester, *Alexandre de Riquer*, 17–18.

18 Colm Tóibín, 'Playboys of the GPO', *London Review of Books,* 18 April 1996, 14.

19 Tóibín, 'Playboys', 14.

20 Maria Campillo, *Contes de guerra i revolució* (Barcelona: Laia, 1982), 10–13.

21 Esther Centelles, *El conte des de 1939* (Barcelona: Edicions 62, 1995), 5–17.

22 Tóibín, 'Playboys', 16.

23 Terence Brown, *Ireland: A Social and Cultural History 1922–1985* (London: Fontana Press, 1985), 17.

24 Ibid., 67.

25 Ibid., 146.

26 Cited in ibid., 200.

27 Cited in ibid., 201–2.

28 Ashcroft, *The Empire Writes Back*, 36.

29 Brown, *Ireland*, 216.

30 John Wilson Foster, 'Who Are the Irish?', *Colonial Consequences: Essays in Irish Literature and Culture* (Dublin: The Lilliput Press, 1991).

31 Protestants are a minority within the whole island of Ireland but a majority within the six-county area which constitutes Northern Ireland.

32 Foster, 'Who Are the Irish?', 259.

33 Brown, *Ireland*, 318–9.

34 Ibid., 325.

35 Joaquim Molas, *Antologia de contes catalans* (Barcelona: Edicions 62, 1987), 5–6.

36 Edgar Allan Poe, 'The Poetic Principle', *The Complete Poetical Works and Essays on Poetry of Edgar Allan Poe*, John H. Ingram, ed. (London: Frederick Warne, 1888), 153–186.

37 Jordi Castellanos, *Antologia de contes modernistes* (Barcelona: Edicions 62, 1987), 5–6.

38 See, for example, the discussions of oral tradition in J.M. Synge, *Aran Islands* (Dublin: Maunsel, 1911) and in Conrad M. Arensberg, *The Irish Countryman: An Anthropological Study* (London: Macmillan, 1937).

39 Castellanos, *Antologia*, 7.

40 Maria Campillo, *El conte de 1911 a 1939* (Barcelona: Edicions 62, 1995), 12.

41 Cited in Alan Yates, *Una generació sense novel.la? La novel.la catalana entre 1900 i 1925* (Barcelona, Edicions 62, 1984), 173.

42 Ibid., 173.

43 Ibid., 109.

44 John Wilson Foster, 'Irish Fiction 1965–1990', *Field Day Anthology of Irish Writing*, Seamus Deane, ed. (Derry: Faber and Faber, 1992), 939–40.

45 Declan Kiberd, 'Story-Telling: The Gaelic Tradition', *The Irish Short Story*, Patrick Rafroidi and Terence Brown, eds (London: Smythe, 1979), 19.

46 Ibid., 19–20.

47 Ibid., 14.

48 Ibid., 15.

49 Vivian Mercier, ed. *Great Irish Short Stories: A Vintage Collection from Somerville and Ross to Samuel Beckett* (London: Abacus, 1992), 15.

50 Seán O'Faoláin, *The Short Story* (London: Collins, 1948), 46.

51 Colm Tóibín, *Martyrs and Metaphors: Letters from the New Island.* (Dublin: The Raven Arts Press, 1987), 6–8.

52 Trevor, *The Oxford Book of Irish Short Stories*, xiv.

53 Brown, *Ireland*, 158–9.

54 Ibid., 158–9.

55 Dermot Bolger, ed., *The Picador book of Irish Contemporary Fiction* (London: Picador, 1992), xv.

56 Reid, *The Short Story*, 27–8.

57 Women short-story writers in Ireland include Edith Somerville and Violet Martin, Mary Lavin, Elizabeth Bowen, Edna O'Brien and Julia O'Faolain. Less well-known are Mary Beckett, Angela Bourke, Ita Daly, Emma Donoghue, Mary Dorcey, Anne Enright, Angela Bourke, Rita Kelly, Val Mulkerns, Eilís Ní Dhuibhne, Anne Devlin, Fiona Barr, Una Woods, Brenda Murphy, Linda Anderson, Clare Boylan and Anne-Marie Reilly. In Catalonia writers include Caterina Albert, Mercè Rodoreda, Anna Murià, Carme Riera, Isabel-Clara Simó, M. Antonia Oliver, Montserrat Roig and Marta Pessarrodona.

58 David Marcus, 'The Irish Short Story's Last Hurrah?', *Ireland and the Arts*, Tim Pat Coogan, ed. (London: Namara Press, 1983), 85.

59 Janet Madden-Simpson, *Woman's Part: An Anthology of Short Fiction by and about Irishwomen 1890–1960* (Dublin: Arlen House, 1984), i.

60 Conversation with Carme Arnau (June 1998).

61 The connection between women and the genre of the short story does not of course mean that many novels have not been written by women writers.

62 Mary Louise Pratt, 'The Short Story: The Long and the Short of It', *The New Short Story Theories*, Charles E. May, ed. (Athens, OH: Ohio University Press, 1994), 108.

63 Rodoreda, *Cartes a L'Anna Murià*, 90.

64 Madden-Simpson. *Woman's Part*, p. i.

65 Marta Nadal, *Vint escriptors catalans* (Barcelona: Publicacions de l'Abadia de Montserrat, 1997), 126.

66 Guillem-Jordi Graells and Oriol Pi de Cabanyes: 'De la requesta que fou feta a Montserrat Roig', *Serra d'Or*, no. 138, 15 March 1971, 28.

67 Madden-Simpson, *Woman's Part*, 8.

68 Nadal, *Vint escriptors catalans*, 78.

69 Mary Beckett, 'The Master and The Bombs', *A Belfast Woman* (Dublin: Poolbeg, 1980), 80.

70 Eilis Ní Dhuibhne, 'The Bright Lights', *Eating Women is Not Recommended* (Dublin: Attic Press, 1991), 24.

71 Colm Tóibín, *Martyrs*, 10.

72 Charles E. May, 'The Nature of Knowledge in Short Fiction', *The New Short Story Theories*, Charles E. May, ed. (Athens, OH: Ohio University Press, 1994), 136–7.

73 Nadine Gordimer, 'The Flash of Fireflies', *The Story and its Writer: An Introduction to Short Fiction*, Ann Charters, ed. (Boston: Bedford Books of St. Martin's Press, 1995), 780.

74 Ibid.

75 Interview with Cristina Peri Rossi, *Avui*, 6 July 2000.

76 May, 'Nature of Knowledge', 133.

77 In this case, Joyce and Woolf are exceptions.

78 Gordimer, 'The Flash of Firefires', 780.

79 Wendy Hollway, 'Gender Difference and the Production of Subjectivity', *Changing the Subject: Psychology, Social Regulation and Subjectivity*, Julian Henrigues *et al.*, eds. (London: Methuen, 1984), 230.

80 Pratt, 'The Short Story', 104.

81 Ibid.

82 Grace Paley, 'A Conversation with Ann Charters', *The Story and its Writer: An Introduction to Short Fiction*, Ann Charters, ed. (Boston: Bedford Books of St. Martin's Press, 1995), 814.

83 In addition there are reasons which are common to many countries, in particular the aesthetic. The short story was a new form and it became fashionable in some circles in Europe and North America.

84 O'Connor, *The Lonely Voice*, 19.

85 Tóibín, *Martyrs*, 5–6.

86 Brown, *Ireland*, 84.

CHAPTER TWO

1 Maria Aurèlia Capmany, *Betúlia: Obres Completes I* (Barcelona: Editorial Nova Terra, 1974), 52–3.

2 Katy Hayes, 'Getting Rid of Him', *Forecourt* (Dublin: Poolbeg, 1995), 89.

3 In this chapter I use the word 'marriage' as a metaphor. Nowadays, in the Western world, marriage might not be compulsory but most people still live in this kind of relationship and many feel pressurised to create traditional families. Of course in the closing decades of the twentieth century rapid social change altered perceptions of marriage and cohabitation is on the increase, but marriage remains the dominant family form in Ireland and Catalonia. Having children outside marriage or engaging in multiple relationships belongs to the 'margins' of Irish and Catalan society.

4 The term has been inspired by the famous essay 'Compulsory Heterosexuality and Lesbian Existence' by Adrienne Rich in *Feminisms: A Reader*, Maggie Humm, ed. (New York: Harvester Wheatsheaf, 1992).

5 Although Ireland, over much of this century, has had the lowest marriage rate in Europe, the great majority of Irish women did marry. The likelihood is that the many women who emigrated had even higher rates of marriage. See Timothy Guinnane, *The Vanishing Irish: Households, Migration, and the Rural Economy in Ireland, 1850–1914* (Princeton: Princeton University Press, 1997) 193–240.

6 Again 'wife' here is used in a metaphoric way. It is used as a woman being defined by her link or belonging to a man.

7 Maria Aurèlia Capmany. *L'altra ciutat* (Barcelona: Selecta, 1955), 36.

8 Mary Nash, *Rojas: Las mujeres republicanas en la Guerra Civil* (Barcelona: Taurus, 1999), 43.

9 An example of a study which views women as a colonised group is Geraldine Moane, 'Legacies of Colonialism for Irish Women: Oppressive or Empowering?', *Irish Journal of Feminist Studies 1,* March 1996, 100–18.

10 George Duby, *El caballero, la mujer y el cura* (Madrid: Taurus, 1992).

11 Art Cosgrove, ed. *Marriage in Ireland* (Dublin: College Press, 1985), 26.

12 Duby, *El caballero*, 20–1.

13 Luce Irigaray, *The Sex Which is Not One* (Ithaca, NY: Cornell University Press, 1985), 32.

14 Concepció Gil and Roser Soler. 'Família i condició social de la dona a la Catalunya moderna', *Més enllà del silenci*, Mary Nash, ed. (Barcelona: Generalitat de Catalunya, 1988), 108.

15 Duby, *El caballero*, 20.

16 Ann Owens Weekes, *Irish Women Writers: An Uncharted Tradition* (Lexington, KY: The University Press of Kentucky, 1990), 23.

17 Anne Charlon, *La condició de la dona en la narrativa femenina catalana (1900–1983)* (Barcelona: Edicions 62, 1990), 12.

18 Maria Lluïsa Julià. 'Les imatges de la dona en Víctor Català', *Actes de les primeres jornades d'estudi sobre la vida I l'obra de Caterina Albert i Paradís 'Víctor Català'*, Enric Prat and Pep Vila, eds, (Barcelona, Publicacions de l'Abadia de Montserrat, 1992), 259.

19 Weekes, *Irish Women Writers*, 214–15.
20 Ibid., 215.
21 Charlon, *La condició*, 39.
22 Irigaray, *The Sex Which is Not One*, 170. Divorce was legalised in Spain in 1980 and in Ireland in 1996. Needless to say there is still no tradition of divorce in either countries. In Spain, the average number of wives killed by their husbands is around 90 to 110 per year ('Mujeres maltratadas', *La Vanguardia*, 26 November 2000), and the number of women abused by their husbands is around 600,000 (Miguel Bayon 'El Instituto de la Mujer reconoce 600.000 malos tratos al año en España' *El País*, 7 November 2000).
23 André Gunder Frank, *Capitalism and Underdevelopment in Latin America: Historical Studies of Chile and Brazil* (New York: Monthly Review Press, 1967).
24 Ashcroft, *The Empire Writes Back*, 33.
25 Rodoreda, 'El parc de les magnòlies,' *Semblava de seda i altres contes* (Barcelona, Edicions 62, 1996), 115.
26 Rodoreda, 'Paral.lisi,' *Semblava de seda i altres contes* (Barcelona: Edicions 62, 1996), 89.
27 Maria-Josep Ragué-Àrias, 'L'amor sense braços', *I tornarà a florir la mimosa* (Barcelona: Edicions 62, 1984), 114.
28 Gil and Soler, *Família i condicío*, 103.
29 The aim here is to sketch the general case. One can conceive of exceptions, for example, the young widow who inherits substantial property.
30 Weekes, *Irish Women Writers*, 15.
31 Caterina Albert, 'Substitució', *La Mare-Balena* (Barcelona: Editorial Catalana, 1920).
32 As I pointed out in the introduction, it is not my intention to write about the specific case of Northern Ireland. However, perhaps it is relevant to mention here that marriage under Catholicism is indissoluble but Protestantism allows divorce.
33 Charlon, *La condició*, 114.
34 Montserrat Roig, 'Amor i cendres', *El cant de la joventut* (Barcelona: Edicions 62, 1989), 24.
35 Hayes, 'Wedding Bells', *Forecourt*, 153.
36 Edna O'Brien, 'Sister Imelda', *Returning* (London: Weidenfeld and Nicolson, 1982), 156.
37 Mary Beckett, 'The Master and the Bombs', *A Belfast Woman* (Dublin: Poolbeg, 1980), 76.
38 Beckett, 'Heaven', *A Literary Woman* (London: Bloomsbury, 1990), 115.
39 Beckett, 'A Farm of Land', *A Belfast Woman*, 32–9.
40 Irigaray, *The Sex Which is Not One*, 170–91.
41 Albert, 'La Pepa', *Vida mòlta* (Barcelona: Selecta, 1987), 15–160.
42 Beckett, 'Theresa', *A Belfast Woman*, 12–23.
43 Núria Pompeia 'Els Aparadors', *Cinc Cèntims* (Barcelona: Edicions 62, 1982), 27.
44 Gil and Soler, *Família i condició*, 104.
45 Isabel-Clara Simó, 'L'airet del mati a Barcelona', *Es quan miro que hi veig clar* (Barcelona: Selecta, 1979), 154.

46 Ibid., 165.

47 Eilís Ní Dhuibhne, 'Lili Marlene', *The Inland Ice and Other Stories* (Belfast: The Blackstaff Press, 1997), 90.

48 O'Brien, 'The Widow', *Lantern Slides* (London: Penguin, 1990).

49 Ibid., 39.

50 Ibid., 39.

51 Ibid., 42.

52 Ibid., 43.

53 Ibid., 43.

54 Carme Riera, 'Es nus, es buit', *Jo pos per testimoni les gavines* (Barcelona: Planeta, 1977), 79.

55 cf. O'Brien, 'The Creature', *A Scandalous Woman and Other Stories* (London: Penguin, 1976), 85.

56 Albert, 'La jove', *Vida mòlta*.

57 Rodoreda, 'Divendres 8 de juny', *Vint-i-dos contes* (Barcelona: Selecta, 1989).

58 Ibid., 193.

59 O'Brien, 'Savages', *Returning*, 102.

60 O'Brien, 'Dramas', *Lantern Slides*, 141.

61 Albert, 'Diàleg Prismàtic', *Jubileu* (Barcelona, Selecta, 1951).

62 Albert, 'Cendres', *Cendres i altres contes* (Barcelona: Tandem edicions, 1995), 89.

63 Ibid., 90.

64 Ibid.

65 Pompeia, 'L'ordre i el matrimoni', *Cinc Cèntims*, 69.

66 Toril Moi, *Sexual/Textual Politics: Feminist Literary Theory* (London: Routledge, 1994), 118.

67 Irigaray, *The Sex Which Is Not One*, 24.

68 Ibid., 186.

69 Ibid., 185.

70 Ibid., 25.

71 Riera, 'Un capvespre', *Jo pos per testimoni les gavines*, 65.

72 Rodoreda, 'Pluja', *Semblava de Seda i altres contes*.

73 O'Brien, 'Christmas Roses', *Mrs Reinhardt and Other Stories* (London: Penguin, 1988).

74 Ragué-Àrias, 'La sang del castell', 18.

75 Charlon, *La condició*, 144.

76 Julia O'Faolain, 'Man in the Cellar', *Man in the Cellar* (London: Faber and Faber, 1974), 22.

77 Angela Bourke, 'Mayonnaise to the Hills', *By Salt Water* (Dublin: New Island Books, 1996), 166–7.

78 Colm Tóibín, *Martyrs and Metaphors* (Dublin: The Raven Arts Press, 1987), 10.

79 Geraldine C. Nichols, *Escribir, espacio propio: Laforet, Matute, Moix, Tusquets, Riera y Roig por si mismas* (Minneapolis: Minnesota University Press, 1989), 179–80.

80 Charlon, *La condició*, 144.

81 O'Faolain, 'Man in the Cellar', 20.

82 Beckett, 'The Master', 80.
83 Ibid., 77.
84 Ibid., 80.
85 Ibid., 83.
86 Beckett, 'The Excursion', *A Belfast Woman*.
87 Ibid., 6.
88 Ibid., 7.
89 Ibid.
90 Ibid., 10.
91 Rodoreda, 'Abans de morir', *Vint-i-dos contes*.
92 Clare Boylan, 'That Bad Woman', *That Bad Woman* (London: Abacus, 1995), 72.
93 O'Brien, 'The Connor Girls', *Returning,* 20.
94 Ibid., 23.
95 Raymone Popot, 'Edna O'Brien's Paradise Lost', *The Irish Novel in Our Time*, Patrick Rafroide and Maurice Harmon, eds (Villeneuve d'Ascq: Publications de l'Universite de Lille, 1975–6), 271.
96 Simone De Beauvoir, *The Second Sex* (London: Jonathan Cape, 1972), 608.
97 Ashcroft, *The Empire Writes Back*, 164.
98 Simó, 'Alfonso', *Contes d'Isabel* (Barcelona: Columna, 1999), 147
99 Mary Dorcey, 'A Sense of Humour', *A Noise from the Woodshed* (London: Only Women Press, 1989), 37.
100 Ibid., 38–9.
101 Monica McWilliams, 'Women in Northern Ireland: An Overview', *Culture and Politics in Northern Ireland: 1960–1990,* Eamonn Hughes ed., (Buckingham: Open University Press, 1991), 84.
102 Brenda Murphy, 'A Social Call', *The Blackstaff Book of Short Stories* (Belfast: Blackstaff Press, 1988), 44.
103 Ibid.
104 Fiona Barr, 'Excursion', *Sisters* (Belfast: Blackstaff Press, 1980), 4.
105 Kate Cruise O'Brien, 'Losing', *Stories by Contemporary Irish Women,* Daniel J. Casey and Linda M. Casey, eds, (Syracuse: Syracuse University Press, 1990), 142.
106 Albert, *Vida mòlta,* 115. His words are full of mistakes to emphasise his ignorance.
107 Isabel-Clara Simó, *Bresca* (Barcelona: Edicions 62, 1997), 63.
108 Rodoreda, 'En el tren', *Vint-i-dos contes*, 251–7.
109 Rodoreda, 'Divendres 8 de juny'.
110 Albert, *Ombrívoles* (Barcelona: Ayma, 1949), 1–12.
111 Albert, *Drames rurals i Caires vius.* Fourth edn (Barcelona: Edicions 62, 1994), 28.
112 Albert, 'Despres de l'amor', *Jubileu,* 36–53.
113 Sandra Gilbert and Susan M. Gubar, *The Madwoman in the Attic: The Woman Writer and the Nineteenth-Century Literary Imagination.* 2nd edn (New Haven: Yale University Press, 1980), 78.
114 Ibid., 20.
115 Ibid., 21.
116 Ibid., 84.

117 Mary Beckett, 'Heaven'.

118 Ibid., 115.

119 Eilís Ní Dhuibhne, 'The Search for the Lost Husband', *The Inland Ice and Other Stories*, 261.

120 O'Faolain, 'Man in the Cellar', *Man in the Cellar*.

121 Ibid., 7.

122 Ibid., 22.

123 Ibid., 11.

124 Ibid., 22.

125 Hayes, 'Wedding Bells', 152.

126 Ibid., 148.

127 Ibid., 150.

128 Ibid., 152.

129 Ventura Gassol, *Les Tombes Flamejants. Poesies patriòtiques* (Barcelona: Galba, 1980), 73.

130 Albert, 'Carnestottes', *Drames rurals i Caires vius*.

131 Ibid., 313.

132 Dorcey, 'A Country Dance', *A Noise*, 55.

133 Dorcey, 'The Husband' *A Noise*, 76.

134 O'Brien, 'Sister Imelda', *Returning.*

135 Ibid., 151.

136 Ibid., 152.

137 Ibid., 139.

138 Riera, 'Te deix, amor, la mar com a penyora', *Te deix, amor, la mar com a penyora* (Barcelona: Planeta, 1994).

139 Ragué-Àrias 'Em recitaves poemes de Safo', *I tornarà a florir la mimosa* (Barcelona: Edicions 62, 1984).

140 Hayes, 'Getting Rid of Him', 89.

141 Riera, 'Quasi a la mancra de fulletous' *Jo pos*, 49–50.

142 Riera, 'Marc-Miquel', *Jo pos*, 71.

143 Clare Boylan, 'That Bad Woman', 77.

144 Ibid.

145 Hayes, 'Something Formal', *Forecourt*, 4.

146 Ibid., 141.

CHAPTER THREE

1 Mary Beckett, 'A Belfast Woman', *A Belfast Woman* (Dublin: Poolbeg, 1980), 89.

2 Isabel-Clara Simó, 'L'airet del matí, a Barcelona', *És quan miro que hi veig clar* (Barcelona: Selecta, 1979), 168.

3 Ashcroft *et al*, *The Empire Writes Back: Theory and Practice in Post-Colonial Literature* (London: Routledge, 1995).

4 Hélène Cixous, 'The Laugh of the Medusa', *Feminisms: An Anthology of Literary Theory and Criticism*, Robyn R. Warhol, Diane Pricew Herndl, (New Brunswick: Rutgers University Press, 1993), 336.

5   Noel Ignatiev, *How the Irish Became White* (London: Routledge,1995).

6   Ailbhe Smyth, 'Declining identities', *Critical Survey. Anglo-Irish Studies: New Developments* 8 (1996), 148.

7   Víctor Alexandre, *No sóc espanyol* (Barcelona: Proa, 2000). It is astonishing yet predictable that of the twenty interviews only three were with women.

8   Declan Kiberd, *Inventing Ireland* (London: Jonathan Cape, 1995), 9.

9   Francesc Ferrer i Gironès, *Catalanofòbia: El pensament anticatalà a través de la història* (Barcelona: Edicions 62, 2000).

10   Ashcroft, *The Empire Writes Back*, 167.

11   Ibid., 168.

12   Ailbhe Smyth, 'The Floozie in the Jacuzzi', *The Irish Review* 6 (1989), 20.

13   Gener Pompeyo, 'De la mujer y sus derechos en las sociedades modernas', *La Vanguardia*, 26 Feb. 1889. Mary Nash, *Rojas: Las mujeres republicanas en la Guerra Civil* (Barcelona: Taurus, 1999), 42.

14   Edna O'Brien, 'Honeymoon', *A Scandalous Woman and Other Stories* (London: Penguin, 1976), 95–6.

15   Geraldine Moane, 'Legacies of Colonialism for Irish Women. Oppressive or Empowering?' *Irish Journal of Feminist Studies* 1, March 1996, 115.

16   Seamus Heaney, *North* (London: Faber and Faber, 1978), 49–50.

17   Ashis Nandy, *The Intimate Enemy: Loss and Recovery of Self Under Colonialism* (Delhi: Oxford University Press, 1983), 4.

18   Ibid., 3.

19   Medbh McGuckian, 'An Attitude of Compassions', *Irish Literary Supplement* 9, 2 (1990), 1.

20   Albert Memmi, *The Colonizer and the Colonized* (London: Earthscan Publications, 1990), 152.

21   Ibid., 153.

22   Maria Mercè Marçal, 'Joc de màscares', *Dones soles* (Barcelona: Planeta, 1995), 81–2, 86.

23   Mercè Rodoreda, 'Abans de morir', *Vint-i-dos contes* (Barcelona: Selecta, 1989), 268.

24   Ibid., 288.

25   Simó, *'L'airet'*.

26   Anne Devlin, 'Naming the Names', *The Way-Paver* (London: Faber and Faber, 1986) 116.

27   Medbh McGuckian, 'An Attitude of Compassions', 1.

28   Toril Moi, *Sexual/Textual Politics: Feminist Literary Theory* (London: Routledge, 1994).

29   Anne Charlon, *La condició de la dona en la narrative feminina catalana (1900–1983)* (Barcelona: Edicions 62, 1990), 214.

30   Anne Charlon, *La condició*, 12. Moreover, since many barriers have been placed in the way of women's participation in politics, so their interest in nationalism has been 'at a distance'.

31   There is, for instance, already some evidence of this in the Irish case: Margaret Ward, *Unmanageable Revolutionaries: Women and Irish Nationalism* (London: Pluto Press, 1995); Ailbhe Smyth, 'Paying Our Disrespects to the Bloody States We're In: Women, Violence, Culture, and the State', *Irish*

Women's Voices: Past and Present, Joan Hoff and Moureen Coulter, eds (Bloomington, IN: Indiana University Press 1995); Carol Coulter, *The Hidden Tradition: Feminism, Women and Nationalism in Ireland* (Cork: Cork University Press, 1993); C. L. Innes, *Woman and Nation in Irish Literature and Society 1880–1935* (New York: Harvester Wheatsheaf, 1993); Gerardine Meaney, 'Sex and Nation: Women in Irish Culture and Politics, *Irish Women's Studies Reader,* Ailbhe Smyth, ed. (Dublin Attic Press, 1993). It should be noted that women's history and women's studies more generally are in their infancy in Catalonia. See Mary Nash, ed., 'Introduction', *Més enllà del silenci* (Barcelona: Generalitat de Catalunya, 1988), 3.

32   Coulter, *The Hidden Tradition*, 3.

33   This is not the impression one forms from R.F. Foster's *Modern Ireland, 1600–1972* (London: Allen Lane, 1989). Joseph Lee in *The Modernisation of Irish Society, 1848–1918* (Dublin: Gill and Macmillan, 1979), shows how women were organised and used briefly during the Land War of 1879–82, and then quickly sidelined.

34   Ward *Unmanageable Revolutionaries*, 2.

35   Ibid.

36   Ibid., 3.

37   Coulter, *The Hidden Tradition*, 3.

38   Ibid., 25.

39   Ailbhe Smyth, 'Ireland', *Bloomsbury Guide to Women's Literature*, Claire Buck ed. (London: Bloomsbury, 1992), 40.

40   Ibid., 155.

41   Rebecca Pelan, *The Contexts and (Dis)contents of Contemporary Irish Women's Fiction*. PHD, University of Queensland, 1995, 134.

42   Eavan Boland, *Object Lessons: The Life of the Woman and the Poet in Our Time* (Manchester: Carcanet Press, 1995), 65–6.

43   Angela Bourke, 'Mayonnaise to the Hills', *By Salt Water* (Dublin: New Island Books, 1996), 166.

44   Gerardine Meaney, 'Sex and Nation', 230–44.

45   Edna O'Brien, 'Irish Revel', *The Love Object* (London: Penguin, 1970), 113.

46   James Joyce, 'The Dead', *Dubliners* (London: Secker and Warburg, 1994), 157.

47   O'Brien, 'Irish Revel', 91.

48   Rebecca Pelan, 'Edna O'Brien's "World of Nora Bernacle"', *The Canadian Journal of Irish Studies* 22, 2 (December 1996), 57.

49   Ibid., 56.

50   C.L Innes, *Woman and Nation in Irish Literature and Society*, 2.

51   Ibid., 18.

52   Ailbhe Smyth, 'States of Change: Reflections on Ireland in Several Uncertain Parts', *Feminist Review* (Summer 1995), 36.

53   Meaney, 'Sex and Nation', 233.

54   Ailbhe Smyth, 'Paying Our Disrespects'.

55   Edna Longley, *From Cathleen to Anorexia: The Breakdown of Irelands* (Dublin: Attic Press, 1990), 9.

56   Mary Dorcey, 'Mary Dorcey Talks to Nuala Archer: "The Spaces Between the Words"', *The Women's Review of Books* December (1990).

57 Longley, *From Cathleen to Anorexia*, 8.
58 Ibid., 9.
59 Ibid., 15.
60 Ibid., 23.
61 Eilís Ní Dhuibhne, 'The Flowering', *Eating Women Is Not Recommended* (Dublin: Attic Press, 1991), 10.
62 Eilís Ní Dhuibhne, 'Love, Hate and Friendship', *The Inland Ice and Other Stories* (Belfast: The Blackstaff Press, 1997), 36–7.
63 Ibid., 37.
64 Ibid., 41.
65 Ibid., 42.
66 Julia O'Faolain, 'It's A Long Way To Tipperary', *We Might See Sights* (London: Faber and Faber, 1968), 65.
67 Ibid., 71.
68 Ibid., 70.
69 Ibid., 71.
70 Ibid., 70.
71 Ibid., 75.
72 Ibid., 71.
73 Ibid., 72.
74 Ibid., 73.
75 Ibid., 75.
76 Ibid., 81.
77 Edna O'Brien, 'Epitaph', *Lantern Slides* (London: Penguin, 1990), 62.
78 Maeve Kelly, *A Life of Her Own* (Dublin: Poolbeg, 1976), 144.
79 Ibid., 144–5.
80 Ibid., 147.
81 Ibid., 144.
82 Ibid., 148.
83 Mary Beckett, 'A Belfast Woman', 84.
84 Ibid.
85 Ibid., 86.
86 Ibid., 97.
87 Ibid., 87.
88 Ibid., 87–88.
89 Ibid., 98–99.
90 Ibid., 93.
91 Ibid., 98
92 Fiona Barr, 'The Wall Reader', *The Wall Reader and Other Stories* (Dublin: Arlen House, 1979), 6.
93 Ibid., 7.
94 Ibid., 8.
95 Ibid., 10.
96 Ibid., 12.
97 Ibid., 3.
98 Ibid., 11.
99 Ibid., 10.

100 Ibid., 1.

101 Ibid., 2.

102 Ibid., 8.

103 Edna O'Brien, 'The Connor Girls', *Returning* (London: Penguin, 1983), 12.

104 Ibid., 9.

105 Ibid.

106 Ibid., 10.

107 Ibid., 12.

108 Ibid., 10.

109 Ibid.

110 Ibid., 11.

111 Ibid., 14.

112 Ibid., 20.

113 Ibid., 21.

114 Joaquim Rubió i Ors, Jacint Verdaguer, Àngel Guimerà, Antoni de Bofarull, Víctor Balaguer, Frederic Soler.

115 Lluïsa Julià, 'Òrfenes i desemparades', 'Quadern', *El País*, 25 March 1993, 8.

116 Cristina Dupláa, 'Les dones i el pensament conservador català contemporani', *Més enllà del silenci,* Mary Nash ed. (Barcelona: Generalitat de Catalunya, 1988), 185.

117 Ibid.

118 Kathleen McNerney and Cristina Enriquez de Salamanca, eds, *Double Minorities of Spain A Bio-Bibliographic Guide to Women Writers of the Catalan, Galician, and Basque Countries* (New York: Modern Language Association of America, 1994), 7.

119 Coulter, *The Hidden Tradition*, 10.

120 Dupláa 'Les dones', 187.

121 Ibid., 176.

122 Mary Nash, 'Política, condició social i mobilització femenina: les dones a la Segona República i a la Guerra Civil', *Més enllà del silenci*, (Barcelona: Genralitat de Catalunya, 1988), 243.

123 Ibid., 248.

124 Ibid., 262.

125 Charlon, *La condició*, 105.

126 Xavier Febres, ed., *Diàlegs a Barcelona: Isabel-Clara Simó i Montserrat Roig* (Barcelona: Laia, 1985), 8.

127 Fiona Barr, Barbara Haycock Walsh and Stella Mahon, *Sisters* (Belfast: Blackstaff Press, 1980), 25–34.

128 Febres, *Diàlegs a Barcelona*, 24.

129 Ibid., 32.

130 Ibid., 49.

131 Ibid., 102.

132 Ibid., 103.

133 Charlon, *La condició*, 215–16. For example, Montserrat Roig's 'La Divisió' in *El cant de la joventut*. The main character is called Aloma, like the one in Rodoreda's most famous novel.

134 For example, Maria Mercè Marçal's 'Joc de Màscares' is a new version of Carme Riera's 'Te deix, amor, la mar com a penyora'.

135 Caterina Albert, *Drames Rurals i Caires vius,* 4th edn (Barcelona: Edicions 62, 1994), 183.

136 Mercè Rodoreda, 'Viatge al poble dels guerrers', *Viatges i Flors* (Barcelona: Edicions 62, 1990), 7.

137 Ibid.

138 Margarida Casacuberta, 'Sobre viatges i flors de Mercè Rodoreda', *Actes del I Simposi* (Barcelona: Publications de l'Abadia de Montserrat, 1998), 377.

139 Simó, 'L'airet', 168–9.

140 Maria Àngels Anglada, *La daurada parmelia i altres contes* (Barcelona: Columna, 1991) 12.

141 Ibid., 18.

142 Rodoreda, 'Viatge al poble del guerrers', 15.

CHAPTER FOUR

1 Mercè Rodoreda, 'La salamandra', *La meva Cristina i altres contes* (Barcelona: Edicions 62, 1974), 104.

2 Anne Enright, '(She Owns) Everything', *The Portable Virgin* (London: Minerva, 1992), 3.

3 I can speak of my own experience. When I was a child at school, not only did we not study our own language but using it was associated with powerlessness.

4 Bill Ashcroft, Gareth Griffiths and Helen Tiffin, *The Empire Writes Back: Theory and Practice in Post-colonial Literatures* (London: Routledge, 1989), 7.

5 Ngugi wa Thiong'o, *Decolonising the Mind: The Politics of Language in African Literature* (London: James Currey, 1986), 16.

6 Ashcroft, *The Empire Writes Back*, 167–8.

7 Thomas Davis, *Selections from his Prose and Poetry* (London: Gresham Publishing Co., 1910), 174.

8 Albert Memmi, *The Colonizer and the Colonized* (London: Earthscan Publications, 1990), 186.

9 Ibid., 187.

10 Ferrer i Gironès, *Catalanofòbia: El pensament anticatalà a través de la història* (Barcelona: Edicions 62, 2000), 23.

11 Víctor Alexandre, *Jo no sóc espanyol* (Barcelona: Proa, 2000). 226.

12 Gearóid Ó Tuathaigh, 'Decolonisation, Identity and State-Formation: The Irish Experience', *Culture and Power: Institutions*, Rosa González ed. (Barcelona: Pomociones y Publicaciones Universitarias, 1996), 30.

13 Ashcroft, *The Empire Writes Back*, 175.

14 Toril Moi, *Sexual/Textual Politics: Feminist Literary Theory* (London: Routledge, 1994), 111.

15 James Joyce, *A Portrait of the Artist as a Young Man* (Harmondsworth: Penguin, 1960), 189.

16 Montserrat Roig, *Digues que m'estimes encara que sigui mentida* (Barcelona: Edicions 62, 1991), 35.

17 Ibid., 35.

18 Alexandre, *Jo no sóc espanyol*, 172.

19 Julia Kristeva, 'Women's Time', *The Feminist Reader: Essays in Gender and the Politics of Literary Criticism*, Catherine Belsey and Jane Moore, eds (London: Macmillan, 1997), 210.

20 Ann Rosalind Jones, 'Writing the Body: Toward an Understanding of *l'Ecriture Feminine*', *Feminisms: An Anthology of Literary Theory and Criticism*, Robyn R. Warhol and Diane Price Herndl, eds (New Brunswick: Rutgers University Press, 1993), 357–8.

21 Toril Moi, *Sexual/Textual Politics*, 158–9.

22 Eilís Ní Dhuibhne, 'The Inland Ice', *The Inland Ice and Other Stories* (Belfast: The Blackstaff Press, 1997), 217.

23 Ní Dhuibhne, 'The Shapeshifters', *Eating Women Is Not Recommended* (Dublin: Attic Press, 1991), 112.

24 Mar has two meanings in Catalan: a woman's name and sea.

25 Montserrat Roig, 'Mar', *El cant de la joventut* (Barcelona: Edicions 62, 1989), 48.

26 Roig, 'Mar', 58.

27 Richard Kearney, ed., *The Irish Mind: Exploring Intellectual Traditions* (Dublin: Wolfhound Press, 1985–7), 11.

28 Toni Morrison, 'Interview with Toni Morrison "Voice of America"' *The Irish Times,* 28 March 1998: 16.

29 Mary Dorcey, 'Mary Dorcey Talks to Nuala Archer: "The Spaces Between the Words"', *The Women's Review of Books,* December 1990, 18.

30 Dorcey, 'Mary Dorcey Talks', 15.

31 Marta Nadal, *Vint escriptores catalans* (Barcelona: Publications de l'Abadia de Montserrat, 1997), 127.

32 Ailbhe Smyth, ed., *Wildish Things: An Anthology of New Irish Women's Writing* (Dublin: Attic Press, 1989), 12.

33 Luce Irigaray, *The Sex Which is Not One* (Ithaca, NY: Cornell University Press, 1985), 132.

34 Thus in 1841, according to the census of population of Ireland, 37% of men could read and write while only 19% of women claimed to have these skills. By 1911 this basic literacy gap had substantially disappeared, the ratios being 81% and 76% respectively. Of course, higher education was still monopolised by males. For Catalonia we have statistics compiled on a different basis, but they tell essentially the same story. In 1855 some 73% of boys were registered in primary schools while only 27% of girls of the same age group were so registered. By the 1930s there was still an advantage in favour of boys but the gender gap had narrowed greatly. However, at university level in Catalonia in the early twentieth century, 94% of students were male while women made up only 6%. See Rosa M. Capel Martínez, *El trabajo y la educación de la mujer en España* (Madrid: Ministerio de Cultura, 1986).

35 Mary Dorcey, 'Mary Dorcey Talks', 15.

36 Ibid., 16.

37 Ibid.

38 There are only a few exceptions: Ana Maria Moix and Ester Tusquets write only in Spanish.

39 Clare-Mar Molinero, 'The Politics of Language: Spain's Minority Languages', Helen Graham and Jo Labanyi, eds, *Spanish Cultural Studies: An Introduction: The Struggle for Modernity* (Oxford: Oxford University Press, 1995), 337.

40 Josep-Anton Fernández, 'Becoming Normal: Cultural Production and Cultural Policy in Catalonia', in Graham and Labanyi, *Spanish Cultural Studies*, 342.

41 Carme Arnau, *Introducció a la narrativa de Mercè Rodoreda: El mite de la infantesa* (Barcelona: Edicions 62, 1982), 12.

42 Fernández, 'Becoming normal', 343.

43 Ibid., 345.

44 Catalan people have traditionally been sensitive to minority languages. Among the Catalans who participated in the colonisation and evangelisation of America, a number wrote grammars of the native languages. Prócoro Hernández, *Els catalans al món indígena* (Barcelona: Generalitat de Catalunya, 1991), 76.

45 Montserrat Roig, *Digues que m'estimes encara que sigui mentida* (Barcelona: Edicions 62, 1991), 38.

46 *Diccionari General de la Llengua Catalana* is the first dictionary of the Catalan language published and still the most prestigious.

47 A second contemporary Catalan writer, Palmira Ventós, used a male pseudonym, that of 'Felip Palma'.

48 Anne Charlon, *La condició de la dona en la narrativa femenina catalana 1900–1983* (Barcelona: Edicions 62, 1990), 216.

49 Xavier Febrers, ed., *Diàlegs a Barcelona: Isabel-Clara Simó i Monserrat Roig* (Barcelona: Laia, 1985), 63.

50 Charlon, *La condició*, 12.

51 Marta Cièrcoles, 'Drets d'autora', *Avui*, 23 April 1998, 18.

52 Kathleen McNerney and Cristina Enríquez de Salamanca, eds. *Double Minorities of Spain: A Bio-bibliographic Guide to Women Writers of the Catalan, Galician and Basque Countries* (New York: Modern Language Association of America, 1994), 7.

53 Rodoreda, 'La salamandra', 98–9.

54 Jean Chevalier and Alain Gheerbrant, *A Dictionary of Symbols*, trans. John Buchanan-Brown (London, Penguin, 1996), 821.

55 Jack Residder, *The Hutchinson Dictionary of Symbols* (Oxford: Helicon, 1997), 175.

56 Rodoreda, 'La salamandra', 100.

57 Carme Gregori, 'Metamorfosi i altres prodigis' *Actes del I simposi internacional de narrativa breu Vincent Alonso, et al., eds,*(Barcelona: Publications de l'Abadia de Montserrat, 1998), 297.

58 Rodoreda, 'La salamandra', 104.

59 Gregori, 'Metamorfosi', 288.

60 Emilie Bergmann, 'Flowers at the North Pole: Mercè Rodoreda and the Female Imagination in exile', *Catalan Review: International Journal for Catalan Culture,* December 1987, 85.

61 Rodoreda, 'En el tren', *Vint-i-dos contes* (Barcelona: Editorial Selecta, 1989), 251.

62 Rodoreda, 'L'elefant', *La meva Cristina i altres contes*, 82.

63 Imma Monsó, 'Neu al cervell', *Si és no és* (Taragona: El Mèdol, 1997), 10.

64 Ibid.

65 Ibid., 11.

66 Ibid., 12.

67 Ibid.

68 Ibid., 21.

69 Maria Mercè Marçal, 'Joc de màscares', *Donas solles* (Barcelona: Planeta, 1995), 84.

70 Ibid., 92.

71 Charlon, *La condició*, 208.

72 Maria Aurèlia Capmany, 'El temps passa sobre un mirall', *Coses i noses* (Barcelona: La Magrana, 1980), 163–71.

73 Caterina Albert', 'La jove', *Vida mòlta* (Barcelona: Selecta, 1987).

74 Ibid., 23.

75 Simó, 'L'airet del matí, a Barcelona', *És quan miro que hi veig clar* (Barcelona: Selecta, 1979), 158.

76 Rodoreda 'Flor Fossil', *Viatges i Flors* (Barcelona: Edicions 62 1982), 127.

77 Isabel Olesti, *Dibuix de dona amb ocells blancs* (Barcelona: Destino, 1995).

78 Ó Tuathaigh, 'Decolonization, Identity and State-Formation', 30.

79 Michele Dowling, '"The Ireland that I would have." de Valera and the creation of an Irish national image', *History of Ireland 5* (Summer 1997), 38.

80 Líam Kennedy, *Colonialism, Religion and Nationalism in Ireland* (Belfast: The Institute of Irish Studies, 1996), 206.

81 Ó Tuathaigh, 'Decolonisation, Identity and State-Formation', 40.

82 Richard Kearney, ed., *The Irish Mind*, 12.

83 Maeve Kelly, 'The Sentimentalist', *The Blackstaff Book of Short Stories*, Éilís Ní Dhuibhne, 144.

84 Ibid., 148.

85 Ibid., 144.

86 Ibid., 145.

87 Ibid.

88 Ann Owens Weekes, *Unveiling Treasures: The Attic Guide to the Published Works of Irish Women Literary Writers: Drama, Fiction, Poetry* (Dublin: Attic Press, 1993), 253.

89 Eilís Ní Dhuibhne, 'The Flowering', *Eating Women is not Recommended* (Dublin: Attic Press, 1991), 11. This might be usefully compared with ideas and sentiments present in Brian Friel's work, in particular *Making History* and *Translations*.

90 O'Brien, 'The Connor Girls', *Returning* (London: Weidenfeld and Nicholson, 1982). 9.

91 Anne Enright, '(She Owns) Everything', 3.

92 Ibid., 6.

93 Ibid., 7.

94 Enright, 'Revenge', *The Portable Virgin*, 38.

95 Enright, 'The House of the Architect's Love Story', *The Portable Virgin*, 58.

96 Katy Hayes, 'War', *Forecourt* (Dublin: Poolbeg, 1995), 8.

97 Hayes, 'Something Formal', *Forecourt*, 139.

98 Angela Bourke, 'Ohio by the Ocean', *By Salt Water* (Dublin: New Island Books, 1996), 156.

99 Ibid., 166–7.

100 Medbh McGuckian, 'An Attitude of Compassions' Q&A with Medbh McGuckian, Interview with Kathleen McCracken, *Irish Literary Supplement* 9, 2 (1990), 20–1.

101 Moi, *Sexual/Textual Politics*, 145.

102 O'Brien, 'Paradise', *The Love Object*, 132.

103 Mary Dorcey, 'Flowers for Easter' *A Noise from the Woodshed* (London: Only Women Press, 1989), 112.

104 Ibid., 120.

105 Ameh Devlin, 'Naming the Names', *The Way-Paver*, (London: Faber and Faber), 105.

106 Moi, *Sexual/Textual Politics*, 158.

107 Devlin, 'Naming the Names', 95.

108 Ibid.

109 Ibid., 103.

110 Ibid.

111 Ashcroft, *The Empire Writes Back*, 183.

112 Devlin, 'Naming the Names', 117.

113 Ibid., 119.

CHAPTER FIVE

1 Katy Hayes, 'Wedding Bells,' *Forecourt* (Dublin: Poolbeg, 1995), 156.

2 Declan Kiberd, *Inventing Ireland* (London: Jonathan Cape 1995), 6.

3 R. Ford, *The Granta Book of the American Short Story* (London: Granta Books, 1992), xvii.

4 Marta Nadal, *Vint escriptors catalans* (Barcelona: Publicacions de l'Abadia de Montserrat, 1997), 14.

5 Eilís Ní Dhuibhne, 'The Search for the Lost Husband', *The Inland Ice and Other Stories* (Belfast: The Blackstaff Press, 1997), 262.

6 How Ulster unionist women might relate to, or dissent from, this statement would itself contitute an interesting point of departure for some further research.

7 Peter Barry, *Beginning Theory: An Introduction to Literary and Cultural Theory* (Manchester: Manchester University Press, 1995), 195.

8 Ibid., 123.

9 Geraldine Moane, 'Legacies of Colonialism for Irish Women: Oppressive or Empowering?', *Irish Journal of Feminist Studies,* March 1996, 2.

10 Ibid., 2.

11 Montserrat Roig, *Molta roba i poc sabó* (Barcelona: Edicions 62, 1995), 10.

12 Edna O'Brien, 'The Connor Girls', *Returning* (London: Weidenfeld and Nicolson, 1982), 9.

13 Geraldine Nichols, *Escribir espacio propio. Laforet, Matute, Moix, Tusquets, Riera, y Roig por si mismas* (Minneapolis: Minnesota University Press, 1989), 109.

14 Eilís Ní Dhuibhne, *'The Inland Ice' and Other Stories* (Belfast: The Blackstaff Press, 1997), 186.

15 Ibid., 188.

16 Hayes, 'Something Formal', *Forecourt*, 139.

17 Hayes, 'Getting Rid of Him', *Forecourt*, 89.

18 Clare Boylan, 'That Bad Woman', *That Bad Woman* (London: Abacus, 1995), 70.

19 Maria Mercè Marçal, 'Joc de màscares', *Dones Soles* (Barcelona: Planeta, 1995), 84.

20 The change women went through in Catalonia in the 1970s and 1980s has been massive. There was a great willingness to break from a fascist ideology which had imprisoned them in the household in Spanish society and which had isolated them from Europe for forty years. But we must not forget the huge obstacles faced by earlier generations of women, including women writers. The life span of some of these writers was untypically short. As Montserrat Roig says in 'Mar', 'The time was too short to realise I could live in a different way, that it wasn't impossible' (88). Helena Valentí, Montserrat Roig, Maria Aurèlia Capmany and Maria Mercè Marçal died of cancer, many at a young age. One might speculate – it is no more than speculation – that the struggles and the stress they experienced, including bouts of depression, contributed to this reduced life expectancy.

21 Colin Graham, '"Liminal Spaces"': Postcolonial Theories and Irish Culture', *The Irish Review*, Autumn/Winter 1994, 39.

22 Líam Kennedy, 'Modern Ireland: Post-colonial Society of Post-colonial Pretensions', *Colonialism, Religion and Nationalism in Ireland* (Belfast: The Institute of Irish Studies: The Queen's University of Belfast, 1996).

23 This would of course be disputed by orthodox economic historians such as L.M. Cullen. See his standard textbook, *An Economic History of Ireland Since 1660* (London: Batsford, 1972).

24 Terry Eagleton, Fredric Jameson and Edward Said, *Nationalism, Colonialism and Literature* (Minneapolis: University of Minnesota Press, 1990), 69–95.

25 Ibid., 43–68.

26 Barry, *Beginning Theory*, 193.

27 Graham, 'Liminal Spaces', 40.

28 Stephen Howe, 'The Empire Strikes Back', *New Stateman and Society*, 25 Sept. 1992, 36.

29 Moi, *Sexual/Textual Politics*, 164.

APPENDIX

1 Kathleen McNerney and Cristina Enriquez de Salamanca, eds. *Double Minorities of Spain: A Bio-Bibliographic Guide to Women Writers of the Catalan, Galician, and Basque Countries* (New York: Modern Language Association of America, 1994), 32.

Bibliography

PRIMARY BIBLIOGRAPHY

Irish Short Stories

Barr, Fiona, Barbara Haycock Walsh and Stella Mahon. *Sisters*. Belfast: The Blackstaff Press, 1980.

Barr, Fiona *et al*. *The Wall Reader and Other Stories*. Dublin: Arlen House, 1979.

Beckett, Mary. *A Belfast Woman*. Dublin: Poolbeg,1980.

—. *A Literary Woman*. London: Bloomsbury, 1990.

Bourke, Angela. *By Salt Water*. Dublin: New Island Books, 1996.

Boylan, Clare. *That Bad Woman*. London: Abacus, 1995.

Devlin, Anne. *The Way-Paver*. London: Faber and Faber, 1986.

Dorcey, Mary. *A Noise from the Woodshed*. London: Only Women Press, 1989.

Enright, Anne. *The Portable Virgin*. London: Minerva, 1992.

Hayes, Katy. *Forecourt*. Dublin: Poolbeg, 1995.

Murphy, Brenda. 'A Social Call', *The Blackstaff Book of Short Stories*. Belfast: Blackstaff Press, 1988.

Ní Dhuibhne, Eilís. *Eating Women Is Not Recommended*. Dublin: Attic Press, 1991.

—. *The Inland Ice and Other Stories*. Belfast: The Blackstaff Press, 1997.

Ní Dhuibhne, Eilís *et al*. *The Blackstaff Book of Short Stories*. Belfast: The Blackstaff Press, 1988.

O'Brien, Edna. *The Love Object*. London: Penguin, 1970.

—. *A Scandalous Woman and Other Stories*. London: Penguin, 1976.

—. *Mrs Reinhardt and Other Stories*. London: Penguin, 1988.

—. *Lantern Slides*. London: Penguin, 1990.

—. *Returning*. London: Weidenfeld and Nicolson, 1982.

O'Faolain, Julia. *Man in the Cellar*. London: Faber and Faber, 1974.

—. *We Might See Sights*. London: Faber and Faber, 1968.

Catalan Short Stories

Albert, Caterina. *La Mare-Balena*. Barcelona: Editorial Catalana, 1920.

—. *Ombrívoles*. Barcelona: Ayma, 1949.

—. *Jubileu*. Barcelona: Selecta, 1951.

—. *Vida mòlta*. Barcelona: Selecta, 1987.

—. *Drames rurals i Caires vius*. Fourth edn, Barcelona: Edicions 62, 1994.

—. *Cendres i altres contes*. Barcelona: Tandem, 1995.

Anglada, Maria Àngels. *La daurada parmelià i altres contes*. Barcelona: Columna, 1991.

Marçal, Maria Mercè. 'Divisa', *Cau de llunes*. Barcelona: Selecta, 1976.

—. 'Joc de màscares' *Dones soles,* Barcelona: Planeta, 1995.

Monsó, Imma. *Si és no és,* Tarragona: El Mèdol, 1997.

Olesti, Isabel. *Dibuix de dona amb ocells blancs.* Barcelona: Destino, 1995.

Pompeia, Núria. *Cinc Cèntims.* Barcelona: Edicions 62, 1982.

Ragué-Àrias, Maria-Josep', *I tornarà a florir la mimosa.* Barcelona: Edicions 62, 1984.

Riera, Carme. *Jo pos per testimoni les gavines.* Barcelona: Planeta, 1977.

—. *Te deix, amor, la mar com a penyora.* Barcelona: Planeta, 1994.

Rodoreda, Mercè. *La meva Cristina i altres contes.* Barcelona: Edicions 62, 1974.

—. *Vint-i-dos contes.* Barcelona: Selecta, 1989.

—. *Viatges i flors.* Barcelona: Edicions 62, 1990.

—, *Semblava de seda i altres contes.* Barcelona: Edicions 62, 1996.

Roig, Montserrat. *El cant la joventut.* Barcelona Edicions 62, 1989.

—. *Molta roba I poc sabó.* Barcelona: Edicions 62, 1995.

Simó, Isabel-Clara. *És quan miro que hi veig clar.* Barcelona: Selecta, 1979.

—. *Bresca.* Barcelona: Edicions 62, 1997.

— 'Alfonso', *Contes d'Isabel.* Barcelona: Columna, 1999.

SECONDARY BIBLIOGRAPHY

Irish Critical Studies

Allen, Walter. *The Short Story in English.* Oxford: Clarendon Press, 1981.

Anderson, Benedict. *Imagined Communities: Reflections on the Origin and Spread of Nationalism.* London: Verso, 1991.

Ashcroft, Bill, Gareth Griffiths and Helen Tiffin. *The Empire Writes Back: Theory and Practice in Post-Colonial Literatures.* London: Routledge, 1989.

—. *The Post-colonial Studies Reader.* London: Routledge, 1995.

Averill, Deborah M. ed. *The Irish Short Story from George Moore to Frank O'Connor.* Lanham, MD: University Press of America, 1982.

Barry, Peter. *Beginning Theory: An Introduction to Literary and Cultural Theory.* Manchester: Manchester University Press, 1995.

Bates, H.E. *The Modern Short Story.* London: Michael Joseph, 1972.

Boland, Eavan. *A Kind of Scar: The Woman Poet in a National Tradition.* Dublin: Attic Press, 1989.

—. *Object Lessons: The Life of the Woman and the Poet in Our Time.* Manchester: Carcanet Press, 1995.

Bolger, Dermot, ed. *The Picador Book of Irish Contemporary Fiction.* London: Picador, 1992.

Boyle Haberstroh, Patricia. 'Literary Politics: Mainstream and Margin'. *The Canadian Journal of Irish Studies,* 18, 1, July 1992, 181–91.

Brown, Terence. *Ireland: A Social and Cultural History 1922–1985.* London: Fontana Press, 1985.

Buck, Claire, ed. *Bloomsbury Guide to Women's Literature.* London: Bloomsbury, 1992.

Carlson, Julia. *Banned in Ireland. Censorship and the Irish Writer.* London: Routledge, 1990.

Casey, Daniel J. and Linda M. Casey. eds, 'Introduction'. *Stories by Contemporary Irish Women*. Syracuse: Syracuse University Press, 1990.

Chevalier, Jean and Alain Gheerbrant, eds. *A Dictionary of Symbols*. Trans. John Buchanan-Brown. London: Penguin, 1996.

Cixous, Hélène. 'The Laugh of the Medusa', *Feminisms: An Anthology of Literary Theory and Criticsm*. Robyn R. Warhol and Diane Price Herndl, eds. New Brunswick: Rutgers University Press, 1993, 334–49.

Cosgrove, Art, ed. *Marriage in Ireland*. Dublin: College Press, 1985.

Coulter, Carol. *The Hidden Tradition: Feminism, Women and Nationalism in Ireland*. Cork: Cork University Press, 1993.

Davis, Thomas. *Selections from his Prose and Poetry*. London: Gresham Publishing Co., 1910.

De Beauvoir, Simone. *The Second Sex*. Trans. H.M. Parshley. London: Jonathan Cape, 1972.

De Salvo, Louise, Kathleen Walsh D'Arcy and Kathleen Hogan. *Territories of the Voice: Contemporary Stories by Irish Women Writers*. London: Virago, 1990.

Donovan, Katie. *Irish Women Writers Marginalised by Whom? Letters From the New Island*. Dublin: The Raven Arts Press, 1988.

Dorcey, Mary. 'Mary Dorcey Talks to Nuala Archer: 'The Spaces Between the Words', *Women's Review of Books*, December 1990, 17–20.

Dowling, Michele. '"The Ireland that I would have": de Valera and the creation of an Irish national image'. *History of Ireland 5*, Summer 1997.

Duby, George. *El caballero, la mujer y el cura*. Madrid: Taurus, 1992.

Eagleton, Terry, Fredric Jameson and Edward Said. *Nationalism, Colonialism and Literature*. Minnesota, University of Minnesota Press, 1990.

Ford, R. *The Granta Book of the American Short Story*. London: Granta Books, 1992.

Foster, John Wilson. 'Who Are the Irish?', *Colonial Consequences: Essays on Irish Literature and Culture*. Dublin: The Lilliput Press, 1991, 245–60.

—. 'Irish Fiction 1965–1990', *Field Day Anthology of Irish Writing*. Seamus Deane, ed. Vol. 3. Derry: Faber and Faber, 1992, 937–43.

Foster, R. F. *Modern Ireland, 1600–1972* London: Allen Lane, 1989.

Gilbert, Sandra M. and Susan Gubar. *The Madwoman in the Attic: The Woman Writer and the Nineteenth-Century Literary Imagination*. 2nd edn, New Haven: Yale University Press, 1980.

Gordimer, Nadine. 'The Flash of Fireflies', *The Story and its Writer: An Introduction to Short Fiction*. Ann Charters ed. Boston: Bedford Books of St. Martin's Press, 1995, 778–81.

Graham, Colin. '"Liminal Spaces": Post-Colonial Theories and Irish Culture, *The Irish Review 16*, 1994, 29–43.

Gittings, Chris. 'Canada and Scotland: Conceptualising 'Postcolonial' Spaces. *Essays on Writing in Canada 95*, Fall 1995, 135–161.

Guinnane, Timothy. *The Vanishing Irish: Households, Migration and the Rural Economy in Ireland, 1850–1914*. Princeton University Press, 1997, 193–240.

Gunder Frank, Andre. *Capitalisms and Underdevelopment in Latin America*. New York Monthly Review, 1967.

Harasym, Sarah. *The Post-colonial Critic: Interviews, Strategies, Dialogues. Gayatry Chakravorty Spivak*. New York: Routeledge, 1990.

Heaney, Seamus. *North*. London: Faber and Faber, 1978.

Hollway, Wendy. 'Gender Difference and the Production of Subjectivity', *Changing the Subject: Psychology, Social Regulation and Subjectivity*. Julian Henrigues *et al*, eds. London: Methuen, 1984, 227–63.

hooks, bell. 'Marginality as a Site of Resistance', *Out There: Marginalisation and Contemporary Culture*. Russell Ferguson *et al*, eds. Cambridge, MA: MIT Press, 1990, 341–43.

Howe, Stephen. 'The Empire Strikes Back', *New Statesman and Society*, 25 Sept. 1992, 36–37.

Ignatiev, Noel. *How the Irish Became White*. London: Routledge, 1995.

Innes, C.L. *Woman and Nation in Irish Literature and Society 1880–1935*. New York: Harvester Wheatsheaf, 1993.

Iremonger, Valentin, ed. 'Introduction', *Irish Short Stories*. London: Faber and Faber, 1960. 9–14.

Irigaray, Luce. *The Sex Which is Not One*. Ithaca, NY: Cornell University Press, 1985.

Jones, Ann Rosalind. 'Writing the Body: Toward an Understanding of *l'Ecriture Feminine*', *Feminisms: An Anthology of Literary Theory and Criticism*. Robyn R. Warhol and Diane Price Herndl, eds. New Brunswick: Rutgers University Press, 1993.

Johnson, Toni O'Brien and David Cairns. *Gender in Irish Writing*. Buckingham: Open University Press, 1991.

Joyce, James. *A Portrait of the Artist as a Young Man*. Harmondsworth: Penguin, 1960.

—. *Dubliners*. London: Secker and Warburg, 1994.

Kearney, Richard, ed. *The Irish Mind: Exploring Intellectual Traditions*. Dublin: Wolfhound Press, 1987.

Kelly, Maeve. *A Life of Her Own*. Dublin: Poolbeg, 1976.

Kenneally, Michael, ed. *Cultural Contexts and Literary Idioms in Contemporary Irish Literature*. Gerrards Cross: Colin Smythe, 1988.

Kennedy, Líam. *Colonialism, Religion and Nationalism in Ireland*. Belfast: The Institute of Irish Studies, The Queen's University of Belfast, 1996.

Kiberd, Declan. 'Story-Telling, The Gaelic Tradition', *The Irish Short Story*. Patrick Rafroidi and Terence Brown, eds. Gerrards Cross: Smythe, 1979, 17–28.

—. *Inventing Ireland*. London: Jonathan Cape, 1995.

Kristeva, Julia. 'Women's Time', *The Feminist Reader: Essays in Gender and the Politics of Literary Criticsim*. Cathererine Belsey and Jane Moore, eds. London: Macmillan, 1997, 201–16.

Lee, Joseph. *The Modernisation of Irish Society, 1848–1918*. Dublin: Gill and Macmillan, 1979.

Lloyd, David. *Anomalous States: Irish Writing and the Post-colonial Moment*. Dublin: The Liliput Press, 1993.

Longley, Edna. *From Cathleen to Anorexia: The Breakdowns of Irelands*. Dublin: Attic Press, 1990.

Loomba, Ania. *Colonialism/Postcolonialism*. London: Routledge, 1998.

Madden-Simpson, Janet. *Woman's Part: An Anthology of Short Fiction by and about Irishwomen 1890–1960*. Dublin: Arlen House, 1984.

Maeve, Kelly. *A Life of Her Own*. Dublin: Poolbeg, 1976.

Marcus, David. 'The Irish Short Story's Last Hurrah?' *Ireland and the Arts*. Tim Pat Coogan, ed. London: Namara Press, A Special Issue of Literary Review, 1983.

—. 'Introduction', *Irish Short Stories*. Dublin: Bodley Head, 1980.

May. Charles E. 'The Nature of Knowledge in Short Fiction', *The New Short Story Theories*. Charles E. May, ed. Athens, OH: Ohio University Press, 1994.

McGuckian, Medbh. 'An Attitude of Compassions: Q&A with Medbh McGuckian', Interview by Kathleen McGracken, *Irish Literary Supplement* 9 (1990).

McWilliams, Monica. 'Women in Northern Ireland', *Culture and Politics in Northern Ireland 1960–1990*, Eamon Hughes ed. Buckingham: Open University Press, 1991, 81–100.

Meaney, Gerardine. 'Sex and Nation: Women in Irish Culture and Politics', *Irish Women's Studies Reader*. Ailbhe Smyth ed. Dublin: Attic Press, 1993.

Memmi, Albert. *The Colonizer and the Colonized*. London: Earthscan Publications, 1990.

Mercier, Vivian, ed. 'Introduction', *Great Irish Short Stories: A Vintage Collection from Sommerville and Ross to Samuel Beckett*. London: Abacus, 1992.

Mills, Lia. 'Irish Women Poets and the Iconic Feminine', *Feminist Review*, Summer 1995, 69–88.

Moane, Geraldine. 'Legacies of Colonialism for Irish Women: Oppressive or Empowering?', *Irish Journal of Feminist Studies* 1, March 1996, 100–18.

Moi, Toril. *Sexual/Textual Politics: Feminist Literary Theory*. London: Routledge, 1994.

Morrison, Toni. 'Interview with Toni Morrison "Voice of America"', *The Irish Times*, 28 March 1998.

Nandy, Ashis. *The Intimate Enemy: Loss and Recovery of Self Under Colonialism*, Delhi: Oxford University Press, 1983.

O'Connor, Frank. 'Introduction'. *The Lonely Voice: A Study of the Short Story*. London: Macmillan, 1962.

O'Faolain, Nuala. 'Irish Women and Writing in Modern Ireland', *Irish Women: Image and Achievement: Women in Irish Culture from Earliest Times*. Eiléan Ní Chuilleanáin, ed. Dublin: Arlen Press, 1985.

O'Faoláin, Seán. *The Short Story*. London: Collins, 1948.

Ong, Walter J. *Orality and Literacy: The Technologizing of the Word* London: Methuen, 1982.

Ó Tuathaigh, Gearóid. 'Decolonisation, Identity and State-Formation: The Irish Experience', *Culture and Power: Institutions*. Rosa González, ed. Barcelona: Promociones y Publicacions Universitarias, 1996, 27–44.

Paley, Grace. 'A Conversation with Ann Charters', *The Story and its Writer: An Introduction to Short Fiction*. Ann Charters, ed. Boston: Bedford Books of St Martin's Press, 1995, 813–16.

Parker, Michael, ed. 'Introduction', *The Hurt World: Short Stories of the Troubles*. Belfast: The Blackstaff Press, 1994.

Pelan, Rebeca. 'The Contexts and (Dis)contents of Contemporary Irish Women's Fiction', PhD, University of Queensland, 1995.

—. 'Edna O'Brien's "World of Nora Barnacle"', *The Canandian Journal of Irish Studies*, December 1996. 49–62.

Poe, Edgar Alan. 'The Poetic Priciple', *The Complete Poetical Works and Essays on Poetry of Edgar Allan Poe*. John H. Ingram, ed. London: Frederick Warne, 1888.

Popot, Raymonde. 'Edna O'Brien's Paradise Lost', *The Irish Novel in Our Time*. Patrick Rafroide and Maurice Harmon, eds. Villeneuve-d'Ascq: Publications de l'Universite de Lille, 1975–6, 253–65.

Pratt, Marie Louise. 'The Short Story: The Long and the Short of It', *The New Short Story Theories*. Charles E. May, ed. Athens, OH: Ohio University Press, 1994, 91–113.

Rafroidi, Patrick and Terence Brown, eds. *The Irish Short Story*. Gerrards Cross: Colin Smythe, 1979.

Reid, Ian. *The Short Story*. London: Methuen, 1977.

Residder, Jack. *The Hutchinson Dictionary of Symbols*. Oxford: Helicon, 1997.

Rich, Adrienne. 'Compulsory Heterosexuality and Lesbian Existence', *Feminisms: A Reader*. Maggie Humm, ed. New York: Harvester Wheatsheaf, 1992, 176–80.

Robinson, Hilary. 'Irish/Woman/Artwork: Selective Readings', *Feminist Review*, Summer 1995, 89–110.

Scott, Bonnie Kime. 'Feminist Theory and Women in Irish Writing', Audrey S. Eyler and Robert F. Garrat, eds. *The Uses of the Past. Essays on Irish Culture*. Newark, DE: University of Delaware Press, 1988, 55–63.

Showalter, Elaine. 'Towards a Feminist Poetics', *Feminisms: A Reader*. Maggie Humm, ed. New York: Harvester Wheatsheaf, 1992, 382–84.

Smyth, Ailbhe. 'The Floozie in the Jacuzzi', *The Irish Review* 6, 1989, 7–24.

—. 'Ireland', *Bloomsbury Guide to Women's Literature*. Claire Buck, ed. London: Bloomsbury, 1992.

—. 'States of Change: Reflections on Ireland in Several Uncertain Parts', *Feminist Review*, Summer 1995, 24–43.

—. 'Paying Our Disrespects to the Bloody States We're In: Women, Violence, Culture, and the State', *Irish Women's Voices: Past and Present*. Joan Hoff and Moureen Coulter, eds (Bloomington, IN: Indiana University Press), 1995.

—. 'Declining Identities', *Critical Survey: Anglo-Irish Studies: New Developments* 8, 1996, 143–57

—, ed. *Wildish Things: An Anthology of New Irish Women's Writing*. Dublin: Attic Press, 1989.

Smyth, Gerry. *The Novel and the Nation: Studies in the New Irish Fiction*. London: Pluto Press, 1997.

Thiong'o, Ngugi Wa. *Decolonising the Mind: The Politics of Language in African Literature*. London: James Currey, 1986.

Tóibín, Colm. 'Playboys of the GPO', *London Review of Books*, 18 April 1996. 14–16.

—, *Martyrs and Metaphors*. Dublin: The Raven Arts Press, 1987.

Trevor, William, ed. 'Introduction', *The Oxford Book of Irish Short Stories*. Oxford: Oxford University Press, 1989.

Ward, Margaret. *Unmanageable Revolutionaries: Women and Irish Nationalism*. London: Pluto Press, 1995.

—. 'Irish Women and Nationalism', *Irish Studies Review*, Winter 1996–7, 8–14.

Weekes, Ann Owens. *Irish Women Writers: An Uncharted Tradition*. Lexington, KY: The University Press of Kentucky, 1990.

—. *Unveiling Treasures: The Attic Guide to the Published Works of Irish Women Literary Writers: Drama, Ficition, Poetry*. Dublin: Attic Press, 1993.

Welch, Robert, ed. *The Oxford Companion to Irish Literature*. Oxford: Clarendon Press, 1996.

Catalan Critical Studies

Alexandre, Víctor, *Jo no sóc espanyol*. Barcelona: Proa, 2000.

Alonso, Vicent. *Entre la poesia en prosa i el conte literari*. València: Universitat de València, Publicacions de l'Abadia de Montserrat, 1992.

— Bernal, Alonso, Vincent, Assumpció Gregori, and Camel eds. *Actes del primer simposi internacional de narrativa breu*. València: Universitat de València, Publicacions de l'Abadia de Montserrat, 1998.

Aranda, Quim. Interview with Mary Nash: 'A les dona encara no se l'escolta', *Avui*, 23 January 2000.

Arnau, Carme. *Introducció a la narrativa de Mercè Rodoreda: El mite de la infantesa* Barcelona: Edicions 62, 1982, 12.

Balcells, Albert. *Catalan Nationalism: Past and Present*. London: Macmillan, 1996.

Bergmann, Emilie. 'Flowers at the North Pole: Mercè Rodoreda and the Female Imagination in Exile', *Catalan Review: International Journal of Catalan Culture*, Dec. 1987, 83–100.

Bou, Enric. 'El premi "Víctor Català": una aproximació al conte catala sota el franquisme', *Els Marges*. no. 12, Jan. 1978, 102–8.

Campillo, Maria. *Contes de guerra i revolució*. Barcelona: Laia, 1982.

—. *El conte de 1911 a 1939*. Barcelona: Edicions 62, 1995.

Capel Martínez, Rosa Maria. *El trabajo y la educación de la mujer en Espana (1900–1930)*. Madrid: Ministerio de Cultura, 1986, 361–96.

Capmany, Maria Aurèlia. *L'altra ciutat*. Barcelona: Selecta, 1955.

—. *Betúlia: Obres Completes I*. Barcelona: Edicio Nova Terra, 1974, 29–233.

—. 'El temps passa sobre un mirall', *Coses i noses*. Barcelona: La Magrana, 1980.

—. *Ara*. Barcelona: Plaza y Janés, 1988.

Casacuberta, Margarida. 'Sobre viatges i flors de Mercé Rodoreda', *Actes de I Simposi*. Barcelona: Publications de l'Abadia de Montserrat, 1998.

Castellanos, Jordi. *Antología de contes modernistes*. Barcelona: Edicions 62, 1987.

Centelles, Esther. *El conte des de 1939*. Barcelona: Edicions 62, 1995.

Charlon, Anne. *La condició de la dona en la narrativa femenina catalana 1900–1983*. Barcelona: Edicions 62, 1990.

—. 'Dona catalana, i a més novel.lista', *Catalan Review* 7, 2, 1993, 41–6.

Cièrcoles, Marta. 'Drets d'autora', *Avui*, 23 April 1998, 17–19.

Cortada, Esther and Montserrat Sebastià. 'La dona i la institució de l'educació' *Més enllà del silenci*. Mary Nash, ed. Barcelona: Generalitat de Catalunya, 1988, 207–26.

Domínguez, Lourdes, 'Interview with Cristina Peri Rossi', *Avui*, 6 July 2000.

Duby, George. *El caballero, la mujer y el cura*. Madrid: Taurus, 1992.

Dupláa, Cristina. 'Les dones i el pensament conservador català contemporani', *Més enllà del silenci*. Mary Nash, ed. Barcelona: Generalitat de Catalunya, 1988, 173–90.

Febrers, Xavier, ed., *Diàlegs a Barcelona: Isabel–Clara Simó i Montserrat Roig*. Barcelona: Laia, 1985.

Fernández, Josep Anton. 'Becoming Normal: Cultural Production and Cultural Policy in Catalonia', *Spanish Cultural Studies: An Introduction: The Struggle for Modernity*. Helen Graham and Jo Labanyi, eds. Oxford: Oxford University Press, 1995.

Ferrer i Gironès, Francesc. *Catalanofòbia. El pensament anticatalà a través de la història*. Barcelona: Edicions 62, 2000.

Gassol, Ventura. *Les tombes flamejants: poesies patriòtiques*. Barcelona: Galba Edicions, 1980.

Gil, Concepció and Roser Soler. 'Família i condició social de la dona a la Catalunya moderna', Mary Nash, ed. *Més enllà del silenci*. Barcelona: Generalitat de Catalunya, 1988, 93–112.

Graells, Guillem-Jordi and Oriol Pi de Cabanyes, 'De la requesta que fou feta a Montserrat Roig', *Serra d'Or*, no. 138, 15 March 1971, 28.

Gregori, Carme. 'Metamorfois i altres prodigis', 297, *Actes de I simposi internacional de narrativa breu*.

Hernández, Prócoro. *Els catalans al món indígena d'Amèrica*. Barcelona: Generalitat de Catalunya, 1991.

Julià, M. Lluïsa. 'Les imatges de la dona en Víctor Català', Enric Prat and Pep Vila. *Actes de les primeres jornades d'estudi sobre la vida i l'obra de Caterina Albert i Paradís 'Víctor Català'*. Barcelona: Publicacions de l'Abadia de Montserrat, 1992, 247–74.

—. 'Òrfenes I desemparades', 'Quadern', *El Païs*, 25 March 1993.

King, Stewart. 'Orquestando la identidad: estrategias postcoloniales en l'Opera Quotidiana de Monserrat Roig' *Proceedings of the First Symposium on Catalonia in Australia*. Robert Archer and Emma Martinell, eds, Barcelona: PPU, 1998, 59–76.

Llovet, Jordi, ed. *Teoria de la literatura*. Barcelona: Columna, 1996.

Lluch, Ernest. 'Esfuerzos inútiles y melancolía', *La Vanguardia*, 31 December 1998.

Marçal, Maria Mercè. 'Divisa', *Cau de llunes*. Barcelona: Selecta, 1976, 32–3.

—, ed. *Cartografies del desig: quinze escriptores i el seu món*. Barcelona: Proa, 1998.

McNerney, Kathleen, ed. *On Our Own Behalf: Women's Tales From Catalonia*. Lincoln: University of Nebraska, 1988.

McNerney, Kathleen and Cristina Enriquez de Salamanca, eds. *Double Minorities of Spain: A Bio-Bibliographic Guide to Women Writers of the Catalan, Galician, and Basque Countries*. New York: Modern Language Association of America, 1994.

Molas, Joaquim. *Antologia de contes catalans*. Barcelona: Edicions 62, 1987.

—. 'Notes per a un comentari de La Pàtria de Bonaventura-Carles Aribau', *Analisis i comentaris de testos literaris catalans I*. Narcis Garolera, ed. Barcelona: Curial, 1982, 209–25.

Molinero, Clare-Mar. 'The Politics of Language: Spain's Minority Languages'. *Spanish Cultural Studies: An Introduction: The Struggle for Modernity*. Helen Graham and Jo Labanyi, eds. Oxford: Oxford Unversity Press, 1995, 336–42.

Nadal, Marta. *Vint Escriptors Catalans*. Barcelona: Publications de l'Abadia de Montserrat, 1997.

Nash, Mary. 'Politica, condició social i mobilització femenina: les dones a la Segona Republica i a la Guerra Civil', *Més enllà del silenci*. Mary Nash, ed. Barcelona: Generalitat de Catalunya, 1988, 243–264.

—. *Rojas: Las mujeres republicanas en la Guerra Civil*. Barcelona: Taurus, 1999.

Nichols, Geraldine. *Escribir espacio propio: Laforet, Matute, Moix, Tusquets, Riera y Roig por si mismas*. Minneapolis: Minnesota University Press, 1989.

Peri Rossi, 'Cristina: Interview', *Avui*, 6 July 2000.

Pessarrodona, Marta. 'Una manera de ser', *Avui*, 16 August 2000.

Pompeyo, Gener. 'De la mujer y sus derechos en las sociedades modernas', *La Vanguardia*, 26 February 1889.

Rodoreda, Mercè. *Cartes a l'Anna Murià 1939–1956*. Barcelona: Edicions l'Eixample, 1991.

Roig, Montserrat. *Digues que m'estimes encara que sigui mentida*. Barcelona: Edicions 62, 1991.

Segura, Isabel, ed. *Literatura de dones: una visió del món*. Barcelona: La Sal, 1988.

Trenc Ballester, Eliseu and Alan Yates. *Alexandre de Riquer: The British Connection in Catalan Modernisme*. Sheffield: The Anglo-Catalan Society, 1988.

Triadú, Joan. 'El conte, gran desheretat de l'edició catalana', *Serra d'Or*, Octubre, 1972, 683–5.

—, 'Panorama de narracio breu'. *Serra d'Or* Setembre (1991), 609–10.

Yates, Alan. *Una generació sense novel.la? La novel.la catalana entre 1900 i 1925*. 3rd edn, Barcelona: Edicions 62, 1984.

Index